W9-CYB-695

Manny J. González, DSW
Gladys González-Ramos, PhD
Editors

Mental Health Care for New Hispanic Immigrants: Innovative Approaches in Contemporary Clinical Practice

Mental Health Care for New Hispanic Immigrants: Innovative Approaches in Contemporary Clinical Practice has been co-published simultaneously as *Journal of Immigrant & Refugee Services,* Volume 3, Numbers 1/2 2005

Pre-publication REVIEWS, COMMENTARIES, EVALUATIONS . . .

"**A** COMPREHENSIVE OVERVIEW of the mental health needs, issues, and barriers confronting the emergent new Latino communities in the United States (i.e., Dominican, Colombian, Peruvian, Nicaraguan). . . . Also provides ample information about the need for culturally effective mental health prevention and treatment models."

Mario De La Rosa, PhD
Associate Professor
School of Social Work
and Director, Center for Research
on US Latinos, HIV/AIDS,
and Drug Abuse,
Florida International University

More Pre-publication
REVIEWS, COMMENTARIES, EVALUATIONS . . .

"TIMELY AND VALUABLE. . . . WELL THOUGHT OUT, SCHOLARLY, AND COMPREHENSIVE . . . LONG OVERDUE. As a Latina academican I am familiar with some of the studies referred to in this text, but I have not seen them organized or conceptualized so well until now. I am struck with how comprehensive these eleven chapters are in addressing such a complex population and its service needs. IN A SCHOOL OF SOCIAL WORK, THIS TEXT WOULD BE EXCELLENT IN A HEALTH AND MENTAL HEALTH POLICY COURSE or in an elective course specifically designed to study Hispanic communities in the US. It will also be informative for doctoral students involved with research on Hispanic communities."

Carmen Oritz Hendricks, DSW, LMSW
Associate Professor
Hunter College School of Social Work

"A MUST-READ FOR EDUCATORS, PROVIDERS, POLICYMAKERS, and anyone in the helping professions. There is a richness in how each author embraces concepts of Latino ethnic identity within a socio-cultural-political and economic context to understand the risk and protective factors facing new immigrants in a global society. The authors explore illness presentations, health beliefs, acculturation processes, help-seeking behaviors, adaptive capacities, cultural meanings, and expressions of psychiatric distress in diverse Latino groups. The uniqueness of this book lies in its analysis of the health and mental health issues of Latino groups within ecological and cultural contexts, and explaining transactional dimensions that influence access, best practices, and treatment preferences for diverse Latino groups."

Catherine Medina, PhD, CSW
Clinical Associate Professor
and Director of Field Learning
and Community Partnerships,
New York University

"**A** MOST APPROPRIATE AND VALUABLE TEXT-BOOK to be used in professional schools of social work, nursing, psychiatry, and psychology. . . . This is a very timely book for mental health professionals providing services to the ever-growing population of recent Hispanic immigrants in the United States. . . . Provides an overview of the major Hispanic groups: Mexican, Puerto Rican, Cuban, and Dominican, and the major mental health issues facing these populations. . . . Provides readers with the opportunity to learn about the intra-group differences among Hispanic immigrants."

Rosa Perez-Koenig, DSW
Assistant Professor
Fordham University
Graduate School of Social Service

The Haworth Social Work Practice Press
An Imprint of The Haworth Press, Inc.

New York • London • Victoria (AU)
www.HaworthPress.com

Mental Health Care for New Hispanic Immigrants: Innovative Approaches in Contemporary Clinical Practice

Mental Health Care for New Hispanic Immigrants: Innovative Approaches in Contemporary Clinical Practice has been co-published simultaneously as *Journal of Immigrant & Refugee Services*, Volume 3, Numbers 1/2 2005.

Mental Health Care for New Hispanic Immigrants: Innovative Approaches in Contemporary Clinical Practice, edited by Manny J. Gonzalez, DSW, and Gladys Gonzalez-Ramos, PhD (Vol. 3, No. 1/2, 2005). *"A COMPREHENSIVE OVERVIEW OF MENTAL HEALTH needs, issues, and barriers confronting the emergent new Latino communities in the United States (i.e., Dominican, Colombian, Peruvian, Nicaraguan). . . . Also provides ample information about the need for culturally effective mental health prevention and treatment models." (Mario De La Rosa, PhD, Associate Professor, School of Social Work, and Director, Center for Research on US Latinos, HIV/AIDS, and Drug Abuse, Florida International University)*

The Health and Well-Being of Caribbean Immigrants in the United States, edited by Annette M. Mahoney, MS, DSW (Vol. 2, No 3/4, 2004). *The Health and Well-Being of Caribbean Immigrants in the United States is a timely addition to the knowledge base concerning the integration of this population into the fabric of American society. On the eve of the fortieth anniversary of the 1965 Immigration Reform Act, this book examines the relationship between immigrants from the Caribbean and the social and economic structures as well as the political culture of the United States. This body of work provides resources for scholars and researchers and provides instrumental strategies for use in practice by counselors/social workers, curriculum developers, and immigration analysts.*

Immigrants and Social Work: Thinking Beyond the Borders of the United States, edited by Diane Drachman, PhD, and Ana Paulino, EdD (Vol. 2, No. 1/2, 2004). *"HIGHLY INFORMATIVE . . . . THE AUTHORS EXPLAIN AND ILLUSTRATE VITAL CONCEPTS such as transnationalism, return migration, and circular migration. Each chapter examines changes in the United States' immigration laws in the aftermath of 9/11 and their respective impacts on the suffering of immigrant populations. Chapters on the establishment of voluntary social services in Armenia and on international social work practice are bonuses for the reader. I thank professors Drachman and Paulino for placing a 'spotlight' on a substantive area fundamental to contemporary social work practice." (Alex Gitterman, EdD, Professor of Social Work, University of Connecticut School of Social Work; Editor of* "The Legacy of William Schwartz: Group Practice as Shared Interaction")

Mental Health Care for New Hispanic Immigrants: Innovative Approaches in Contemporary Clinical Practice

Manny J. González, DSW
Gladys González-Ramos, PhD
Editors

Mental Health Care for New Hispanic Immigrants: Innovative Approaches in Contemporary Clinical Practice has been co-published simultaneously as *Journal of Immigrant & Refugee Services*, Volume 3, Numbers 1/2 2005.

The Haworth Social Work Practice Press
An Imprint of The Haworth Press, Inc.

New York • London • Victoria (AU)
www.HaworthPress.com

Published by

The Haworth Social Work Practice Press, 10 Alice Street, Binghamton, NY 13904-1580 USA

The Haworth Social Work Practice Press is an imprint of The Haworth Press, Inc., 10 Alice Street, Binghamton, NY 13904-1580 USA.

Mental Health Care for New Hispanic Immigrants: Innovative Approaches in Contemporary Clinical Practice has been co-published simultaneously as *Journal of Immigrant & Refugee Services*, Volume 3, Numbers 1/2 2005.

The development, preparation, and publication of this work has been undertaken with great care. However, the publisher, employees, editors, and agents of The Haworth Press and all imprints of The Haworth Press, Inc., including The Haworth Medical Press® and The Pharmaceutical Products Press®, are not responsible for any errors contained herein or for consequences that may ensue from use of materials or information contained in this work. Opinions expressed by the author(s) are not necessarily those of The Haworth Press, Inc.

Cover design by Marylouise E. Doyle

Library of Congress Cataloging-in-Publication Data

Mental Health Care for New Hispanic Immigrants: Innovative Approaches in Contemporary Clinical Practice / Manny J. González, DSW, and Gladys González-Ramos, editors.
    p. cm.
    "Co-published simultaneously as Journal of Immigrant & Refugee Services, volume 3, numbers 1/2, 2005."
    Includes bibliographical references and index.
    ISBN 13: 978-0-7890-2307-0 (hc : alk.paper)
    ISBN 10: 0-7890-2307-5 (hc. : alk.paper)
    ISBN 13: 978-0-7890-2308-7 (pbk. : alk.paper)
    ISBN 10: 0-7890-2308-3 (pbk. : alk.paper)
    1. Latin Americans–Mental health–United States. 2. Latin Americans–Mental health services–United States. 3. Immigrants–Mental health–United States. 4. Immigrants–Mental health services–United States. 5. Hispanic Americans–Mental health. 6. Hispanic Americans–Mental services. 7. Psychiatry, Transcultural–United States. I. González, Manny J. II. González-Ramos, Gladys.
  RC451.5.H57M455 2005
  362.1′08968073–dc22   2004021154

Indexing, Abstracting & Website/Internet Coverage

This section provides you with a list of major indexing & abstracting services and other tools for bibliographic access. That is to say, each service began covering this periodical during the year noted in the right column. Most Websites which are listed below have indicated that they will either post, disseminate, compile, archive, cite or alert their own Website users with research-based content from this work. (This list is as current as the copyright date of this publication.)

(continued)

*Exact start date to come.

Special Bibliographic Notes related to special journal issues (separates) and indexing/abstracting:

- indexing/abstracting services in this list will also cover material in any "separate" that is co-published simultaneously with Haworth's special thematic journal issue or DocuSerial. Indexing/abstracting usually covers material at the article/chapter level.
- monographic co-editions are intended for either non-subscribers or libraries which intend to purchase a second copy for their circulating collections.
- monographic co-editions are reported to all jobbers/wholesalers/approval plans. The source journal is listed as the "series" to assist the prevention of duplicate purchasing in the same manner utilized for books-in-series.
- to facilitate user/access services all indexing/abstracting services are encouraged to utilize the co-indexing entry note indicated at the bottom of the first page of each article/chapter/contribution.
- this is intended to assist a library user of any reference tool (whether print, electronic, online, or CD-ROM) to locate the monographic version if the library has purchased this version but not a subscription to the source journal.
- individual articles/chapters in any Haworth publication are also available through the Haworth Document Delivery Service (HDDS).

To my wife, Mildred; my sons, Jeremy John and Elijah Gabriel; and in memory of my mother, Elisa Grau

Dr. Manny J. González

To my husband, Ernesto Loperena; and in memory of my parents, Juan González and Modesta Ramos; and friend, Dr. Lucretia J. Phillips

Dr. Gladys González-Ramos

Mental Health Care for New Hispanic Immigrants: Innovative Approaches in Contemporary Clinical Practice

CONTENTS

ABOUT THE EDITORS

Manny J. González, DSW, is Associate Professor at Fordham University Graduate School of Social Service. He received his Master's degree in Clinical Social Work from New York University and his Doctoral degree from Adelphi University. At Fordham University, Dr. Gonzalez teaches MSW courses in clinical practice, advanced assessment and diagnosis (psychopathology), and the treatment of children. He also teaches in the Graduate School of Social Service's PhD program courses in research issues with children and families, mental health, and practice theory. Dr. Gonzalez is currently conducting psychotherapy intervention research with depressed Hispanic preadolescent children.

Dr. Gonzalez's professional background is in the field of mental health. He has practiced in diverse clinical settings including primary health care centers, teaching hospitals, school-based mental health clinics, child welfare, and community mental health centers. Dr. Gonzalez has provided direct clinical services to patients of different immigrant and ethnic-racial minority groups, principally Hispanics and African Americans. He has also held positions in the area of mental health administration, consultation and supervision.

Dr. Gonzalez has published articles and chapters specific to clinical practice with Hispanic immigrants and evidence-based practice. He is co-author (together with Elaine Congress, DSW) of the second edition of an edited book on cross-cultural direct practice issues: *Multicultural Perspectives in Working with Families* (forthcoming), New York: Springer.

Gladys González-Ramos, PhD, is Associate Professor at the New York University School of Social Work, and Adjunct Associate Professor of Neurology at the New York University School of Medicine. She received her Master's and Doctoral degrees in Social Work from NYU. She holds a certificate in psychoanalytic psychotherapy with adults and one with children and families.

Dr. Gonzalez-Ramos has worked in the field of mental health for over twenty-five years, practicing in a variety of community and hospital settings with children and families. She has been particularly interested in access to services and developing community-based services for Hispanic and other diverse families. Her primary areas of research and publications have been in the provision of culturally competent services and the study of cultural child-rearing values of Hispanic mothers.

For the past several years, Dr. Gonzalez-Ramos has been expanding her work to the field of service delivery to persons and family caregivers from culturally diverse backgrounds affected by Parkinson's disease. Through her work with the National Parkinson Foundation, she has been working on several grant funded programs to create numerous nationally based educational and care initiatives that are responsive to underserved persons affected by Parkinson's disease and the allied health professionals who provide care.

Foreword:
Culturally Competent Mental Health Care with New Hispanic Immigrants

Ian A. Canino

In the modern world where transportation, global markets, and communication have so rapidly evolved, and concomitantly there has been an ethnic and religious displacement of millions of people due to wars, political persecution, and large economic gaps between the wealthy and poor nations, understanding the impact of the highly complex and multi-variable patterns of migration has become a necessity.

Migration is a dynamic and complex process. The reasons for migration may be political, educational, economic, and often highly personal or family induced. The process may be fraught with stress, it may be smooth and easy, or it may be forced or voluntary. Migration may include a shift from rural to urban or vice versa or within or between similar or different geographical and-or cultural ecologies. It may include people of all ages and both genders with different levels of adaptive capacities and skills who may come as part of intact or segmented families. Some migrants may choose to stay for different periods of time and may be able to travel back and forth to their native countries. Others return when they are older and others never return.

Ian A. Canino, MD, is Clinical Professor of Psychiatry, College of Physicians and Surgeons, Columbia University.

[Haworth co-indexing entry note]: "Foreword: Culturally Competent Mental Health Care with New Hispanic Immigrants." Canino, Ian A. Co-published simultaneously in *Journal of Immigrant & Refugee Services* (The Haworth Social Work Practice Press, an imprint of The Haworth Press, Inc.) Vol. 3, No. 1/2, 2005, pp. xix-xxiv; and: *Mental Health Care for New Hispanic Immigrants: Innovative Approaches in Contemporary Clinical Practice* (ed: Manny J. González, and Gladys González-Ramos) The Haworth Social Work Practice Press, an imprint of The Haworth Press, Inc., 2005, pp. xv-xx. Single or multiple copies of this article are available for a fee from The Haworth Document Delivery Service [1-800-HAWORTH, 9:00 a.m. - 5:00 p.m. (EST). E-mail address: docdelivery@haworthpress.com].

For those migrants arriving at host countries that are receptive and welcoming the experience may be different to those arriving at hostile countries. Levels of differences in documentation, language, religious practices, cultural expectations, and resources may predict how well and how fast the migrant adapts to the new environment. The inter-change between the migrant and the new society may enrich both, enrich one, or elicit prejudicial and discriminatory policy patterns.

In this book, for example, Fuertes et al. address those difficulties experienced by South American immigrants but that are applicable to many other groups. These include discrimination, poverty, acculturation, and language acquisition. They discuss a wide and diverse spectrum of reactions to the adjustment process in a new country and review well the theoretical approaches to acculturation and social support literature.

Countries experience and respond to migration in their own particular manner. In the United States, as in many other countries, waves of different immigrant groups have characterized its history. It has affected its culture, influenced its economy, it has had an impact on resource allocation and politics, and has triggered new governmental policies and legislative incentives. As a consequence, policy makers, economists, politicians, sociologists, public health officials, and increasingly mental health professionals have been requested to address and explain this old and historic process in new ways.

The first chapter in this book (González-Ramos and González) explores reported health disparities observed in minority groups, many of whom are migrants, in this country. It discusses the fact that these groups, due to a variety of personal and socio-economic barriers to health services, do not access or receive quality care in a timely fashion, thus potentially affecting their productivity. Obviously the first step, once the physical and mental health needs have been identified for a specific population, is to identify those cultural norms that determine health-seeking behavior and the health literacy patterns of the consumer group. This in turn strongly interacts with service accessibility, structural issues in health care, and the efficacy and specificity of treatment interventions.

In order to establish outreach services and community partnerships, González-Ramos and González state that it is necessary to understand those specials barriers to care that often characterize the migrant groups addressed in this book, such as stigma, health beliefs, discrimination, language utilization, and lack of medical insurance. The authors underline the need to address the heterogeneity within each specific population, the special strengths and vulnerabilities of each group, and the particular needs of the at risk sub-groups constituted by rural migrants and youth as a necessary step to diminish these disparities.

As time has evolved, older immigrant groups have consolidated their differential impact in the United States. New groups continue to arrive constantly in various numbers and influence and are influenced by our increasingly multi-cultural society. They often bring enriching cultural and labor resources and often require services that support their special physical and psychological well-being.

Fuertes et al. discuss social supports and underline two leading hypotheses, the buffering and the main effect hypothesis, and they address the complexity of these mechanisms. They state that "different types and sources of support may be required as a function of need and may change in the short or long term." They review studies that find ethnic differences among the participants who ask for assistance in stress situations and in the levels of susceptibility that affect resource deterioration.

This book, nevertheless, specifically addresses the psychological and cultural profiles that distinguish migrant Latino groups in this country. In doing so it informs mental health clinicians about competent interventions.

Latino immigrants and their descendants have become one if not the largest group of migrants in this country. Mexican Americans, Puerto Ricans, and Cubans in the United States have constituted the largest members in this category. Many clinical articles have been published about their unique characteristics and service needs and better and more research-based findings have been published in respected journals regarding their health and mental health profiles.

Guarnaccia et al. offer an overview of the demographic and mental health profiles of these migrant communities. They underline those special characteristics and events that need to be known in order to identify and deliver services to these groups. They state that the values of personalismo, respeto, the somatization of distress, expressed emotion, and concerns about psychotropic medications have been endorsed as important factors for service delivery providers. Findings suggest that in the Mexican American population, risk groups consist of the elderly and widowed Mexican women, farm workers, and Mexican individuals who have stayed longer in this country.

The authors describe differences in service utilization within these groups. Puerto Ricans and Cubans indicate high service utilization rates and Mexicans indicate low utilization rates. They mention the importance of espiritistas and santeros in the Puerto Ricans and Cubans, and of curanderos in Mexicans as alternative folk resources. They state that ecological family therapy for Cuban Americans and cognitive behavioral approaches for depressed Latinos have been described as effective interventions.

The authors critically review the findings of major epidemiological studies that include these three major Latino groups in this country. They state that the findings suggest higher rates of symptoms of depression and depression cases in Puerto Ricans and Cubans from Mariel, and an increased risk for developing alcohol and abuse/dependence disorders in acculturated Mexican Americans.

Barrio and Yamada review the special treatment interventions described in the literature for chronically mentally ill Mexican-American adults. Focusing on family and community based approaches the authors underline the importance of those family patterns that relate to perceptions of mental illness and mental health providers, expectations of social adjustment, religious attributions, rules of mutual obligation, and supportive networks.

They mention findings in Mexican Americans that suggest lower utilization of case management services, lower levels of expressed emotion with lack of family warmth as a better predictor of relapse, and increased service utilization and attendance when a community based comprehensive approach is implemented. They underline that caution needs to be considered with other approaches. For example, they mention a study of BFT (Behavioral Family Treatment) that indicated a greater risk of symptom exacerbation for the less acculturate immigrant Mexican sample.

In view of the heterogeneity of this population the authors mention the different clinical variables that need to be considered and the need to understand a cultural orientation along a continuum. They underline the risk and protective factors, and mention the need for more bilingual and bicultural services.

This book, in addition to describing these three groups, addresses an increasingly large sub-group of Latinos–those of Central American and Dominican origin–whose special and specific characteristics and mental health needs have been under-represented in the literature. González et al., for example, underscore the family reunification issues that are unique to the Mariel and balsero Cuban immigrant. In addition, González-Ramos and González discuss a school-based approach that may be used in addressing the mental health needs of Hispanic immigrant children.

Engstrom and Piedra underline the importance of macro-systems in the service delivery to a particular sub-group in this category. The authors address those Central American refugees who have been exposed to political persecution, torture and loss. The authors adopt a human rights framework to discuss the appropriate interventions.

They describe citizenship, undocumented status, and health insurance as primary barriers to access of care and insufficient translators and a confusing bureaucracy as impeding adequate utilization. Through a case vignette they illustrate the special factors of fear of deportation, survival guilt, recurrent traumatic memories, acculturative stress, and poor access to safe and consistent employment. For those immigrants who flee political persecution and enter this country as illegal migrants, they mention interventions that include help with a complicated asylum-seeking process and ethno-medical community based services.

Pérez and Fortuna discuss the special considerations that need to be addressed for undocumented immigrant Latinos. They mention how specific political and economic factors, poverty, and illegal status interact with legislation and policy measures to create limited access to health care and other problems.

The authors describe their own chart review study of mostly male undocumented Latinos and conclude that they have a specific diagnostic profile (i.e., higher rates of substance abuse, anxiety, depression, and adjustment disorders), have a larger number of reported stressors, have a lower rate of attended appointments, and have lower lifetime mental health utilization rates than other Latinos.

Baez describes the special demographics and cultural patterns of the Dominican population. As a young and relatively recent migrant group they are characterized by the centrality of the family, by both Christian and complimentary spiritual beliefs, by hijos de crianza and compadres, and by back and forth migration patterns.

Mental health strategies should include concrete services, a present and directive orientation, and a focus on solutions. Baez urges clinicians to be aware of immigration stress, "ethnic lumping," the strengths of the patient, and to educate patients about the therapeutic process. She addresses other factors that include the occasional discontinuities of treatment because of the back and forth migration, and the occasional need to give token gifts by the patients to the therapist.

Berkman et al. discuss older New York City Puerto Ricans' and Dominicans' conceptions of mental health as important in understanding the impact of beliefs in service utilization, social acceptability, and symptom interpretation.

Implementing the Illness Self Regulation Model (ISRM) they collected their information thru three focus groups following a qualitative research method and semi-structured interviews. The items included questions about the conceptions and causes of emotional health and problems, of depression, of anxiety, and of the distinction between the two.

The authors state that the findings suggest the expressed importance of social relations in order to maintain emotional health, that the symptoms of depression are perceived as including anhedonia and physical symptoms, and that anxiety is perceived as an outcome of loss and stress.

The impact on mental health of migration has triggered many research incentives. In this book, Fuertes et al. underline the importance of these concepts in understanding the immigrant experience and promote further studies of the instruments and research methodology that specifically address this population sample. They conclude that individual differences need to be considered and that there is probably no one right intervention approach. Perez et al. discuss the limitations of their study and urge clinicians, in the meantime, to consider these preliminary findings in their clinical interventions with this population. Citing the limitations of their study and recommending further research incentives, Berkman et al. underline the need to consider findings within the context of severity of psychopathology and of cultural and social variations in prevalence and distress expression and interpretation.

Finally, this book concludes with a compelling chapter by Vega on the future of culturally competent health and mental health care for Latino immigrants. He stresses the importance of understanding the organizational context and culture of the health/mental health service delivery system while concomitantly appreciating the socio-economic-political factors that are presently affecting health care in the 21st century. Vega notes that culturally competent care for Latino patients must–whenever possible–be consistent with the operational realities that health/mental health care organizations continually confront: professional education requirements, cost effectiveness expectations, reaccrediting and licensure standards and improved patient care.

Chapter 1

Health Disparities
in the Hispanic Population:
An Overview

Gladys González-Ramos
Manny J. González

SUMMARY. Closing the gap on health and mental health disparities has been receiving increasing attention, coming at a time of
growing diversity in the U.S. population. There have been several
reports, from the U.S. government and others, calling for increased
focus on disparities and proposing the elimination of these (IOM,
2001, 2003; USDHHS, 2001). Despite all these efforts, health and
mental health disparities are quite pronounced in the Hispanic population. There are a myriad of reasons for these inequalities that seem
to include an interplay of social, personal, and environmental factors. This manuscript examines health and mental health disparities

Gladys González-Ramos, PhD, is Associate Professor, New York University
School of Social Work.
Manny J. González, DSW, is Associate Professor, Fordham University Graduate
School of Social Service.

[Haworth co-indexing entry note]: "Health Disparities in the Hispanic Population: An Overview."
González-Ramos, Gladys, and Manny J. González. Co-published simultaneously in *Journal of Immigrant &
Refugee Services* (The Haworth Social Work Practice Press, an imprint of The Haworth Press, Inc.) Vol. 3,
No. 1/2, 2005, pp. 1-19; and: *Mental Health Care for New Hispanic Immigrants: Innovative Approaches in
Contemporary Clinical Practice* (ed: Manny J. González, and Gladys González-Ramos) The Haworth Social
Work Practice Press, an imprint of The Haworth Press, Inc., 2005, pp. 1-19. Single or multiple copies of this
article are available for a fee from The Haworth Document Delivery Service [1-800-HAWORTH, 9:00 a.m. -
5:00 p.m. (EST). E-mail address: docdelivery@haworthpress.com].

Digital Object Identifier: 10.1300/J191v3n01_01

in the Hispanic population and suggests some future directions to be considered. *[Article copies available for a fee from The Haworth Document Delivery Service: 1-800-HAWORTH. E-mail address: <docdelivery@haworth press.com> Website: <http://www.HaworthPress.com> © 2005 by The Haworth Press, Inc. All rights reserved.]*

KEYWORDS. Health, Hispanics, mental health disparities

INTRODUCTION

Closing the gap on health and mental health disparities has been receiving increasing attention, coming at a time of growing diversity in the U.S. population. With the prediction that by 2050 (U. S. Census Bureau, 2001), ethnic and racial minorities will represent the majority of the U.S. population, the need to eliminate such disparities seems imperative.

There have been several recent reports from the U.S. government and others (Geiger, 2003; IOM, 2002, 2003; Mayberry, Mili & Ofili, 2000) calling for increased focus on health disparities and proposing recommendations for the elimination of such inequalities. Among these, and specific to the issue of mental health, is the 2001 Surgeon General's Supplement Report on Mental Health examining the role of ethnicity, culture and race. After a careful analysis of national and international data, the report states that "minorities bear a greater burden of unmet mental health needs and thus suffer a greater loss to their overall health and productivity" (USDHHS, 2001, p. 3). The more recent July 2003 report from the New Freedom Commission on Mental Health also highlights the existing disparities and sets national goals for how to close the gap.

While health disparities were noted as far back as 1944 (Myrdal, 1944), and many have written about them, eliminating them remains elusive. In looking at causality, research points to complex interactions among variables that can include personal, social and environmental factors. Despite this being an area that has been extensively written about, there is a widespread awareness that the reasons for such health disparities are still not well understood.

While there are reported health disparities among Hispanics, most of what has been studied about Hispanics and mental health is about Puerto Ricans and Mexican-Americans in the Los Angeles region, with relatively little about more recent Hispanic immigrants living in the U.S. Without knowledge about the demographic and history of the more recently arrived groups, including their patterns of immigration, sources of stress, strengths and cultural values, patterns of assimilation in the U.S. and cultural protective factors, clinicians face great challenges in providing appropriate and responsive mental health treatment. This lack of knowledge can contribute to provision of care that is less than responsive and thus, can create a situation of greater disparity in the delivery of mental health services.

Among various recommendations from the Institute of Medicine for elimination of health disparities, education of health care providers in culturally competent care is cited as an important vehicle for reducing disparities (IOM, 2003). This manuscript is therefore but one attempt to address the need for greater knowledge about some of the newer Hispanics and delivery of mental health services.

HEALTH DISPARITIES IN THE U.S.

The U.S. Department of Health and Human Services (USDHHS), as a leading government agency and author of *Healthy People 2010*, defines disparities as an "inequality or gap that exists between two or more groups," with the reasons understood as being due to an interplay of personal, social and environmental factors (USDHHS, 2001, p. 3). The Institute of Medicine (IOM), for the purposes of their own review of disparities, offers a more specific definition, and thus, define them as "a racial or ethnic difference in the quality of health care that are not due to access-related factors, clinical needs, preferences and appropriateness of intervention" (IOM, 2003, pp. 3-4). So that disparities are said to exist when groups have similar health insurance, same access to care, when there are no differences between groups in terms of preferences and need for treatment (IOM, 2003) As will be discussed, no matter how global or specific the definition is, health disparities are consistently found across most illnesses and health care services.

Health disparities have long been studied in the United States. In the classic 1944 book, *An American Dilemma*, Gunnar Myrdal pointed out that "area for area, class by class, Negroes cannot get the same advantage in the way of prevention that whites can." Forty years later, the Report of the U.S. Department of Health and Human Services Secretary's Task Force on Black and Minority Health highlighted that, despite the growth of both scientific knowledge and medical treatment, blacks, Hispanics and other minorities "have not benefited fully or equitably from the fruit of science or from systems responsible for translating and using health services technology" (USDHHS, 1985)

Acknowledging that health disparities were being increasingly noted, in 1999, Congress asked the Institute of Medicine of the National Academy of Sciences to assess differences in the kinds and quality of health care received by both minorities and non-minorities. In response, the Institute undertook an exhaustive review of work published in the last 10 years in order to assess evidence of health disparities. The Institute's work and conclusions are reported in *Unequal Treatment: Confronting Racial and Ethnic Disparities in Healthcare*. Among their more powerful conclusion was that "Racial and ethnic disparities in healthcare exist. These disparities are consistent across a range of medical conditions and healthcare services, are associated with worse health outcomes and occur independently of insurance status, income, and education, among other factors that influence access to healthcare. These disparities are unacceptable" (IOM, 2003, p. 79). While discrepancies were clearest in cardiovascular care, evidence of health disparities were found among a range of diseases, including cancer care, diabetes, end-stage renal disease, pediatric and maternal care, mental health, rehabilitation and nursing home services. (IOM, 2003).

In another attempt to carefully examine the extent of health disparities, Mayberry, Mili and Ofili (2000) reported their findings, after a review of 400 articles published from 1985 to October 1999, which looked at the nature of racial and ethnic differences in preventive, diagnostic and therapeutic services. They found that racial and ethnic disparities continued to exist to a significant extent in several diseases and service types. Most consistent findings were in invasive cardiac care, while cancer, HIV and mental health needed careful interpretation as results were inconsistent. In regards to mental health, studies from the use of outpatient services, inpatient admissions and drug therapy, showed racial and ethnic disparities, though the findings were inconsistent and therefore the implications have not been clear. In their review of the data, the authors also raised the possibility of misdiagnosis occurring. Given these inconclusive findings about the use of mental health services by racial and ethnic groups, and the numerous methodological problems noted in many of the studies, the authors recommended further research to understand the issues of access to mental health care by ethnic and racial minority groups.

More recent efforts to draw attention to health disparities by the Department of Health and Human Services are outlined in the report *Healthy People 2010*, health promotion and a disease prevention initiative. This report puts forth a set of health objectives for the nation for the upcoming decade and proposes two goals. The goals are that of increasing the quality and years of healthy life, and that of eliminating health disparities in the U.S.

The report establishes 427 objectives that are organized into 28 focus areas, including mental health and mental disorders. This ambitious plan, to be achieved by 2010, guides all federal, state and local health services planning. The report puts forth the imperative that every person in the U.S. "deserves equal access to comprehensive, culturally-competent, community-based health care systems that are committed to servicing the needs of the individual and promoting community health." This principle of equal access clearly sets the tone of inclusiveness for all by stating that, "regardless of age, gender, race or ethnicity, income, education, geographic location, disability or sexual orientation," all persons have equal rights to comprehensive care (USDHHS, 2000).

The National Alliance for Hispanic Health (2002) has been very proactive in advocating the inclusion of Hispanic health concerns in the Healthy People reports. In their analysis of the most recent report, they note that there continues to be significant gaps in gathering Hispanic baseline and tracking data for various diseases including mental health and mental disorders. Without establishing the needed baselines, objectives cannot be measured for the Hispanic community. So, in spite of some possible progress that may be made, at the end of the next decade, we may not be much further along in understanding Hispanic health. Included in the missing data for Hispanic adults is the area of mental health and mental disorders, occupational safety and health, nutrition and overweight, heart disease and stroke and oral health, all clearly health concerns for the Hispanic community. With the continuing gaps in data about Hispanics, we need to continue to rely on the Hispanic Health and Nutrition Examination Survey, which is now more than ten years old.

In addition, the Alliance, in its analysis of the recent report found that only 14% of the various recommendations they made to the USDHHS, prior to the final report being finalized, were fully implemented (The National Alliance for Hispanic Health, 2002). According to the Alliance, the final *Healthy People 2010* report contains important gaps in the attention to Hispanic health issues, which will make it impossible for the goal of eliminating health disparities to be met.

DISPARITIES IN MENTAL HEALTH

In the area of mental health, evidence of disparities has been highlighted by some researchers (Alderete et al., 1999; Escobar, 1998; Vega and Alegria, 2001). The 1999 Surgeon General's Report on Mental Health, and the 2001 Supplement that examines culture, race and ethnicity in mental health, highlights the inequality that exists for minority groups needing mental health services (USDHHS, 1999, 2001). The Supplement to Mental Health (2001) extensively documents the "striking disparities" that exist for racial and ethnic minorities in mental health. After a careful analysis, they found that "racial and ethnic minorities have less access to mental health services than do whites. They are less likely to receive needed care. When they receive care, it is more likely to be poor in quality." Most recently in July 2003, the New Freedom Commission on Mental Health report *Achieving the Promise: Transforming Mental Health Care in America,* through their review, came to the conclusion that minorities are underserved or inappropriately served in the current system of mental health care.

As the Hispanic population continues its rapid growth, greater attention to ways to deliver effective mental health treatment seems imperative. In the 2000 census, the number of Hispanics rose to 35.3 million (U.S. Census Bureau, 2001), with projection made that by 2050 they will increase to 97 million, almost one-fourth of the U.S. population.

One of the most vexing problems in looking to understand disparities among Hispanics is the lack of sufficient recognition of the diversity of cultures gathered under the label of Hispanics or Latinos. To group all Hispanic cultures together obscures differences that can, in fact, be very important in understanding the health and mental health needs, the barriers to services and the most effective delivery of services for different Hispanic groups. While there are commonalities across the various groups, such as the central role of the family and the use of the Spanish language, there are also important differences which may hold direct implications for health care. For example, to group all Hispanics together obfuscates important differences that are raised when carefully examining migration status and acculturation of Hispanic groups.

Vega et al. (1998) reported results from the Mexican-American Prevalence and Services study that Mexicans living in the U.S. for 13 years or less had half the rate of mental illness of Mexicans born in the U.S. Vega and Amaro (2002) report on the fact that with increased acculturation, Hispanic individuals might be at greater vulnerability because of the disruption to the networks that provide support at the same time that they are needing to adapt to new systems in the host country. Certain behaviors also seem to increase with acculturation, such as use of cigarettes, alcohol, particularly among young women, while obesity and diabetes seem to lower with increased acculturation. The rate of adolescent pregnancy is twice as high among Hispanics born in the U.S. as those born outside of the U.S. Some have reported a positive correlation between rates of depression and acculturation, though the relationship between these two factors is still not clear. Similar findings about increased rates of mental illness and acculturation were reported from a study of Mexican-Americans in Fresno, California (Alderete et al., 1999). Canino et al. (1987) found similarly that Puerto Ricans living in New York had higher frequency of depression than those living on the island. Findings such as these raise the question, already noted by others such as Escobar (1998), about whether the process of acculturation appears to make the groups studied vulnerable to higher rates of health and mental health problems. As Vega and Alegria (2001) point out, generally the mental health of Hispanics is good, particularly for those living 13 years or less in the U.S. However, we do not understand the ways in which the Hispanic culture serves as a protective factor, and why it seems that acculturation places Hispanics at higher risk for mental health problems.

There is also a need to recognize that, because of the limited studies of the many cultures labeled Hispanic in the U.S., we are mainly drawing from knowledge based on Mexican-Americans and Puerto Ricans. We are still at an infancy stage in knowing about newer Mexican groups, Dominicans, Salvadorans, Columbians, Ecuadorians and others from both Central and South America. By not examining closely the issues of health disparities and service use for each of the myriad of Hispanics in the U.S., we can conclude with generalizations about the state of mental health and use of services which ultimately do not sufficiently clarify these issues, and thus do not help in making health and mental health care more responsive. It can easily be argued that to study all the specific cultures that are grouped under the Hispanic category in the U.S. is unrealistic, since it will be impossible to set up different services for each unique group. However, not looking further into the differences and similarities among groups, only risks leading us into a state of making generalizations, which may not only be incorrect, but which may actually create services that are not responsive and will be underutilized.

In addition to drawing on limited knowledge gained from a few Hispanic groups in the U.S., the Surgeon General's Supplement Report on Mental Health (2001), in examining delivery of mental health services for Hispanics, points to the fact that much of our current understanding of mental health status among Hispanics comes from epidemiological studies derived from prevalence rates according to the psychiatric entities outlined by the Diagnostic and Statistical Manual for Mental Disorders (DSM-IV). While such rates can be more easily compared to findings from other studies using the DSM-IV, there are some disadvantages to this method. The current diagnostic entities do not have sufficient flexibility to account for culturally patterned ways of expressing distress and disorders. Thus, the need for treatment may not be recognized or may be mislabeled. Another problem is that individuals may experience such distress to the point that it disrupts their daily life, but it may fall short of the diagnostic threshold.

In looking specifically at what is known about the incidence of mental health among Hispanics, studies consistently show that Hispanic youth seem to be particularly vulnerable. Psychiatric epidemiological studies of children and adolescents appear to suggest that Hispanic youth experience a significant number of mental health problems, and in most cases, more problems than Caucasian youth (U.S. Department of Health and Human Services, 2001). Glover and colleagues (1999), for example, found that Hispanic youth of Mexican descent in the southwest reported more anxiety-related problem behaviors than white students. Lequerica and Hermosa (1995) also found that 13% of Hispanic children screened for emotional-behavioral problems in pediatric outpatient settings scored in the clinical range on the Childhood Behavior Checklist (CBCL). Similarly, other studies (e.g., Achenbach et al., 1990; Chavez et al., 1994; Vazsonyi & Flannery, 1997) appear to indicate a greater frequency of delinquency behaviors among Hispanic youth in middle schools as compared to Caucasian youth.

In addition to anxiety and behavioral problems, depression is a serious mental health predicament affecting the psychosocial functioning and adjustment of Hispanic youth. Studies of depressive symptoms and disorders have revealed more psychosocial distress among Hispanic youth than Caucasian adolescents (USDHHS, 2001). This finding may be related to the fact that about 40% of African American and Hispanic youth live in poverty, often in chaotic urban settings that disrupt family life and add considerable stress to their already fragile psychological condition (Allen-Mears & Fraser, 2004; Canino & Spurlock, 1994). Nationally, for example, Roberts and Chen (1995) and Roberts and Sobhan (1992) have empirically noted that Hispanic children and adolescents report more depressive symptomatology than do Caucasian youth. In a later study that relied on a self-report measure of major depression, Roberts and colleagues (1997) found that Hispanic youth of Mexican descent attending middle school were found to have a significantly higher rate of depression than Caucasian youth at 12% versus 6%, respectively. These findings held constant even when level of psychosocial impairment and socio-demographic variables were taken into account.

BARRIERS TO MENTAL HEALTH SERVICES

Some of the specific barriers that have been cited for Hispanics in the use of mental health services are lack of knowledge about specialty mental health services, their mistrust and fear of treatment, the different cultural ideas about illness and health, differences in health seeking behaviors, lack of insurance, undocumented status with attendant fear of deportation, stigma felt in seeking care and discrimination by individuals and institutions (Echeverry, 1997; IOM, 2003). In addition, it has been documented that there is a serious shortage of racial and ethnic minorities represented in the mental health professions, and many who are serving the population are not adequately trained in the delivery of culturally competent care (IOM, 2003; Woodward et al., 1992).

In addition to these issues, geography also plays a role in accessibility of services. Hispanics, like all others, who live in rural areas of the U.S., are particularly underserved. It has been found that rural residents with mental health needs tend to seek care later in the progression of their disease, seek care with more disabling problems and therefore require more expensive and extensive services. Adding to the complexity of this issue is the fact that rural populations have lower income levels and lower rates of insurance than their urban counterparts. In addition, the shortage of mental health professionals is even more significant in rural areas (Wagenfeld et al., 1994). Many newer Hispanic groups settle in rural areas of the U.S. where they become migrant workers. In that Hispanics currently represent 71% of all seasonal agricultural workers and 95% of migrant farm workers in the U.S. (The National Alliance for Hispanic Health, 2001), it seems important to find ways to do better health and mental health outreach in these areas. As part of the USDHHS *Healthy People 2010*, there is special attention to the needs of the rural population and the need to better serve this population.

There have been many research efforts trying to tease out the reasons for health disparities. While health disparities are often associated with socio-economic differences, The Institute of Medicine (2003) and others (Dziekan & Okocha, 1993; Zea et al., 1997) whose research shows that racial and ethnic disparities remain, even after adjustments are made for socio-economic status.

Geiger (2003), in close review of the reasons for health disparities, cites several variables that have consistently been listed. Among them are socio-economic status (income, low level of education and unemployment), lifestyle choices and behavior, poor nutrition, different cultural beliefs about health and illness, and lack of access to health care, particularly lack of insurance. He also points to the racial and ethnic discrimination that might contribute to health disparities, not just in the way of persistent disadvantage faced by minorities, but in health care bias–at a conscious, unconscious, individual or institutional level.

The Institute of Medicine (2003) also found in their own review, that healthcare practitioner's attitudes, both conscious and unconscious, their prejudices, stereotypes and clinical uncertainty was one of the factors that contribute to healthcare disparities. In addition, when the patient-provider communication is hampered due to linguistic and cultural differences, no appropriate translator, and ambiguity of the interpretation of clinical data, less than ideal communication can result making for barriers in the clinical encounter and access to service.

Carrillo et al. (2001) have sought to understand issues of access and barriers to care for Hispanics on three different dimensions. Primary access is defined as having health insurance. Secondary access looks at those who have health insurance but face institutional or structural barriers and tertiary access looks at persons who have health insurance, have been able to make a medical appointment but face linguistic or cultural barriers during the medical appointment.

In closely examining primary access issues, we have seen that a large percentage of Hispanics in the U.S. do not have health insurance, a main reason being that employers do not provide health insurance. Almost 40% of Hispanics under the age of sixty-five have no health insurance, making them twice as likely as the rest of the U.S. population to have no coverage. Only 43% of Hispanics, compared to 73% of white non-Hispanics, are covered via their workplace (USDHHS, 2001, p. 142). Carrillo et al. (2001) cite that almost 9 million out of the 11 million Hispanics are in families where at least one person works, with this proportion being similar to other ethnic groups. However, if the worker is not a U.S. citizen, they are less likely than U.S. citizens to be insured by their employer. Many Hispanics are also employed in industries such as agriculture, domestic or construction work that may not cover workers, or they may work in smaller businesses that again do not provide coverage. The impact of this may be related to not seeing a doctor when sick, or going without medications or treatment. By not being covered, Hispanics often cannot take advantage of medical advances, particularly in the area of prevention and access to primary care, and thus, may tend to wait until there is a significant health problem to seek care from emergency rooms.

Looking at secondary access barriers to health care requires examining institutional, organizational or structural issues in the delivery of health care. Factors such as the lack of sufficient racial and ethnic diversity in the health care workforce and in the organization's administration, lack of trained Spanish speaking interpreters, lack of appropriate health education materials, bureaucratic and complicated intake procedures, long waits for appointments, and limited operating hours are among the barriers considered. Barriers such as these make it more difficult for Hispanics to seek quality health care. Even though some Hispanics may have health coverage, they may be less dissatisfied, have poor comprehension of health promotion and may not comply with recommendations given by well-intentioned clinicians (Echeverry, 1997). Unfortunately, at times, the client may be blamed for "non-compliance" when, in fact, the reasons may be a complex set of systemic problems.

Tertiary barriers to health care examine those variables that impede Hispanics who are insured and have been able to get a medical appointment but face significant barriers. Racial and ethnic discrimination, as seen in providers' bias, has been cited in the literature (Geiger, 2003). In keeping with this, the American Medical Association (AMA) in 1990 noted the black-white health disparities and acknowledged that "disparities in treatment decisions may reflect the existence of subconscious bias . . . The health care system, like all other elements of society, has not fully eradicated prejudice" (Council on Ethical and Judicial Affairs, 1990).

In examining factors for persons having difficulty accessing health care services, health care communication has recently been looked at as an area needing further understanding. Health promotion materials, even with English language materials, have been found to be a major problem, in that many people in need of care, have low literacy rates, may not understand what services are available, may not be able to access the care, or may not understand the communication from written materials, including prescriptions, informed consent forms or intake forms (USDHHS, 2003).

Health literacy relates to the capacity to obtain process and understand basic health information, enough for people to make the best decisions for themselves. Poor health literacy is therefore seen when persons cannot understand health materials, instructions on prescription bottles, informed consent forms, or the communication from a health care professional. People with poor health literacy have been reported as having poorer health outcomes, as being less likely to go for health screenings, as more likely to present at later stages of illness and as more likely to be hospitalized (USDHHS, 2003).

According to the 1993 National Adult Literacy Survey (NALS), which surveyed 26,000 adults representative of a wide range of backgrounds, only 17% of Americans have adequate literacy skills to understand and use health care information, with the remaining 83% of the population not having the adequate skills to understand health education materials. While in 2002 a more detailed study was carried out by NALS, the results are not yet available. The 1993 NALS survey did not look at health literacy; it did study factors that are related to understanding how persons seeking health care may or may not be able to understand health communication materials.

In the 1993 survey, NALS divided literacy and math tasks into five levels, with level 1 being least proficient and level 5 being most proficient. They found that 54% of Mexicans/Hispanics and 56% of Central and South Americans were at level 1, the least proficient level of literacy, compared to only 20% of the total population being at level 1. As most health related printed materials are written at a high school to college level, it would seem, given the levels reported by NALS, that most Hispanics are not likely to understand such materials, even if the client population is sufficiently fluent in English. The National Academy on an Aging Society 1988 report cites, as the consequences and costs of poor health literacy, less preventive care, more medication and treatment errors and lack of informed consent. In response to some of the problems, Pfizer through their program "Clear Health Communication Initiative," the Institute of Medicine and the American Medical Association have all started initiatives to help improve both written and spoken health communication, between professionals and consumers.

FUTURE DIRECTIONS

Closing the gap on health and mental health disparities will require sustained, multi-level efforts. While the situation is not hopeless, and things have slowly changed in some ways over the years, eliminating disparities is still far from our reach. There are several thoughts we would like to share as future directions, particularly as they pertain to Hispanics and mental health.

1–Making Care More Accessible

In looking to future directions, it is important to note that over half of the population seeking mental health care, not just the Hispanic population, receives treatment via primary care clinics. Perhaps it is time that we listen to what clients are telling us, as to where they think care needs to be delivered. However, there is also growing recognition that mental health problems go undiagnosed, untreated and under-treated in primary care settings. "A significant percent of patients in primary care show signs of depression, yet up to half go undetected and untreated" (New Freedom Commission on Mental Health, 2003, p. 60).

We need to consider not only the quality of our services, but also where we physically situate services, thus helping to make them more physically accessible. The education of those working in primary care settings also needs to be considered as well as provision of services that are delivered in non-fragmented ways, so that physicians can readily recognize depression and refer to a mental health specialist member of an in house team who can assess and treat the depression.

Seeking care in more naturalistic settings, such as through primary care centers, makes sense for many Hispanics, given the close association between the body and the mind in the culture. Hispanics have long been recognized to have a holistic understanding of health; even the language reflects the close ties between the body and the mind. *Estar sano* (to be healthy) usually denotes both health and mental health, without the split that can exist between both in our delivery of services. Emotional problems often manifest themselves in somatic complaints and physical illness, and also carries emotional aspects. Indeed, as chronic illnesses manifest themselves in the growing Hispanic aging population, we need to see how the physical and emotional are closely interwoven, and how illness affects not just the individual but the family as well. While most clinicians readily recognize this overlap, our service delivery is far from reflecting the close tie that exists between both aspects.

Fragmentation of care at different levels, from the financial to the existing split between the physical and emotional, has been cited by consumers as a problem in seeking care (IOM, 2003). Not only is there a general lack of understanding of mental health services and how to seek care, but, even for those seeking care, fragmentation is at the core of service delivery. This may point to the fact that, while the medical establishment has tended to divide the body from the mind, the client knows differently, and perhaps better. Care was not always as fragmented as it is today, and the body and mind split did not always exist.

The notion that one might get care for emotional distress or mental health problems in a more naturalistic environment such as a school, or a setting that is connected to the rest of a person's well being, like a primary care clinic, is not new. Rather, the problem may be that we have not sufficiently listened to what clients seem to be telling us for years; that is, the system of delivery perhaps had its own resistances to change to more client-centered, holistic care. In fact, the beginning of the social work profession was based in community settlement houses where care was provided in a holistic manner, attending to the psychological, biological and social/environmental aspects of families (Trattner, 1992). Throughout the years, there have been a multitude of programs based in the community in naturalistic settings that have been successful in reaching out to Hispanic children and adults. Yet, the core of much of mental health treatment continues to be provided in mental health clinics that are typically separate from the rest of health care and from the clients' natural environment, adding to the physical and psychological distance and to the stigma that can be felt.

There is also growing attention to the need to close the unnatural divide between health and mental health services. The USDHHS and the New Freedom Commission call for the need to have greater collaboration between these services in a seamless continuum from outreach to diagnosis to treatment of mental health for all populations. They call for an understanding of greater intersection between the mind and body that have been divided for too long.

Similarly, children's emotional and social problems often manifest themselves in the school setting. Schools are the largest referral source of children for mental health treatment, yet many never make it to the clinic. Why has there been such a split between a child's natural environment and where they are sent for help?

In trying to understand more clearly Puerto Rican mothers' perception of mental health problems in school-age children, and how to best make services accessible, Gonzalez-Vucci (1985) conducted a study of 40 Puerto Rican mothers in NYC. The study examined the mothers' understanding of mental health problems in school-aged children, according to vignettes presented to the mothers, and assessed their preferences as to where to seek treatment for children's problems.

Unless the problem was deemed "severe" by the mother's rating (such as a drug problem), mothers significantly preferred services for their children to be at the school and, as a second choice, at the pediatrician's clinic. These mothers chose the school site to be their primary preference, regardless of socio-economic status, acculturation level or even prior experience with mental health clinic services, suggesting an even stronger support for the conclusion. The mothers stated seeing the school as a "second home" to the children and a sense of familiarity and trust with the place and school personnel. The pediatrician was chosen as the second most preferred site to take child for mental health problems, with mothers again citing familiarity and trust of the doctor as reasons for their preference. Many mothers in this study cited unfamiliarity with mental health clinics. In fact, when asked, one said that mental health clinics were "a place where they take x-rays of your head," a place she did not want to take her child.

It is also interesting to note from this study discrepancies between how clinicians rated children's mental health problems as compared to the mothers' ratings. In one vignette, mothers are presented with a story of a six-year old boy who was having difficulty accepting the birth of his two-week old sister. For example, he tended to squeeze her a bit too hard when kissing her. The clinician's rated his problems as "mild," with some comment on his not needing any mental health treatment as he was just having a normal developmental reaction. However, the mothers rated his problem as "severe," noting that he was the older brother who needed to protect the younger baby sister. To the mothers, it was of concern that he was not following the expected cultural role for the male.

Likewise, clinicians rated a seven-year-old girl's several behavioral problems as "severe," with some concluding she might even be psychotic. By contrast, the mother's rated this girl's problems as "mild," saying that she was having delayed separation difficulties from her mother. This starts to point out the gap that can exist between clinicians' perceptions of behaviors and Puerto Rican mothers understanding, as well as how culture impacts a mother's perception of appropriate role behavior. Among the various implications of this study is that clinicians need to be culturally-competent in their care, recognize how persons have different understanding of behaviors; the study also points to the fact that, for some mothers, placing mental health services at the school might make most sense to them, and therefore may be less stigmatizing and perhaps result in better utilization of services.

The recent reports government reports (New Freedom Commission on Mental Health, 2003; USDHHS, 2001) on mental health emphasize the importance of school-based mental health settings. Evidence has been growing for years that school mental health programs help decrease truancy, discipline problems and early identification of emotional distress (Jennings, Pearson, & Harris, 2000). Again, this notion is not new, and certainly has been used, proven to be helpful and effective, yet it is very much underutilized.

2–Delivery of Care in a Culturally Competent Manner

While medical anthropologists and others such as Kleinman (1980) have been writing for years about how culture dictates a person's ways of being, our current services do not sufficiently reflect this knowledge. The gap between research and practice is indeed wide. The Institute of Medicine's report (2003) *Unequal Treatment* powerfully highlighted the findings on the necessity to educate healthcare professionals about delivery of care to patients from different cultures in the U.S. They found evidence that socio-cultural differences between clinicians and patients influenced communication and clinical decision-making. When these differences are not explored, appreciated, understood and communicated about in the clinical encounter, the result they found was patient dissatisfaction, poor adherence and poorer outcomes. At worst, failure to take into account differences can lead to generalizations and stereotypes of patients that can result in biased treatment.

Education to deliver culturally competent care seems to necessitate a three level approach. Clinicians need to *examine their attitudes, gain knowledge* about cultural ways of understanding and communicating about illness and *learn skills* about how to deliver care. While this has become clearer, we still lack evidence-based research to show what works best in education for cultural competence (IOM, 2003). Professional schools in healthcare have made great strides in calling for the need to educate students to be culturally competent, but few have reported on evidence based best practices, which has hampered the field from moving forward in such a critical area. "Despite the recognized importance of culturally relevant services, training curricula generally lack an adequate focus on developing cultural competence" (New Freedom Commission on Mental Health, 2003, p. 70).

Part of the problem has been the slow buy-in for the need for culturally competent services. There has been and continues to be great ambivalence about the need to do for care of this nature. Indeed, it was not until the present edition of the *Healthy People 2010* that elimination of health disparities was made a high priority goal.

Clearly much more research will need to be done to find best practices in the field of cultural competence and best practices for the education of healthcare professionals. The ongoing ambivalence faced at all levels responsible for healthcare, from government levels down to clinicians who do not recognize and/or accept the relevance of cultural competence will need to be tackled.

3–Need to Increase Work Force from Diverse Backgrounds

The recommendation made by the Institute of Medicine to "increase the proportion of underrepresented U.S. racial and ethnic minorities among health professionals" (IOM, 2003, pp. 186), comes from evidence about the benefits of having a larger pool of diverse practitioners delivering care. The intention is not necessarily that patients and clinicians be matched for race and ethnicity, but rather that by having increasing numbers of diverse clinicians in the work force, they can help to make overall delivery of services more responsive.

It has been shown that minority clinicians are more likely than their non-minority colleagues to see patients from minority backgrounds. It has also been seen that, when there is concordance of race and ethnicity, patients are more likely to be satisfied and to adhere to treatment recommendations (IOM, 2003).

These facts emphasize the importance, noted previously in the second point of this section, of the need for education to help clinicians become culturally competent. Perhaps patients would rather see clinicians from their own background, since the clinician may be more familiar with cultural norms, language and communication patterns. However, that is not to say that clinicians from non-minority backgrounds cannot become culturally competent and able to deliver effective services with which patients are satisfied.

Beyond these three points, our future efforts will need to include research that casts a wider net, and seeks to understand newer Hispanic immigrants. We cannot rely on older studies examining the Mexican-American and the Puerto Rican population, we need to recognize the rich diversity of groups called Hispanic and seek to understand the similarities and differences. Research about the newer groups can yield best practices that will impact our care delivery. We will also need to closely examine the policy issues, and understand the on-going ambivalence towards closing the gap on mental health disparities. To not be much further along in collecting base line data on Hispanic health by the year 2010, is to be wasting time and precious resources of a large part of the work force and the well being of the largest "minority" group in the U.S. None of these are easy goals to achieve. The choice is ours to make in how we choose to guide future policies, research and practice.

REFERENCES

Achenbach, T.M., Bird, H.R., Canino, G. and Phares, V. (1990). Epidemiological comparisons of Puerto Rican and U.S. mainland children: Parent, teacher, and self-reports. *Journal of the American Academy of Child and Adolescent Psychiatry*, 29 (1), 84-93.

Alderete, E., Vega, W.A., Kolody, B. and Aguilar-Gaxiola, S. (1999). Depressive symptomatology prevalence and psychological risk factors among Mexican migrant farmworkers in CA. *Journal of Community Psychology*, 27, 457-471.

Allen-Meares, P. and Fraser, M.W. (2004). *Intervention with children and adolescents: An interdisciplinary perspective*. New York: Allyn and Bacon.

Canino, G.J., Bird, H.R., Shrout, P.E., Rubio-Stipec, M., Bravo, M., Martinez, R., Sesman, M. and Guevara, L.M. (1987). The prevalence of specific psychiatric disorders in Puerto Rico. *Archives of General Psychiatry*, 44, 727-735.

Carillo, J.E., Trevino, F.M., Betancourt, J.R. and Coustasse, A. (2001). Latino access to health care: The role of insurance, managed care, and institutional barriers. In M. Aguirre-Molina, C. Molina and R. E. Zambrana (Eds.) *Health issues in the Latino Community.* San Francisco: CA.

Chavez, E.L., Oetting, E.R. and Swain, R.C. (1994). Dropout and delinquency: Mexican-American and Caucasian non-Hispanic youth. *Journal of Clinical Child Psychology*, 23, 47-55.

Council on Ethical and Judicial Affairs AMA. (1990). Black-White disparities in healthcare. *Journal of the American Medical Association*, 263, 2344-2346.

Dziekan, K.I. and Okocha, A.G. (1993). Accessibility of rehabilitation services: Comparisons by racial-ethnic status. *Rehabilitation Counseling Bulletin*, 36, 183-189.

Echeverry, J.J. (1997). Treatment barriers: Accessing and accepting professional help. In J. Garcia and M.C. Zea (Eds.) *Psychological interventions and research with Latino Populations.* Boston: Allyn and Bacon.

Escobar, J.I. (1998). Immigration and mental health: Why immigrants better off? *Archives of General Psychiatry*, 55, 781-782.

Geiger, H.J. (2003). Racial and ethnic disparities in diagnosis and treatment: A review of the Evidence and a consideration of causes. In Institute of Medicine (Eds.) Unequal Treatment Washington, DC: The National Academies Press.

Glover, S.H., Pumariega, A.J., Holzer, C.E., Wise, B.K. and Rodriguez, M. (1999). Anxiety Symptomatology in Mexican-American adolescents. *Journal of Family Studies*, 8 (1), 47-57.

Gonzalez-Vucci, G. (1985). Puerto Rican mothers' preferences for delivery of mental health Services. (unpublished dissertation) New York University.

Jennings, J., Pearson, G. and Harris, M. (2000). Implementing and improving school-based Mental health services in a large, urban school district. *Journal of School Health*, 70, 201-205.

Institute of Medicine (2003). *Unequal Treatment: Confronting racial and ethnic disparities in Healthcare.* Washington, DC: The National Academies Press.

Institute of Medicine (2001). *Crossing the quality chasm: A new health system for the 21st Century.* Washington DC: National Academy Press.

Kleinman, A. (1980). *Patients and healers in the context of culture: An exploration of the Borderland between Anthropology, medicine and psychiatry.* Berkeley: University of CA Press.

Lequerica, M. and Hermosa, B. (1995). Maternal reports of behavior problems in preschool Hispanic children: An exploratory study in preventive pediatrics. *Journal of the National Medical Association*, 87 (12), 861-868.

Mayberry, R., Mili, F. and Ofili, E. (2000). Racial and ethnic differences in access to medical Care. *Medical Care Research and Review*, 57 (1), 108-145.

Myrdal, G. (1944). *An American Dilemma.* New York: Harper & Brothers Publisher.

New Freedom Commission on Mental Health (2003). *Achieving the promise: Transforming Mental health care in America.* Rockville, MD: Department of Health and Human Services.

Roberts, R.E., Roberts, C.R. and Chen, R. (1997). Ethnic differences in levels of depression among adolescents. *American Journal of Community Psychology*, 25 (1), 95-110.

Roberts, R.E., Chen, Y.W. and Solovitz, B.L. (1995). Symptoms of DSM-III-R major depression Among Anglo, African, and Mexican American adolescents. *Journal of Affective Disorders*, 36 (1-2), 1-9.

Roberts, R.E. and Sobhan, M. (1992). Symptoms of depression in adolescence: A comparison of Anglo, African, and Hispanic Americans. *Journal of Youth and Adolescence*, 216 (6), 639-651.

The National Alliance for Hispanic Health (2001). *A primer for cultural proficiency: Towards quality health services for Hispanics.* Washington, DC: Estrella Press.

The National Alliance for Hispanic Health. (2002). *Healthy People 2010: Hispanic concerns go unanswered: Policy brief.* Washington, DC: Arthur.

Trattner, W.I. (1994). *From poor law to welfare state.* 5th Edition. New York: Macmillian.

U.S. Census Bureau. (2001). The Hispanic population: Census 2000 brief. Retrieved June 12, 2003, from www.census.gov/population/www/cen2000/briefs.html

U.S. Department of Health and Human Services. (1985). *Report on the Secretary's Task Force on Black and Minority Health: Vol. 2. Crosscutting issues in minority health.* Washington, DC: U.S. Government Printing Office.

U.S. Department of Health and Human Services (1999). *Mental Health: A report of the Surgeon General.* Rockville, MD: Author.

U.S. Department of Health and Human Services (2000). *Healthy People 2010: Understanding And improving health*, 2nd edition. Washington, DC: U.S. Government Printing Office.

U.S. Department of Health and Human Services (2001). *Mental health: Culture, race, and Ethnicity–A supplement to mental health: A report of the Surgeon General.* Rockville, MD: Author.

U.S. Department of Health and Human Services (2001). *Healthy people in healthy communities* Washington, DC: U.S. Government Printing Office.

U.S. Department of Health and Human Services (2003). *Communicating health: Priorities and Strategies for progress.* Washington, DC: U.S. Government Printing Office.

Vazsonyi, A.T. and Flannery, D.J. (1997). Early adolescent delinquent behaviors: Associations with family and school domains. *Journal of Early Adolescence*, 17 (3), 271-293.

Vega, W.A. and Alegria, M. (2001). Latino mental health and treatment in the United States. In M. Aguirre-Molina, C. Molina and R.E. Zambrana (Eds.) Health issues in the Latino Community. San Francisco: Jossey-Bass.

Vega, W.A. and Amaro, H. (2002). Latino Health: Good health, uncertain prognosis. In T. A. La Veist (Eds.) *Race, ethnicity and health: A public health reader.* San Francisco, CA: Jossey-Bass.

Vega, W.A., Kolody, B., Aguilar-Gaxiola, S., Alderate, E., Catalano, R. and Carveo-Anduaga, J. (1998). Lifetime prevalence of DSM-III-R psychiatric disorders among urban and rural Mexican Americans in California. *Archives of General Psychiatry*, 55, 771-778.

Vega, W.A., Kolody, B., Aguilar-Gaxiola, S. and Catalano, R. (1998). Gaps in service utilization by Mexican Americans with mental health problems. *American Journal of Psychiatry*, 156, 928-934.

Vega, W.A., Kolody, B., Aguilar-Gaxiola, S. and Catalano, R. (1999). Gaps in service utilization by Mexican-Americans with mental health problems. *American Journal of Psychiatry,*156, 928-934.

Wagenfeld, M.O., Murray, J.B., Mohatt, D.F. and De Bruyn, J.C. (1994). *Mental health and Rural America, 1980-1993: An overview and annotated bibliography.* NIH publication #94-3500. Washington, DC: DHHS, U.S. Public Health Service.

Woodward, A.M., Dwinell, A.D. and Arons, B.S. (1992). Barries to mental health care for Hispanic Americans: A literature review and discussion. *Journal of Mental Health Administration,* 19 (3), 224-236.

Zea, M.C., Belgrave, F.Z., Garcia, J.G. and Quezada, T. (1997). Socioeconomic and cultural factors in rehabilitation of Latinos with disabilities. In J. Garcia and M.C. Zea (Eds.) *Psychological interventions and research with Latino Populations.* Boston: Allyn and Bacon.

Chapter 2

Mental Health
in the Hispanic Immigrant Community:
An Overview

Peter J. Guarnaccia
Igda Martinez
Henry Acosta

SUMMARY. This chapter addresses the mental health status of Hispanics in the United States. The prevalence and incidence of mental health disorders among different Hispanic ethnic subgroups is examined. Patterns of mental health services utilization and barriers to mental health care are also reviewed. Research specific to best mental health practices with Hispanics is stressed. *[Article copies available for a fee from The Haworth Document Delivery Service: 1-800-HAWORTH. E-mail address: <docdelivery@haworthpress.com>*

Peter J. Guarnaccia, PhD, is Professor and Medical Anthropologist, Institute for Health, Health Care Policy and Aging Research, Rutgers, The State University of New Jersey.

Igda Martinez, BA, is Research Assistant, Center for State Health Policy, Rutgers, The State University of New Jersey.

Henry Acosta, MA, MSW, LSW, is Project Director, *Changing Minds, Advancing Mental Health for Hispanics.*

The writing of this chapter was made possible through funding for *Changing Minds, Advancing Mental Health for Hispanics* by the Eli Lilly and Company Foundation.

[Haworth co-indexing entry note]: "Mental Health in the Hispanic Immigrant Community: An Overview." Guarnaccia, Peter J., Igda Martinez, and Henry Acosta. Co-published simultaneously in *Journal of Immigrant & Refugee Services* (The Haworth Social Work Practice Press, an imprint of The Haworth Press, Inc.) Vol. 3, No. 1/2, 2005, pp. 21-46; and: *Mental Health Care for New Hispanic Immigrants: Innovative Approaches in Contemporary Clinical Practice* (ed: Manny J. González, and Gladys González-Ramos) The Haworth Social Work Practice Press, an imprint of The Haworth Press, Inc., 2005, pp. 21-46. Single or multiple copies of this article are available for a fee from The Haworth Document Delivery Service [1-800-HAWORTH, 9:00 a.m. - 5:00 p.m. (EST). E-mail address: docdelivery@haworthpress.com].

KEYWORDS. Hispanics, mental health services, mental health utilization

SOCIAL AND CULTURAL BACKGROUNDS OF LATINOS IN THE UNITED STATES

Latinos are a diverse cultural group; the use of a general label is both conceptually and practically inappropriate. Latino groups differ in national origin and history; in the particular social formations within each country that shape age, gender and class relationships; in the pressures within each country that have led to migration and the differing waves of migration; and the differing relationships with the United States through time that have affected how those migrants were received (Bean & Tienda, 1987; Melville, 1994; Molina & Aguirre-Molina, 1994; Molina, Aguirre-Molina & Zambrana, 2001; Portes & Bach, 1985; Grenier & Stepick, 1992). These features have not only created marked differences among the Latino groups, but considerable intra-cultural variation within groups as well. At the same time, changes within United States society and cultures have affected where migrants have gone, how they have been received, the opportunities they have had to develop themselves as individuals and groups, and the cultures of the United States with which the migrants have interacted (Pedraza-Bailey, 1985; Portes & Bach, 1985; Portes & Rumbaut, 1990; Portes & Stepick, 1993; Rogler, 1994). This overview focuses on the four largest Hispanic groups: Mexican Americans, Puerto Ricans, Cuban Americans and Dominicans.

Mexican Americans

People of Mexican origin make up the largest portion of Latinos in the U.S. Current population estimates are that there are 35.3 million Latinos in the United States and that 58.5% of them are of Mexican origin (U.S. Census Bureau, 2000). Mexican diversity results from differences in the generation that migrated, length of residence, legal status, social status, ethnic background, and reasons for migration. A significant portion of the Mexican origin population cannot be considered immigrants. This group, who often refer to themselves as *Hispanos*, established themselves in the southwestern states during the period of Spanish colonialism and were incorporated into the U.S. through colonial expansion of the U.S. At the same time, Mexicans overwhelmingly make up the largest group of new immigrants to the United States.

Wide variations exist in educational level, occupational status and income within the Mexican American community. Mexican Americans differ in their knowledge of and preference for use of Spanish and English. While some Mexican Americans actively work in agricultural occupations and make up the largest ethnic group among migrant farm laborers (Chavez, 1992), the overwhelming majority of Mexican Americans now work in the services and industrial sectors of large Southwest cities such as San Antonio and Los Angeles [the second largest Latino city in the Americas]. At the same time, Mexican Americans, because of their proximity to Mexico, their large communities throughout the Southwest, and their continued high rates of immigration, have a strong cultural base from which to reinforce their cultural identity.

Mexican migrants largely leave economically depressed rural areas, although a significant portion of migrants first go to cities within Mexico. Government policies since World War II that have favored the urban working class over rural populations, economic restructuring programs imposed on Mexico by international lending agencies, and development of an industrial zone in northern Mexico further facilitated by the NAFTA all have created an economic situation which disadvantages the rural sector. The severe poverty in rural areas has led to the exodus of those most able to organize and finance a trip to the U.S. and the first waves of migration include a preponderance of young men. The migration process has transformed local social structures at the same time as it has injected more cash and brought more consumer goods into the local economy in Mexico. The magnitude of the Mexican migration means that many migrants can get information and contacts for making the trip, and even with increased border patrols, the number of possible crossings make the trip relatively certain (Massey, 1987). The major stressors of the trip are its cost, dealing with unscrupulous *coyotes* and sometimes exploitative Mexican border police (Conover, 1987), and the fears and reality of apprehension by the U.S. border patrol (Cervantes et al., 1989).

Mexican immigrants have found large communities in the U.S. where they have large numbers of co-ethnics, frequent kin and people from their home communities to whom they can turn for aid. Given the poor state of the Mexican economy, Mexican immigrants find a considerable earnings differential, making frequent trips or prolonged stays very attractive. At the same time, the long hours of work, difficult working conditions, and isolation due to work schedules take their toll on immigrants' mental health. In particular, Mexican American farm workers are at particular risk of psychological problems from the combination of stressful work and living conditions, toxic exposures to pesticides with neurological effects, and substance abuse. Another high risk group are older Mexican women from lower social class backgrounds, particularly those who have experienced marital disruption and lost the economic and social support marriage continues to afford.

Second and later generation Mexican Americans are at higher risk for developing psychological disorders than new immigrants. By the second generation, issues such as ethnic discrimination, lack of job mobility, economic decline in the southwest, and frustrated social and material aspirations lead to a rise in psychological distress and disorder. Also, acculturation to the larger society increases the risk of developing substance abuse disorders, as both drugs and drug abuse are more prominent in the U.S. These social stressors create higher rates of disorder in second generation Mexican Americans (Vega et al., 1998).

There has been considerable debate about the under-utilization of mental health services by Mexican Americans. While the growth of large Mexican communities in major cities throughout the southwest has led to the development of bilingual/bicultural mental health services, access issues are still significant. Lack of health benefits in the jobs and industries where Mexican immigrants are concentrated, the high cost of services and relatively low wages, pressures of work, and legal status issues all act as barriers to service utilization. Within the community, the stigma of mental illness also acts as a barrier to help-seeking in the mental health sector. The extended family system, Catholic and Protestant churches active in the community, and folk sector resources such as *curanderos* and *espiritualistas* all provide alternative sources of support for those in distress (Casas & Keefe, 1978; Chavez & Torres, 1994). However, most recent research indicates that use of alternative resources does not deter formal mental health services use. Rather, structural barriers in gaining access to services and in the service system are more prominent (Treviño & Rendón, 1994). Ethnographic work suggests that those who use multiple sectors may be the most active help-seekers (Chavez & Torres, 1994).

Puerto Ricans

Puerto Ricans account for 10% of the mainland Latino population and number 3.4 million individuals. New York City (PMSA) is the largest mainland Puerto Rican city with over 800,000 Puerto Ricans (2000 census). However, this metropolitan area now accounts for less than a third of the mainland Puerto Rican population. While New York City was at one time the largest Puerto Rican city, the rates of return migration and growth of the metropolitan area now make the San Juan-Bayamon PMSA larger at 1.8 million people. Additionally, Chicago, Philadelphia, Newark (NJ), Hartford (CT) and a number of smaller industrial cities throughout New Jersey, Connecticut, Massachusetts and Eastern Pennsylvania all have sizable Puerto Rican communities.

Puerto Ricans experience the lowest socio-economic status of the major Latino groups. Puerto Ricans are United States citizens, ensuring free movement from the Island of Puerto Rico to the mainland. The United States government plays an active role in controlling the economy and the social life of the Island, including a major effort to industrialize the Island starting in 1947 and several attempts to make English the language of instruction in schools and of daily life. In cities like New York, at least a generation of Puerto Ricans have lived all of their lives on the mainland, many of whom use English as their primary language. While Puerto Ricans have easier access to social ties on the Island, their ties to an autonomous culture are more tenuous than other Latino groups, because Puerto Rican culture has been more dramatically transformed by almost a century of American dominance.

The major push to emigrate is the lack of employment on the Island due to long term economic policies which destroyed small-scale agriculture and encouraged high-technology industrial development which created few entry-level jobs for lower skill workers. For many years, the majority of those who left were poorer Puerto Ricans, many of whom migrated through the San Juan metropolitan area. The exodus of professionals seeking better job opportunities and salary structures in the U.S. increased in the 1970s and 80s, particularly to the urban northeast, but also to Florida and Texas.

Puerto Ricans have concentrated in the urban northeast in New York City and surrounding smaller urban centers. A declining employment base with the broad de-industrialization of the northeast and a rise in poorly paid and limited benefit jobs in the service sector are the major stressors Puerto Ricans face on the mainland. While there are significant Puerto Rican communities in several northeast cities, Puerto Ricans still experience high levels of discrimination. Urban renewal processes have continued to disrupt Puerto Rican communities so that social networks and community organizations have had to be rebuilt. These social transformations have pushed Puerto Ricans to the least desirable neighborhoods of New York City and to other urban centers in decline such as Bridgeport, CT and Reading, PA. At the same time, a recent study by Rivera-Batiz and Santiago (1994) indicates that Puerto Ricans born on the mainland are improving their economic status, although a significant proportion (30%) of mainland Puerto Ricans remain in poverty. It is not surprising that the group with the highest rate of psychological distress and disorder is the poorest segment of the population regardless of where they reside (Vera et al., 1991), as Puerto Ricans are exposed to the same politico-economic system on the mainland and on the Island. Better educated Puerto Ricans have done well on both the Island and mainland and their mental health profile resembles that of the general U.S. population (Canino et al., 1987).

Loss of cultural identity is a prominent issue related to Puerto Rican mental health (Flores, 1993). Decades of efforts to Americanize Puerto Rico have taken their toll on the sense of cultural autonomy Puerto Ricans experience relative to other Latino groups, who draw renewal from relatively intact home cultures. The development of a Nuyorican culture, while a vibrant force on the mainland, has led to discrimination when migrants return to Puerto Rico to live (Flores, 1993). The high rates of circular migration have created a sub-population who are "neither here nor there." While the implications of these issues are difficult to document in terms of specific mental health outcomes, they provide an important context for understanding the Puerto Rican migrant experience in comparison to that of other Latino immigrants.

Puerto Ricans are relatively high utilizers of health services, particularly the general medical sector. Access to a widespread public health system (until very recently) in Puerto Rico and eligibility for health benefits and federal health programs on the mainland make financial access issues less of a barrier than for other Latinos. Given the high use of the medical sector both in Puerto Rico and the mainland (Treviño & Rendón, 1994; Vera et al., 1991), recognition of mental health problems by primary care providers is a significant issue. Recognition of the idioms of *nervios* and *ataque de nervios* as important signs of psychological distress among many Puerto Ricans, especially those from working class and poor backgrounds, can contribute to recognition of psychosocial problems in primary care. At the same time, there are not simple translations of these idioms of distress into psychiatric diagnoses; rather they cut across a range of distress and disorder requiring careful assessment of both the symptoms and contexts of experience (American Psychiatric Association, 1994; Guarnaccia et al., 1993, 2003). Both *espiritismo* and *santeria* continue to flourish in Latino neighborhoods of New York City; their presence is more variable in smaller cities in the northeast where Puerto Ricans have spread. In epidemiological studies, the use of the folk sector appears limited for mental health problems; however, the long history of rich ethnographic reports of the use of these resources argue for the continued importance of this sector in mental health help-seeking (Garrison, 1977; Harwood, 1977; Koss-Chioino, 1992). Less studied, but potentially as important, is the role of both the Catholic and newer Protestant churches, their clergy, and lay organizations in support of people in psychological distress.

Cuban Americans

Cuban Americans, who are concentrated in Miami, Florida with secondary centers in other parts of Florida and the New York metropolitan area, make up

3.5% of the mainland Latino population, reflecting a relative decline in the Cuban population relative to the growth of other Latino groups in the U.S. (Census 2000).

While some Cubans migrated to the U.S. prior to the Cuban Revolution in 1960, the establishment of a large Cuban community post-dates the Revolution. Much of the intra-group diversity among Cubans mirrors the different waves of emigration from Cuba. The first migrants, who were more educated and professional, received considerable aid from the U.S. government to secure loans to start businesses and to transfer their professional credentials as doctors, lawyers, etc. (Pedraza-Bailey, 1985; Portes & Bach, 1985; Grenier & Stepick, 1992). As a group, Cubans have the highest levels of socioeconomic status of all Latino groups. They also have the highest rate of retention of Spanish as their primary language. Cubans have developed a vibrant ethnic enclave in Miami, where Cubans have become a dominant force in the political and cultural life of the city (Portes & Stepick, 1993).

Strong family ties that serve as the basis for bringing new family members to the U.S. and a strong ethnic enclave in Miami have made the migration for many Cubans less stressful than for some other Latino groups. U.S. government aid for the resettlement of Cubans has also been decisive in their successful adaptation (Grenier & Stepick, 1992). The relatively lower rates of distress and disorder in studies of Cuban mental health result in part from this aid, as well as from the higher pre-migration social status of Cuban immigrants. One of the most potent sources of emotional distress for Cuban immigrants is the separation of families between the U.S. and Cuba and the great difficulties of returning to Cuba for important family transitions. However, the epidemiological data does not provide evidence of the impact of this source of psychological distress in symptoms or disorder.

For Cubans, the development of a public and private medical and mental health care system staffed by and, in the case of the private sector, owned and operated by Cubans greatly facilitated access to services. At least in Miami, language barriers have been alleviated significantly. In the early phases of migration, financial access was guaranteed by the U.S. government's support package for Cuban refugees. The general high socioeconomic status of settled Cubans makes financial access unproblematic as well. Both *santeria* and *espiritismo* are active in the Latino communities of Miami, though their on-going role in mental health care is less well documented than for Puerto Ricans.

Dominicans

Migrants from the Dominican Republic comprise another important Latino group from the Caribbean (Garrison & Weiss, 1987; Grasmuck & Pessar, 1991). The 2000 Census counted approximately 750,000 Dominicans, accounting for 2% of the Latino population in the U.S. Dominicans have concentrated heavily in the New York metropolitan area, particularly in the neighborhood of Washington Heights. Dominicans come primarily from urban centers of the Dominican Republic, though there is also a significant rural population, many of whom step-migrated through the capital city of Santo Domingo.

The Dominican migration began after the assassination of the dictator Trujillo in 1961 and the U.S. occupation in 1965. The U.S. government facilitated the emigration of political dissidents as a political safety valve to reduce the level of protest against the U.S. occupation and the imposition of a pro-U.S. government (Grasmuck & Pessar, 1991). Dominican emigrants were often middle class individuals who had been frustrated by the lack of jobs and economic under-development in the Dominican Republic; more recent waves have come from the poorer sectors of Dominican society. The earlier waves of migrants created a base of legal residents who could bring relatives in a chain migration from the island. While earlier waves of Dominican migrants often experienced downward mobility in terms of job status, the wage differentials between New York and the Dominican Republic were so great that even less prestigious jobs provided the income for acquiring a middle class lifestyle which would be unattainable at home.

The Dominican experience is mixed in terms of the reasons for migrating. Extreme poverty in the Dominican Republic pushes many Dominicans to migrate. Like Cubans, some Dominicans fled political persecution, although from a right-wing rather than left-wing government. However, unlike Cubans, Dominican political refugees were not officially recognized and did not receive the same aid. Some Dominicans left the Dominican Republic because of high unemployment on their island. Many Dominicans come as a result of family reunification efforts as well. Those Dominicans who are undocumented suffer stress due to their precarious status in the U.S. The Dominican enclave in Washington Heights is quite large, but cannot match Miami in its social and economic development.

Sources of psychological distress prominently appear in both Dominicans' home communities and in the neighborhoods of New York City where they have settled. However, there is a need for systematic community studies of the mental health of the Dominican community in the U.S.

LATINO MENTAL HEALTH STATUS

Several major studies have examined the mental health of Latinos in the U.S. These include: the Hispanic Health and Nutrition Examination Survey [HHANES] (National Center for Health Statistics, 1985; Moscicki, Rae, Regier & Locke, 1987); the Los Angeles site of the NIMH Epidemiologic Catchment Area Program [ECA] (Regier, Meyer, Kramer, Robins, Blazer, Hough, Eaton & Locke, 1984; Karno, Hough, Burnham, Escobar, Timbers, Santana & Boyd, 1987); the Mexican American Prevalence and Services Study [MAPSS Study] (Vega, Kolody, Aguilar-Gaxiola, Alderete, Catalano & Caraveo-Anduaga, 1998); and studies in Puerto Rico of mental health and mental health service utilization (Canino, Bird, Shrout, Rubio-Stipec, Bravo, Martinez, Sesman & Guevara, 1987, 1990; Vera, Alegria, Freeman, Robles, Rios & Rios, 1991). The major instruments in these studies were the NIMH Center of Epidemiological Studies Depression Scale (CES-D), the NIMH Diagnostic Interview Schedule (DIS), and the Composite International Diagnostic Interview (CIDI). All of these studies included large samples of Mexican Americans. The HHANES included samples of Mexican Americans, Puerto Ricans and Cuban Americans. No major mental health studies have included Dominicans or some of the other rapidly growing Latino groups such as Colombians and Ecuadorians. The National Latino and Asian American Study [NLAAS] of the mental health of these rapidly growing ethnic groups will provide U.S. national data on the mental health of the Latino population. While again the focus will be on the three largest Latino groups, there will be a sample of "Other Latinos" that should include a sizeable sample of Dominicans.

Hispanic Health and Nutrition Examination Survey

The Hispanic Health and Nutrition Examination Survey [HHANES], a major national study developed to assess health conditions and health needs of the Latino population in the U.S., incorporated the CES-D and the depression section of the DIS. Using self-identified ethnicity, the researchers sampled 7,462 Mexican Americans in the five Southwestern states; 2,834 Puerto Ricans in the New York metropolitan area; and 1,357 Cubans in Miami, Florida. The age range of those included in the study was six months to 74 years of age. These data are, to date, the best available on the physical and mental health of large representative samples of Latinos in the U.S., though the NLAAS will finally provide an updated picture of the mental health of Latinos.

Compared to Cuban and Mexican-Americans, Puerto Ricans had much higher rates of both symptoms of depression and depression "cases" using the CES-D and a greater prevalence of Major Depressive Episode using the DIS.

Compared to Cuban and Mexican-Americans, Puerto Ricans had much higher rates of depression cases using the CES-D and a greater prevalence of Major Depressive Episode using the DIS. Using the standard CES-D caseness criteria of a score of 16 or higher, 28% of Puerto Ricans met this criteria compared to 13% of Mexicans and 10% of Cubans. CES-D scores are not equivalent to a diagnosis of depression; rather, they indicate the likelihood that the person would meet depression criteria. The prevalence of Major Depressive Episode was assessed using the depression module of the Diagnostic Interview Schedule. Puerto Ricans also had higher rates of Major Depressive Episode. Nine percent of Puerto Ricans met criteria for Major Depressive Episode in their lifetime, compared to 4% of Mexicans and Cubans (Moscicki et al. 1987). The higher rates of CES-D scores need to be interpreted with some caution. Analyses by Angel and Guarnaccia of the Hispanic HANES indicate consistent differences in the way Latinos conceptualized depression, as reflected in the conflation of poor physical health with psychological distress (Angel & Garnaccia, 1989) and differing factor structures of the CES-D from those found in other studies using these measures (Guarnaccia, Angel & Worobey, 1989).

The higher rates of CES-D scores need to be interpreted with some caution. Analyses by Angel and Guarnaccia of the Hispanic HANES indicate consistent differences in the way Latinos conceptualized depression, as reflected in the conflation of poor physical health with psychological distress (Angel & Guarnaccia, 1989) and differing factor structures of the CES-D from those found in other studies using these measures (Guarnaccia, Angel & Worobey, 1989).

The Los Angeles ECA Study

The Los Angeles site of the NIMH Epidemiologic Catchment Area Program [LA-ECA Study] over-sampled Mexican-Americans to allow for a comparison of their mental health with the Anglo-American sample there and in the other four sites of the national study. The researchers carefully translated the DIS into Spanish for this study (Karno et al., 1987). They collected information on migration history to compare the mental health of recent arrivals from Mexico to longer term residents and those born and raised in the U.S. The overall rates of psychiatric disorder for Mexican-Americans were strikingly similar to those of non-Latino Whites in Los Angeles and to respondents in the other ECA sites. For example, only 3% of Mexican Americans met criteria for Major Depression. This is slightly lower than Mexican Americans in the Hispanic HANES and much lower than the rates for Puerto Ricans. The researchers have argued that these results contradict earlier studies showing higher rates of distress for Mexican-Americans using symptom scales rather than diagnostic interviews. At the same time, a finding of the LA-ECA suggests that cultural factors and migration issues played important roles in response to the DIS.

In comparing native born Mexican-Americans to immigrants from Mexico, native born populations had higher rates of disorder (Burnham, Hough, Karno, Escobar & Telles, 1987). The immigrants might have been expected to experience greater stress due to migration and lower economic and educational levels. The authors argued that recent immigrants are often the hardiest members of their communities and experience a significant improvement in living conditions compared with their home communities in Mexico. Over time, longer term residents and U.S.-born Mexican-Americans respond with a sense of deprivation after they compare their status to the standards of living in the U.S. Furthermore, they found that acculturation to U. S. society increased the risks of developing both alcohol and drug abuse/dependence disorders; problems which were more prevalent in the non-Latino white population. These findings raise important questions about past studies comparing Latinos in their home countries and in the U.S. without carefully analyzing migration status and acculturation interactions. The study shows the varied impacts of immigration and acculturation processes across different psychiatric disorders, arguing for more complex and heterogeneous models of ethnicity and of the relation of migration to mental health. These findings were more strongly supported by the research of Vega and colleagues (1998) in the MAPSS Study.

Mexican American Prevalence and Services Study (MAPSS)

The MAPSS study was a large (3,000 adults) study of a Mexican origin sample in Fresno, California (Vega et al., 1998). It used a similar methodology to the National Co-Morbidity Study (Kessler et al., 1994). The study utilized a translated and culturally adapted version of the Composite International Diagnostic Interview (CIDI). The study particularly examined rates of mental illness by immigration status and rural/urban residence in Fresno country. The most important finding of this study was that as Mexican immigrants acculturated to U.S. society, their mental health worsened. Recent Mexican immigrants (those in the U.S. for 13 years or less) had almost half the rate of mental illnesses of Mexican Americans born in the U.S. That is, those people who were recently immigrated from Mexico had the lowest rates of mental illness, similar to those of Mexican nationals, while those who had been born in the U.S. had the highest rates of mental illness, similar to rates in the National Co-Morbidity Study. These findings were particularly true for alcohol and substance use disorders, though they cut across all the major depressive, anxiety and substance abuse disorders. This study suggests that longer residence in the U.S. is deleterious to the mental health of persons of Mexican origin.

Studies in Puerto Rico

Canino and colleagues (1987) designed and implemented the Puerto Rico Island Study at the same time as the ECA studies and used a parallel methodology. This study developed a stratified random sample for all of Puerto Rico. The researchers developed a translation of the DIS specifically for Puerto Rico (Bravo, Canino & Bird, 1987). The Puerto Rico Island Study, similar to the LA-ECA study, found that there were no major differences between the rates of mental disorder on the Island compared to the five Epidemiologic Catchment Area studies carried out on the mainland U.S. (Regier et al., 1984). Puerto Ricans in Puerto Rico were found to suffer from similar levels of mental disorder compared to people from a variety of ethnic and social class backgrounds on the mainland U.S. Similar to the LA-ECA study, 3% of Puerto Ricans in Puerto Rico met criteria for Major Depression.

The differences, reported earlier between Puerto Ricans and other Latinos in the HHANES using the DIS depression schedule and the CES-D, indicate more frequent disorder for Puerto Ricans living in the New York metropolitan area than those living in Puerto Rico. The significant social disadvantage experienced by Puerto Ricans in New York (compared to other ethnic groups in New York, to Puerto Ricans on the Island and to other Latino groups) indicate that social factors play a prominent role in the production of psychological distress. At the same time, many of those who migrate from Puerto Rico to Manhattan lack the human and social capital to succeed on the Island. Because of their lack of human and social capital, they encounter problems in New York as well. A more macro-social analysis argues that Puerto Ricans suffer both on the mainland and the Island from the same economic forces which marginalize low skill workers and which leave migration as one of the few economic options available. At this level, the same social stressors are causative of psychological distress in this group regardless of where they reside.

Research by Alegria and colleagues (Alegria et al., 1991) on the use of mental health services by poor Puerto Ricans on the Island provides an additional comparison. These researchers used the CES-D and DIS depression schedule in their study allowing for comparisons with the Hispanic HANES. By standardizing the comparison to poor populations both in Puerto Rico and New York, they found similar rates of depressive symptoms and diagnoses (Vera et al., 1998). These findings further strengthen the argument that poverty has a direct impact on psychological distress, regardless of where Puerto Ricans live.

Study of Cuban Refugees

An epidemiological study comparing Mariel Cuban and Haitian refugees from the early 1980s provides further insights into the effects of different characteristics of immigrants, their migration experience, and the nature of the sending and receiving contexts on their mental health and service utilization (Eaton & Garrison, 1992; Portes, Kyle & Eaton, 1992). These researchers argue that the comparison between these two groups of refugees who arrived in large numbers to Miami during the same period provide a valuable contrast in the contexts of the sending and receiving societies as well as characteristics of the refugees themselves. The researchers used a design similar to the Epidemiologic Catchment Area Studies to examine the mental health consequences of migration and they used a modified version of the DIS to measure Major Depressive Disorder, Anxiety Disorders, Alcohol Disorder, and a psychosis screen. Their sample included 452 Mariel Cubans and 500 Haitians who entered the U.S. during the same period. The Mariel Cubans experienced more disorder than the Haitians or than other Latino groups. Approximately 4% of Cubans met criteria for Major Depressive Disorder in the Hispanic HANES. Mariel Cubans had the highest rates of disorder of any of the comparison groups; with 8.3% meeting criteria for Major Depressive Disorder; this is parallel to the rates of Major Depression among Puerto Ricans in New York and poor Puerto Ricans on the Island.

Summary: Comparison of Rates of Disorder Across the Major Studies

Table 1 summarizes the data from these studies. The Mariel era Cubans generally had the highest rates of disorder, comparable to mainland Puerto Ricans in the Hispanic HANES. Mexicans and Cubans had higher rates of alcohol problems. The high rates of phobia should be interpreted with some caution. Many of the individuals in these studies were undocumented and had valid concerns about immigration issues. Their fears may have been less a sign of mental illness than a reflection of their precarious status in the U.S.

TABLE 1. Rates of Psychiatric Disorders Across Major Studies of Latino Mental Health

Diagnosis	LA-ECA Mexican Americans (1243)	Island Study Puerto Ricans (1513)	Mariel Cubans (452)	MAPSS (3012)
Major Depression	3.0%	3.0%	8.3%	9.0%
Panic Disorder	1.0	1.1	4.3	1.7
Phobia	7.3	6.3	15.6	7.4
Alcohol Disorders	5.3	2.7	6.0	3.3

[Sources: Canino et al., 1987; Karno et al., 1987; Portes et al., 1992; Vega et al., 1998]

National Latino and Asian American Study (NLAAS)

The NLAAS, which is being carried out in 2003, is the first nationally representative study of the mental health of Latinos and Asian Americans in the U.S. This study will include large samples of Puerto Rican, Mexican and Cuban subjects and a significant group of other Latinos. The NLAAS will also use the CIDI, culturally and linguistically adapted for different Latino groups. The NLAAS is designed to be parallel to two other national mental health studies: the follow-up to the National Co-Morbidity Study of the general U.S. population and a national study of the mental health of African Americans.

LATINO MENTAL HEALTH UTILIZATION

Latinos, particularly Mexican Americans, have very low rates of use of mental health services (Briones et al., 1990; Hough et al., 1987; Wells et al., 1987; Pescosolido et al., 1998; Vega et al., 1999; Peifer et al., 2000; Vega & Alegria, 2001; Vega et al., 2001; U.S. Department of Health and Human Services [USDHHS], 2001). Lack of health insurance and language barriers are the most commonly cited problems in Latino's utilization of mental health services. Immigrants are even less likely to use mental health services than U.S. born Latinos. When Latinos do seek help for mental health problems, they are more likely to do so in the general medical sector than in specialty mental health services.

The most robust findings of the underutilization of mental health services by Mexican-Americans come from the Los Angeles site of the Epidemiologic Catchment Area Study and from the MAPSS. In the LA-ECA Study, non-Hispanic whites were seven times more likely to use outpatient mental health services than Mexicans who spoke mostly Spanish. Mexicans who were less acculturated had very low use of any services that might address mental health problems, either in the specialty mental health sector or in general human services. Hospitalization rates were more similar across the groups, probably because hospitalizations involve more serious problems and because they are often initiated by third parties. Mexican Americans with a diagnosed mental disorder in the LA-ECA were half as likely as non-Hispanic whites to make a mental health visit.

The MAPSS study also found that Mexican Americans were low users of outpatient mental health services and identified even more striking differences between people of Mexican origin born in the U.S. and those born in Mexico. Overall, only a quarter of those with an identified DSM disorder sought mental health services. In looking within this group of those with a need for mental health care, immigrants used 40% of the services that Mexicans born in the

U.S. did. When Latinos seek help for mental health problems, they are more likely to seek help in general medical care settings than in specialty mental health care. This finding came out particularly strongly in the MAPSS for Mexican Americans, but was also true of the LA-ECA studies.

Studies among Puerto Ricans in Puerto Rico and Cubans in Miami provide a different picture for somewhat different reasons (Vega & Alegria, 2001; Burnette & Mui, 1999). Rates of utilization of outpatient mental health services in Puerto Rico are similar to findings among the general population in the U.S. Once barriers of language and culture are removed (and to some extent insurance status), Puerto Ricans in Puerto Rico seem to use similar amounts of mental health services as European Americans in the U.S. Cubans in Miami also have higher rates of utilization that Mexican Americans in California. The predictors of this utilization among Cuban Americans appear to include higher socio-economic status, special supports from government programs to provide health insurance, the presence of a large number of Cuban professionals, and the reproduction of the Cuban system of clinics in Miami. These studies indicate that for some Latinos, when cultural, linguistic and financial barriers are removed or lessened, rates of utilization of outpatient mental health services increase significantly.

LATINO MENTAL HEALTH BARRIERS

There are a wide range of barriers to seeking mental health care that have been identified in the Latino mental health literature (Hough et al., 1987; Pescosolido et al., 1998; Vega et al., 1999; Vega & Alegria, 2001; Vega et al., 2001; U.S. Department of Health and Human Services [USDHHS], 2001). These barriers can be organized into several dimensions: provider barriers, barriers in the service system, community-level barriers, barriers in the social networks of people in the community, and person-centered barriers. The most important system level barriers include lack of health insurance, language barriers, discrimination from the system and lack of information about services (especially in Spanish). Community centered barriers include the stigma of mental illness and the density of family and other support networks. Person-centered barriers include lack of recognition of mental health problems, stigma of mental illness, and a self-reliant attitude.

The major barriers to mental health service use among Latinos are lack of health insurance and citizenship/immigration status (USDHHS, 2001; Vega & Alegria, 2001). Thirty-seven percent of Latinos are uninsured; this is double the rate among European-Americans. A significant part of the reason for these high rates of lack of insurance is the low rates of provision of insurance by employers of Latinos. Forty-three percent of working Latinos received health insurance from their employers compared to 73% of European Americans.

Language barriers also figure prominently in Latino's use of mental health services (Vega & Alegria, 2001; Prieto et al., 2001; USDHHS, 2001). A large proportion of the Latino population in the U.S. speaks Spanish as their primary language, though this differs among the major Latino groups and across studies (in part, depending on how fully they include undocumented individuals). While some mental health programs, particularly in the Southwest and Northeast, have developed specific Latino-focused programs with large numbers of bilingual/bicultural mental health professional staff, the norm is that there are few, if any, bilingual/bicultural staff in mental health agencies and fewer masters and doctoral level professionals. The Miami area is somewhat of an exception given the large number of Cuban health and mental health professionals in the area. Thus, a major barrier for Spanish-speaking Latinos is the lack of providers who can offer mental health services in Spanish.

A related concern is discrimination against Latinos in mental health services. This discrimination results from both racial and cultural bias against Latinos. While there is more evidence of discrimination for medical conditions (Institute of Medicine, 2002), it is likely these factors operate in the mental health sector as well. Again, the issues differ for different Latino groups. Mexicans have been the focus of English only laws and propositions to limit their access to health and social services in California. Cubans in Miami experience less discrimination because of their dominance in the city, though the Mariel refugees appear to have been more stigmatized than earlier waves. Although Puerto Ricans have been citizens since the beginning of the last century, there is still considerable misunderstanding about their status. Some Latinos from the Caribbean are subjected to the double stigma of being Black and being Spanish speaking.

Lack of information about where to seek mental health services can also be a barrier, particularly lack of information in Spanish. Given that most mental health services are offered in separate settings from general medical services, it is not always clear even to the general population where to get these services.

The stigma of mental illness is particularly powerful as a barrier to seeking care. In particular, the label of *locura* or madness carries strong negative connotations. Someone who is *loco* is seen as severely mentally ill, potentially violent and incurable. Labeling a family member with mental illness as suffering from *nervios* serves to destigmatize that person's experience both in the family and the community (Jenkins, 1988a,b).

Latinos tend to have large family networks which are very important sources of social support and problem solving at times of crisis. The centrality of Latino families to social life is captured in the concept of *familismo*. However, it is important to recognize that many recently immigrated Latinos have fractured family systems as a result of the migration process. Those family members who are in the U.S. are often working long hours and have limited financial resources. Thus the reality of family support may be considerably less than the ideal. A potent source of potential stress is the gap between what Latinos expect in terms of family support and what is actually available to them. In the second generation, families are often fractured by the strains of acculturation and low socioeconomic status. Some researchers have argued that extended family support systems among Latinos may serve as a barrier to seeking mental health care because the resources are available to deal with the problem in the community and because problems like mental illness are dealt with in the privacy of the family. Pescolido and colleagues in Puerto Rico (1998) did find that larger support networks led to longer and more complex pathways to care. Puerto Ricans in Puerto Rico consulted a number of informal advisors about what to do and received support from these family members that kept them out of the mental health system unless the problem was quite severe. Less work has been done in the U.S. on these factors. For those without supports, third parties, such as police or emergency workers, may intervene to bring Latinos to care.

Recent research in Puerto Rico has highlighted a self-reliant attitude as a barrier to seeking care (Ortega & Alegria, 2002). People who felt they should be able to cope with mental health problems themselves were less likely to seek care, even when they reported symptoms indicative of mental illness. This self-reliant attitude was recently expressed in a focus group of Latinos in Spanish as *ponerse de su parte* (contributing one's part). This attitude reflects the feeling that one should be strong enough to cope with life's problems on their own and with the help of family and not need to depend on the mental health system.

LATINO MENTAL HEALTH BEST PRACTICES

There is a serious lack of research on best practices for mental health treatment of Latinos (Garcia & Zea, 1997; Rosenthal, 2000; USDHHS, 2001). The literature contains many suggestions about Latino values (such as *respeto, personalismo, familismo*) that should be incorporated into mental health treatment. Articles also suggest that therapies that are more directive rather than insight oriented and more family rather than individual focused will be more effective with Latinos. However, the research base for these assertions is lacking.

Given the significance of the Latino population in the United States, the reification of bits of stereotypic misinformation on practice with Latinos, and the paucity of rigorous practice outcome research, ascertaining which treatments are relevant and effective and what areas remain to be explored is an important endeavor. (Rosenthal 2000: 219)

This section will follow the stages of providing care to summarize best practices for serving Latinos (from a *Framework for Research on Hispanic Mental Health*, see Rogler, Malgady and Rodgriguez, 1989). These stages include engaging the client in care, assessment and diagnosis, and providing treatment to both the ill individual and the family. Organista (2000) and Lopez and colleagues (2002) address the engagement phase of providing treatment. It is at this stage, that Latino values such as *respeto* and *personalismo* are particularly important. The balancing of respect for the client (as evidenced in forms of address that are age and gender appropriate) with warmth and personal interest (that are more engaging than the typical therapist stance with Anglo American clients) are important for establishing an effective therapist-client relationship. The importance of these values in bringing Latino patients into care are so often repeated that they have significant face validity. While there have not been specific empirical tests of the impact of *respeto* and *personalismo* on engagement, the ethnic matching literature provides indirect evidence for this assertion. Latino clients who see Latino providers are more likely to return for follow-up visits, stay in care longer and are more satisfied with their care. Another critical factor in engagement is being able to communicate effectively with the client in her/his preferred language or combination of Spanish and English. Language use also affects diagnosis. Earlier research (Marcos, 1973a,b, 1976) indicated that bilingual Latinos tended to look more ill when interviewed in English than in Spanish.

In terms of assessment and diagnosis, there are issues at the level of recognition of symptoms and syndromes and issues related to the overall approach to clinical assessment. Issues of misdiagnosis of Latinos are an increasing area of concern. There are particular experiences of Latinos that frequently lead to misdiagnosis in the mental health system. Latinos tend to be very expressive of their physical and emotional pain, often through rich somatic idioms. This "somatization" of distress is misunderstood as either hypochondriasis or a lack of ability to express the psychological dimensions of emotional distress– neither of which is accurate (Angel & Guarnaccia, 1989; Escobar et al., 1987, 1989). Rather Latinos express depression and anxiety through a mix of physical and emotional complaints. Spiritual and religious experiences of visions (Guarnaccia et al., 1992), of hearing one's name called (often by a recently deceased relative) and perceiving presences (sometimes in the form of *celajes*) are relatively common and non-pathological experiences for some Latinos. These same symptoms get misinterpreted by mental health professionals as signs of psychosis. The cultural syndrome of *ataques de nervios* is a dramatic expression of deep sadness and distress among Caribbean Latinos. Some *ataques* that occur at culturally appropriate times such as at a funeral are culturally normative ways of expressing deep sadness; other *ataques* may signal the presence of an anxiety or depression disorder (Guarnaccia et al., 1989, 1993, 1996; Lewis-Fernandez, 1996; Liebowitz et al., 1994).

The systematic adaptation and testing of treatments for Latinos is in its beginning phases. The most work has been done in adapting Cognitive Behavioral Therapy for Latinos (Organista, 2000; Miranda & Munoz, 1994; Wells et al., 2000), especially for the treatment of depression. CBT manuals have been successfully translated and adapted for Latinos and treatments have been shown to be effective. Organista (2000) provides a detailed discussion of the cultural issues in adapting CBT for Latinos in San Francisco and provides details on how they carried out the adaptation. He notes that family themes are predominant in the kinds of problems Latinos bring to mental health treatment. In addition, issues of stress and acculturation, particularly differential rates of acculturation between children and parents, are prominent areas to work on in therapy. Activity schedules, particularly identifying pleasurable activities accessible to low income Latinos, need to be modified from standard CBT protocols. Assertiveness training aspects of CBT need to be adapted to the cultural styles and gender issues prominent among Latinos. Organista also provides useful strategies for approaching cognitive restructuring tasks with Latino clients. CBT has been shown to work well for Latinos. A key issue is insuring that Latinos are offered therapeutic interventions in conjunction with medications.

Family interventions have been proposed to be particularly effective for Latinos because of the strong value placed on family ties, often glossed in Spanish as *familismo*. Much of the work on evaluating the effectiveness of family interventions has been carried out by Szapocznik and colleagues (1997) in Miami with Cuban American families. The focus of this work has been on helping families deal with intergenerational conflicts and acculturative stresses faced by adolescents and has been shown to be quite effective.

The other area of family work has been done with Mexican American families with a relative with schizophrenia (Lopez et al., 2002). Much of this work has been informed by research on the role of expressed emotion in re-hospitalization of a family member with schizophrenia and on adaptation of mutli-family psychoeducational approaches. Jenkins (1988a,b) found that those Mexican Americans families who saw their family member's schizophrenia as a form of *nervios* were more likely to be more accepting of their relative's illness and less likely to express negative emotions towards their family member than European American families who identified the problem as mental illness. Lopez and colleagues (2002) found that expressed warmth was most protective for Mexican American relatives with schizophrenia, while lack of critical comments was most protective for European American family members. Lopez and colleagues (2002) identify a number of modifications which they recommend for developing culturally congruent family interventions for Latino families with a relative with schizophrenia. These adaptations include appropriate translation of family education materials both in terms of language and reading level; engaging families as helpers in improving outcomes for their ill relative; starting education about mental illness by eliciting families' understandings of the problem rather than with standard lectures on the medical model of mental illness; integrating biological and social dimensions of mental illness; and building supports for families and their ill relatives using naturally existing support systems in Latino communities rather than creating support systems among families who are strangers but share the problem of mental illness.

Ethnic matching, that is having Latino clients see Latino therapists, has been shown to be effective in some aspects of mental health treatment and for some Latino groups. The most comprehensive work has been done by Sue and colleagues (1991). Their work shows that when Latino patients are seen by Latino therapists who speak their language, they are more likely to return for follow up appointments and to remain in treatment over longer periods of time. This effect has mostly been studied for Mexican Americans in Los Angeles. The effects were most powerful for Spanish speaking clients. While the impacts on retention in these studies are clear, the effects of matching on outcomes are less strong, though part of the problem is identifying appropriate and sensitive outcome measures.

There are a number of issues surrounding medication treatment for Latinos with mental health problems. One area of concern is that even when Latinos get into care, they do not receive the most recent medications at therapeutic levels (Marin & Escobar, 2001; IOM, 2002). Latinos appear to have significant concerns about psychotropic medications. These include both the strength and the addictive potential of those medications. At the same time, psychotropic medications may be more easily available in Latino's home countries. Those migrants who have been treated for mental illness in their home countries may continue to receive medications from relatives there; this is an important area for assessment in initial visits with Latino clients. There is very limited information that some Latinos may respond differently to psychotropic medications, particularly anti-psychotics, than European Americans (Marin & Escobar, 2001; USDHHS, 2001). Latinos may metabolize some medications differently and be more sensitive to the side effects of medications than European Americans.

Overall, the studies show that once in treatment, Latinos benefit from it. The limited reviews of practice outcome research (Rosenthal, 2000; USDHHS, 2001; Wells et al., 2001) indicate that once Latinos are in care, they benefit greatly from both psychotherapeutic and medication interventions. The limited number of studies available show that the benefits accrue across several modalities, both those specifically adapted for Latinos and more standard approaches. The key issue appears to be getting Latinos into treatment and keeping them there. Getting them into treatment involves addressing the barriers discussed above. Providing bilingual/bicultural therapists to Latinos keeps them in care longer so that they can benefit from the range of modalities available.

CONCLUSION

Latino mental health research has matured significantly and we know considerably more than we did even a decade ago. At the same time there are major questions left to be answered. One key area is to better understand what protects some Latino groups from developing mental illness and puts others at significant risk. Even more important is to identify which Latino subgroups are most at risk and to try preventive interventions to intervene in the onset of disorder. There are also groups of Latinos whose numbers have expanded markedly in the last decade, but about whom we know little in terms of their mental health. These include Dominicans, Colombians, Ecuadorians, Peruvians and Salvadorans. While the NLAAS will provide an updated and more diverse profile of Latino mental health, it is not clear that sufficient samples of these new groups will be represented to provide details on their mental health. Focused, local studies may be more appropriate.

We also know a great deal about the barriers Latinos face in accessing mental health care. These barriers exist at the individual, community, service system, and broader societal levels. What we know much less about is how to effectively overcome these barriers. The next generation of services research needs to test strategies for effectively bringing Latinos in need into mental health treatment.

As the Surgeon General's report (USDHHS, 2001) notes, the area of treatment effectiveness is probably the least studied. While there have been important strides in the area of cognitive behavioral therapy for depression, other areas of treatment are much less developed. These include both therapeutic and medication interventions. There are significant opportunities for the growing number of Latino mental health professionals to make important contributions in these areas.

REFERENCES

Aguirre-Molina, M. & Molina, C. (1994). Latino populations: Who are they? In C. W. Molina & M. Aguirre-Molina (Eds.), *Latino health in the U.S.: A growing challenge* (pp. 3-22). Washington, DC: American Public Health Association.

Aguirre-Molina, M., Molina, C. & Zambrana, R. (Eds.) (2001). *Health Issues in the Latino Community.* San Francisco: Jossey-Bass.

Alegria, M. et al. (1991). Patterns of mental health utilization among island Puerto Rican poor. *American Journal of Public Health, 81,* 875-879.

Angel, R. & Guarnaccia, P.J. (1989). Mind, body and culture: Somatization among Hispanics. *Social Science and Medicine, 28,* 1229-1238.

Bean, F.D. & Tienda, M. (1987). *The Hispanic Population of the United States.* New York: Russell Sage Foundation.

Bravo, M., Canino, G.J. & Bird, H. (1987). El DIS en Español: su traducción y adaptación en Puerto Rico. *Acta Psiquiatrica Psicológica de America Latina, 33,* 27-42.

Briones, D.F., Heller, P.L., Chalfant, H.P., Roberts, A.E. et al. (1990). Socioeconomic status, ethnicity, psychological distress, and readiness to utilize a mental health facility. *American Journal of Psychiatry, 147,* 1333-1340.

Bureau of the Census. (2000). *U.S. Census 2000.* Washington, DC: Department of Commerce.

Burnette, D. & Mui, A.C. (1999). Physician utilization by Hispanic elderly persons: National perspective. *Medical Care, 37,* 362-374.

Burnham, M.A., Hough, R.L., Karno, M.,Escobar, J.J. & Telles, C.A. (1987). Acculturation and lifetime prevalence of psychiatric disorders among Mexican Americans in Los Angeles. *Journal of Health and Social Behavior, 28,* 89-102.

Canino, G.J., Bird, H.R., Shrout, P.E., Rubio-Stipec, M., Bravo, M., Martinez, R., Sesman, M. & Guevara, L.J. (1987). The prevalence of specific psychiatric disorders in Puerto Rico. *Archives of General Psychiatry, 44,* 727-735.

Canino, G.J., Bravo, M., Rubio-Stipec, M. & Woodbury, M. (1990). The impact of disaster on mental health: Prospective and retrospective analyses. *International Journal of Mental Health, 19,* 51-69.

Casas, J.M. & Keefe, S.E. (1978). *Family and mental health in the Mexican American community.* Monograph number seven. Los Angeles: Spanish Speaking Mental Health Research Center.

Cervantes, R.C., Salgado de Snyder, V.N. & Padilla, A.M. (1989). Posttraumatic stress in immigrants from Central America and Mexico. *Hospital and Community Psychiatry, 40,* 615-619.

Chavez, L.R. (1992). *Shadowed lives: Undocumented immigrants in American society.* Fort Worth, TX: Holt, Rhinehart and Winston.

Chavez, L.R. & Torres, V.M. (1994). The political economy of Latino health. In T. Weaver (Ed.), *Handbook of Hispanic cultures in the United States: Anthropology.* (pp. 226-243). Houston: Arte Público Press.

Conover, T. (1987). *Coyotes: A journey through the secret world of America's illegal aliens.* New York: Vintage Books.

Eaton, W.W. & Garrison, R. (1992). Mental health in Mariel Cubans and Haitian boat people. *International Migration Review, 26*, 1395-1415.

Escobar, J.I., Burnham, M.A., Karno, M., Forsythe, A. & Goulding, J.M. (1987). Somatization in the community. *Archives of General Psychiatry, 44*, 713-718.

Escobar, J.I., Rubio-Stipec, M., Canino, C. & Karno, M. (1989). Somatic Symptom Index (SSI): A new and abridged somatization construct. *Journal of Nervous and Mental Disease, 177*, 140-146.

Flores, J. (1993). *Divided borders: Essays on Puerto Rican identity.* Houston, TX: Arte Publico Press.

Garcia, J.G. & Zea, M.C. (Eds.). (1997). *Psychological Interventions and Research with Latino Latino Populations.* Boston: Allyn & Bacon.

Garrison, V. (1977). Doctor, espiritista or psychiatrist?: Health-seeking behavior in a Puerto Rican neighborhood of New York City. *Medical Anthropology, 1*, 65-180.

Garrison, V. & Weiss, C.I. (1987). Dominican family networks and United States immigration policy: A case study. In C.R. Sutton & E.M. Chaney (Eds.), *Caribbean life in New York City: Sociocultural dimensions* (pp. 236-254). New York: Center for Migration Studies of New York, Inc.

Grasmuck, S. & Pessar, D.P. (1991). *Between two islands: Dominican international migration.* Berkeley: University of California Press.

Grenier, G.J. & Stepick, A. (1992). *Miami now! Immigration, ethnicity and social change.* Gainesville, FL: University Press of Florida.

Guarnaccia, P.J., Angel, R. & Worobey, J.L. (1989a). The factor structure of the CES-D in the Hispanic Health and Nutrition Examination Survey: The influences of ethnicity, gender, and language. *Social Science and Medicine, 29*, 85-94.

Guarnaccia, P.J., DeLaCancela, V. & Carrillo, E. (1989b). The multiple meanings of *ataques de nervios* in the Latino community. *Medical Anthropology, 11*, 47-62.

Guarnaccia, P.J., Guevara-Ramos, L.M., Gonzales, G., Canino G.J. & Bird, H. (1992). Cross-cultural aspects of psychotic symptoms in Puerto Rico. *Research in Community and Mental Health, 7*, 99-110.

Guarnaccia, P.J. Canino, G. Rubio-Stipec, M. & Bravo, M. (1993). The prevalence of *ataque de nervios* in Puerto Rico: The role of culture in psychiatric epidemiology. *Journal of Nervous and Mental Disease, 181*, 157-165.

Guarnaccia, P.J., Rivera, M., Franco, F. & Neighbors, C. (1996). The experiences of *ataques de nervios*: Towards an anthropology of emotions in Puerto Rico. *Culture, Medicine and Psychiatry, 20*, 343-367.

Guarnaccia, P.J., Lewis-Fernandez, R. & Rivera Marano, M. (2003). Toward a Puerto Rican Popular Nosology: *Nervios* and *Ataques de Nervios. Culture, Medicine and Psychiatry.*

Harwood, A. (1977). *RX: Spiritist as needed.* New York: John Wiley & Sons.

Hough, R.L., Landsverk, J.A., Karno, M., Burnam, M.A. et al. (1987). Utilization of health and mental health services by Los Angeles Mexican Americans and non-Hispanic Whites. *Archives of General Psychiatry, 44*, 702-709.

Institute of Medicine. (2002). *Unequal Treatment: Confronting racial and ethnic disparities in treatment.* Washington, DC: The National Academies Press.

Jenkins, J.H. (1988a). Conceptions of schizophrenia as a problem of nerves: A cross-cultural comparison of Mexican-Americans and Anglo-Americans. *Social Science and Medicine, 26*, 1233-1244.

Jenkins, J.H. (1988b). Ethnopsychiatric interpretations of schizophrenic illness: The problem of *nervios* within Mexican-American families. *Culture, Medicine and Psychiatry, 12*, 303-331.

Karno, M., Hough, R.L., Burnham, M.A., Escobar, J.I., Timbers, D.M., Santana, F. & Boyd, J.H. (1987). Lifetime prevalence of specific psychiatric disorders among Mexican Americans and Non-Hispanic Whites in Los Angeles. *Archives of General Psychiatry, 44*, 695-701.

Kessler, R. McGonagle, K.A., Zhao, S. et al. (1994). Lifetime and 12-month prevalence of DSM-III-R psychiatric disorders in the United States: Results from the national comorbidity survey. *Archives of General Psychiatry, 51*, 9-19.

Koss-Chioino, J. (1992). *Women as healers, women as clients.* Boulder: Westview Press.

Lewis-Fernández, R. (1996). Diagnosis and treatment of *nervios* and *ataques* in a female Puerto Rican migrant. *Culture, Medicine and Psychiatry, 20*, 155-163.

Liebowitz, M.R. et al. (1994). Ataque de nervios and Panic Disorder. *American Journal of Psychiatry, 151*, 871-875.

Lopez, A.G. & Carrillo, E. (Eds.). (2001). *The Latino Psychiatric Patient: Assessment and Treatment.* Washington, DC: American Psychiatric Publishing, Inc.

Lopez, S.R., Kopelowicz, A. & Canive, J.M. (2002). Strategies in developing culturally congruent family interventions for schizophrenia: The case of Hispanics. In H.P. Lefley & D.L. Johnson (Eds.), *Family interventions in mental illness: International perspectives*, (pp. 61-90). Westport, CT, US: Praeger Publishers/Greenwood Publishing Group, Inc.

Marcos, L.R., Alpert, M., Urcuyo, L. & Kesselman, M. (1973a). The effect of interview language on the evaluation of psychopathology in Spanish-American schizophrenic patients. *American Journal of Psychiatry, 130*, 549-553.

Marcos, L.R., Urcuyo, L., Kesselman, M. & Alpert, M. (1973b). The language barrier in evaluating Spanish-American patients. *Archives of General Psychiatry, 29*, 655-659.

Marcos, L.R. (1976). Bilinguals in psychotherapy: Language as an emotional barrier. *American Journal of Psychotherapy, 30*, 552-560.

Marin, H. & Escobar, J.I. (2001). Special issues in the psychopharmacologic management of Hispanic Americans. *General Psychopharmacology, 35*, 197-222.

Massey, D., Alarion, R., Durand, J. & Gonzalez, H. (1987). *Return to Aztlan.* Berkeley: University of California Press.

Melville, M. (1994). "Hispanic" ethnicity, race and class. In T. Weaver (Ed.), *Handbook of Hispanic cultures in the United States: Anthropology.* (pp. 85-106). Houston: Arte Público Press.

Moscicki, E.K., Rae D., Regier D.A. & Locke, B.Z. (1987). The Hispanic Health and Nutrition Examination Survey: Depression among Mexican-Americans, Cuban-Americans, Puerto Ricans. In M. Gaviria & J.D. Arana (Eds.), *Health and Behavior: Research Agenda for Hispanics.* Chicago: University of Chicago at Illinois.

National Center for Health Statistics. (1985). *Plan and operation of the Hispanic Health and Nutrition Examination Survey 1982-1984.* Washington, DC: U.S. Government Printing Office.

Organista, K.C. (2000). Latinos. In J.R. White & A.S. Freeman (Eds.), *Cognitive-behavioral group therapy: For specific problems and populations* (pp. 281-303). Washington, DC, US: American Psychological Association.

Ortega, A. & Alegria, M. (2002). Self-reliance, mental health need and use of mental healthcare among island Puerto Ricans. *Mental Health Services Research, 4,* 131-140.

Pedraza-Bailey, S. (1985). *Political and economic migrants in American: Cubans and Mexicans.* Austin: University of Texas Press.

Peifer, K., Hu, T. & Vega, W. (2000). Help seeking by persons of Mexican origin with functional impairments. *Psychiatric Services, 51,* 1293-1298.

Pescosolido, B.A., Wright, E.R., Alegria, M. & Vera, M. (1998). Social networks and patterns of use among the poor with mental health problems in Puerto Rico. *Medical Care, 36,* 1057-1072.

Portes, A. & Bach, R.L. (1985). *Latin journey: Cuban and Mexican immigrants in the United States.* Berkeley: University of California Press.

Portes, A. & Rumbaut, R.G. (1990). *Immigrant America.* Los Angeles: University of California Press.

Portes, A., Kyle, D. & Eaton, W.W. (1992). Mental illness and help-seeking behavior among Mariel Cuban and Haitian refugees in South Florida. *Journal of Health and Social Behavior, 33,* 283-298.

Portes, A. & Stepick, A. (1993). *City on the edge: The transformation of Miami.* Berkeley: University of California.

Prieto, L., McNeill, B.W., Walls, R.G. & Gomez, S.P. (2001). Chicanas/os and mental health services: An overview of utilization, counselor preference, and assessment issues. *Counseling Psychologist, 29,* 18-54.

Regier, D.A., Myers, J.K., Kramer, M., Robins, L.N., Blazer, D.G., Hough, R.L., Eaton, W.W. & Locke, B.Z. (1984). The NIMH Epidemiologic Catchment Area Program. *Archives of General Psychiatry, 41,* 934-941.

Rivera-Batiz, F.L. & Santiago, C. (1994). *Puerto Ricans in the United States: A changing reality.* Washington, DC: The National Puerto Rican Coalition.

Rogler, L.H. (1994). International migrations: A framework for directing research. *American Psychologist, 49,* 701-708.

Rogler, L.H., Malgady, R.G. & Rodriguez, O. (1989). *Hispanics and mental health: A framework for research.* Malabar: Robert E. Krieger Publishing Company.

Rosenthal, C. (2000). Latino practice outcome research: A review of the literature. *Smith College Studies in Social Work, 70,* 217-238.

Sue, S. et al. (1991). Community Mental Health Services for ethnic minority groups: A test of the cultural responsiveness hypothesis. *Journal of Consulting and Clinical Psychology,* 59, 533-540.

Szapocznik, J. & Kurtines, W. (1980). Acculturation, biculturalism, and adjustment among Cuban Americans. In A.M. Padilla (Ed.), *Acculturation: Theory, models and some new findings* (pp. 139-159). Boulder: Westview Press.

Treviño, F. & Rendón, M. (1994). Mental illness/mental health issues. In C. W. Molina & M. Aguirre-Molina (Eds.), *Latino health in the U.S.: A growing challenge* (pp. 447-475). Washington, DC: American Public Health Association.

U.S. Department of Health and Human Services. (2001). Mental Health: Culture, Race, and Ethnicity–A Supplement to Mental Health: A Report of the Surgeon General. Rockville, MD: U.S. Department of Health and Human Services, Public Health Services, Office of the Surgeon General.

Vega, W.A., Kolody, B. & Valle, J.R. (1987). Migration and mental health: An empirical test of depression risk factors among immigrant Mexican women. *International Migration Review, 21*, 512-529.

Vega, W.A., Kolody, B., Aguilar-Gaxiola, S. Alderate, E., Catalano, R. & Carveo-Anduaga, J. (1998). Lifetime prevalence of DSM-III-R psychiatric disorders among urban and rural Mexican Americans in California. *Archives of General Psychiatry, 55*, 771-778.

Vega, W. A., Kolody B., Aguilar-Gaxiola, S. & Catalano, R. (1999). Gaps in service utilization by Mexican Americans with mental health problems. *American Journal of Psychiatry, 156*, 928-934.

Vega, W.A., Kolody, B. & Aguilar-Gaxiola, S. (1991). Help-seeking for mental health problems among Mexican Americans. *Journal of Immigrant Health, 3*, 133-140.

Vega, W.A. & Alegria, M. (2001). Latino Mental Health and Treatment in the United States. In: Aguirre-Molina, M., Molina C. & Zambrana, R. (Eds.), *Health Issues in the Latino Community*. San Francisco: Jossey-Bass, pp. 179-208.

Vera, M., Alegria, M., Freeman, D., Robles, R., Rios, R. & Rios, C. (1991). Depressive symptoms among Puerto Ricans: Island poor compared with residents of the New York City area. *American Journal of Epidemiology, 134*, 502-510.

Wells, K.B., Hough, R.L., Golding, J.M., Burnam, M.A. et al. (1987). Which Mexican-Americans underutilize health services? *American Journal of Psychiatry, 144*, 918-922.

Chapter 3

Mental Health Care
of Hispanic Immigrant Children:
A School-Based Approach

Gladys González-Ramos
Manny J. González

SUMMARY. This chapter addresses the mental health care of Hispanic immigrant children within a school-based context. The school system is presented as a natural support agent that is psychologically, culturally and geographically accessible for the delivery of culturally competent mental health services. The development of a multifaceted New York City public school-based program created, by the first author of this chapter, in response to the psychosocial needs of Hispanic immigrant children is discussed as a viable approach that may be used in the provision of ethnic-sensitive mental health care. *[Article copies available for a fee from The Haworth Document Delivery Service: 1-800-HAWORTH. E-mail address: <docdelivery@haworthpress.com> Website: <http://www.HaworthPress.com> © 2005 by The Haworth Press, Inc. All rights reserved.]*

Gladys González-Ramos, PhD, is Associate Professor, New York University, School of Social Work.

Manny J. González, DSW, is Associate Professor, Fordham University, Graduate School of Social Service.

[Haworth co-indexing entry note]: "Mental Health Care of Hispanic Immigrant Children: A School-Based Approach." González-Ramos, Gladys, and Manny J. González. Co-published simultaneously in *Journal of Immigrant & Refugee Services* (The Haworth Social Work Practice Press, an imprint of The Haworth Press, Inc.) Vol. 3, No. 1/2, 2005, pp. 47-58; and: *Mental Health Care for New Hispanic Immigrants: Innovative Approaches in Contemporary Clinical Practice* (ed: Manny J. González, and Gladys González-Ramos) The Haworth Social Work Practice Press, an imprint of The Haworth Press, Inc., 2005, pp. 47-58 . Single or multiple copies of this article are available for a fee from The Haworth Document Delivery Service [1-800-HAWORTH, 9:00 a.m. - 5:00 p.m. (EST). E-mail address: docdelivery@haworthpress.com].

KEYWORDS. Children, Hispanics, immigrants, mental health, schools

INTRODUCTION

When immigrant parents dream of bringing their children to the United States, they usually do so with the intention that their quality of life will improve. They flee political persecution, extreme economic desperation and look to the "land of opportunity," with the expectation that living in a democratic society will result in educational and employment opportunities. On arrival to the United States, however, the reality of sheer survival often becomes paramount. Finding housing and some type of employment become primary goals. Igoa (1995) has observed that, "In low-income immigrant families, it may be difficult for parents to nurture their children because the uprooting experience itself saps the parents' energy" (p. 40). The children in the family often are left to cope on their own, with the hope that they both (parent and child) learn English and acculturate as quickly as possible. The multiple losses the children and their families have gone through, the fears, confusion, sadness, and alienation they may feel often are left unattended. Urrabazo (2000), for example, has noted the multiple traumas that undocumented Hispanic families have been exposed to in their attempt to cross the border into the United States: robbery, sexual assault, and physical and psychological torture. Yet it is these losses and "unspoken" traumas that immigrant children carry with them into their new schools and that teachers, educational administrators, and school mental health personnel (e.g., guidance counselors, school social workers, school psychologists) are confronted with.

Various biopsychosocial factors have been identified as placing children at risk for the development of mental health problems (U.S. Department of Health and Human Services, 1999, 2001). These factors can be grouped into three categories and include health factors (e.g., poor nutrition, limited access to pediatric care), family-social variables (e.g., substandard housing, parental unemployment) and educational variables (e.g., overcrowded schools, high level of dropout rate within ethnic minority groups). Hispanic immigrant children and adolescents must deal with the toxic effects of these identified factors on a continual basis. Yet, when we consider that the school is probably, for most children, the second most significant agent, after the family in the formation of positive self-esteem, optimal mental health, personality and adaptive coping mechanisms (Bronfenbrenner, 1979; Dryfoos, 1994; González-Ramos, 1990; Winters Glasgow, 1983), intervention directed at the mental health concerns of Hispanic immigrant children in school systems throughout the country has not been sufficient (McDonnell and Hill, 1993). Therefore, the primary aim of this chapter is to address the mental health care of Hispanic immigrant children within a school-based context. The school system is presented as a natural support agent that is psychologically, culturally and geographically accessible for the delivery of culturally competent mental health services. The development of a multifaceted New York City public school-based program created, by the first author of this chapter, in response to the mental health needs of Hispanic immigrant children is discussed as a viable approach that may be used in the provision of ethnic-sensitive mental health care.

HISPANIC IMMIGRANT CHILDREN: DEMOGRAPHIC OVERVIEW

Immigrant students enrolled in public school education constitute an ever-increasing proportion of the school-age population, particularly at the secondary high school level (Lucas, 1996). Spenser and Dornbush (1990) have noted that for immigrant students at the high school level, the difficult transitions of adolescence combined with the challenge of learning to express thoughts, develop a personality, and master academic content in a language they are still learning can be emotionally overwhelming. For Hispanic immigrants, the number of children and adolescents in public schools in the United States is steadily increasing. Presently, close to 33% of the Hispanic population is under age 18. Hispanic students comprise 15% of K-12 students overall, a proportion projected to increase to 25% by 2025 (Institute for Urban and Minority Education, 2001). Even though, Hispanic students have educational aspirations, their academic attainment is consistently lower than that of other students (The White House Initiative on Educational Excellence for Hispanic Americans, 1999). The literature (e.g., Glenn, 1992; McDonnell and Hill, 1993; Ogbu, 1991; Suarez-Orozco and Marcelo, 1995) appears to suggest that the educational achievement of Hispanic students is affected by a variety of factors, including poverty, lack of participation in preschool or head-start programs, attendance at poor quality elementary, middle and high schools, and for the recently arrived Hispanic immigrant child, limited proficiency in the English language.

Thirty-nine percent of Hispanics in the United States are immigrants (Therrien and Ramirez, 2000). Eighteen percent of Hispanic youth (children and adolescents) are immigrants, half (48%) were born in the United States to at least one foreign-born parent, and one-third (35%) are the offspring of U.S. born parents (Jamieson, Curry and Martinez, 2001). Among Hispanic families parental educational attainment increases with generation as does mean family income. Third generation Hispanic parents, however, have less education and lower incomes as compared to non-Hispanic whites (Kao, 1999). Because millions of adult Hispanic immigrants will little education have arrived in recent decades to the United States, Hispanics are the least well educated segment of the American population (Vernez and Abrahamse, 1996). High school completion is one of the greatest educational problems confronting Hispanic youth. Statistics (U.S. Department of Education, 2002) suggest that about 15% of native Hispanic adolescents drop out of high school compared with 44% of immigrant Hispanic youth. For some Hispanic immigrant youth this reflects their experience in the United States school systems, but many others, especially older Hispanic immigrant adolescents, never enroll in school because they immediately seek some type of employment in order to assist their families in economic survival.

As mentioned earlier in this chapter, the Hispanic youth (children and adolescents) immigrant population is progressively increasing in the United States and in major urban cities like New York. In the United States, Hispanic children are now the second largest group after white non-Hispanic children (González-Ramos and Sanchez-Nester, 2001). Over 6 million Hispanic students, of approximately 50 million students, are in grades K to 12 in the United States schools. It is estimated that nearly 2 million of these students speak Spanish as their primary language and are not fluent in English. At a time when the size of the general school population has remained essentially stable, the number of limited English proficiency (LEP) students (three-fourths of whom are Spanish speaking) grew by 85 percent between 1985 and 1992 (Goldenberg, 1996). Hispanics represent 27 percent of the total New York City population (Center for Puerto Rican Studies, 2000). The Caribbean continues to account for the largest number of immigrants, representing 29 percent of all immigrants settling in New York City. Within the Caribbean most immigrants emigrated from the Dominican Republic (New York City Department of City Planning, 1999). In the City of New York, Hispanic children make up 37.8 percent of the elementary public school population. This percentage is in comparison to 35.7 percent for black children and 17.4 percent for white non-Hispanic children attending elementary public schools (Board of Education of the City of New York, 1996).

HISPANIC IMMIGRANT CHILDREN AND SCHOOL-BASED MENTAL HEALTH SERVICES

School-based mental health programs have the best potential for the delivery of preventive mental health services with minimal risk of stigmatization (i.e., parental fear or concern of having a child labeled as mentally ill) (Dryfoos, 1994). Just like school-based health clinics (or school-based health centers) have been instrumental in addressing important pediatric health concerns, such as child maltreatment, asthma, teen pregnancy, violence, and childhood depression (Hutchinson and Poole, 1998), school-based mental health services may be also be influential in reducing behavioral problems and increasing the adaptive coping capacities of Hispanic immigrant children. The School Development Program of the Yale Child Study Center (Comer, 1980) and Project Self-Esteem in California (McDaniel and Bielin, 1990) are excellent examples of how school mental health services can make it possible for children from urban poor and vulnerable backgrounds–like Hispanic immigrant children–to achieve high levels of education and gain the necessary problem-solving skills required for adaptive living. School-based mental health services further reduce the fear of stigmatization by encouraging parental involvement in the treatment of children and by empowering parents to become agents of change on behalf of their children. The empowerment model in mental health practice promotes interventions that will reduce patient's "powerlessness stemming from the experience of negative valuations and discrimination" (Solomon, 1982, p. 89).

Although some attempts have been made at a national and local level (Dryfoos, 1994; González-Ramos, 1990; González-Ramos and Nester-Sanchez, 2001; Igoa, 1995; Suarez-Orozco and Suarez-Orozco, 2001) to address the mental health needs of Hispanic immigrant children within a school context, knowledge of these children's experiences in adjusting to the mainland United States, their unique issues, the socio-emotional tensions they face, and the impact of immigration on their educational experiences have not been sufficiently addressed. Even though migration and immigration do not necessarily result in maladjusted behaviors (indeed, some immigrant children have been identified as "invulnerable"), there are many children who are susceptible to the multiple pressures that are typical of being an immigrant. Many researchers (Igoa, 1995; Pawliuk et al., 1996; Short and Johnson, 1997; Thomas, 1992) agree that there is considerable acculturation stress associated with migration, which is a confusing and disconcerting time as the new immigrant family seeks to resettle into a new environment and new set of cultural values. Such culture shock or migration readjustment experiences often are misunderstood, or worse, not even recognized by service professionals and educators. Researchers (Rousseau, Drapeau and Corin, 1996) have found that the major negative effects of stress from migration experiences on these children are often expressed in the schools, especially by behavioral problems and identity conflicts. Because leaving one's homeland often brings about a disruption in support networks–friends, extended family, and religious and social institutions–immigrants often deal with a tremendous amount of stress without the buffer of these supports. Compounding matters, it has been found that immigrant and refugee children and their families tend to underuse health and social services (Kopala, Esquivel and

Baptiste, 1994). The school system, as one of the main institutions that comes in contact with these children, is an ideal setting in which to identify and provide early assistance to immigrant children and their families.

In view of the many areas of potential stress for Hispanic immigrant children and their families, mental health clinicians need to look at how such families cope with overwhelming pressures. The literature shows repeatedly that Hispanic families often underutilize mental health services (Gil, 1980; González, 2002). Rogler et al. (1983), in their study of help-seeking behavior, suggested two theories to explain underutilization by Hispanic families: the alternate resource theory and the barrier theory.

The alternate resource theory of Rogler et al. (1983) suggests that the Hispanic family uses familiar social organizations within its cultural milieu to deal with its problems. The extended family and folk healers are two of the most important resources cited. However, as has been noted, the extended family often is disrupted in the process of migration. In addition, folk healers rarely are used as substitutes for mental health professionals and even may be used in addition to conventional services.

Another possible explanation is the barrier theory (Rogler et al., 1983), which faults the service delivery system for lack of cultural understanding and sensitivity. Barriers include the lack of Spanish-speaking, culturally aware mental health clinicians, Spanish-speaking receptionists, and trained translators. In addition, administrative forms are often not translated into Spanish, and services are costly and geographically inaccessible.

To better comprehend Hispanic mothers' understanding of their children's mental health problems and their preferences for the delivery of culturally sensitive services, the first author of this chapter (González-Vucci [Ramos], 1985) conducted a study of Puerto Rican mothers. The goal of the study was to examine the view and preferences of the consumers of services.

González-Vucci [Ramos] (1985) carried out in-depth structured interviews with 40 Puerto Rican mothers, most of whom were of low socioeconomic status. They were given 10 vignettes of Puerto Rican boys and girls ages 6 to 12 that posed a range of learning difficulties and behavioral problems and were asked numerous questions about how they would handle the problems. Regarding preference for site of service, the mothers overwhelmingly chose the school setting, regardless of whether they or their children had previously gone to a traditional mental health clinic. Contrary to the literature, mothers did not choose a spiritualist as the person from whom they would seek help with the child's problem. It is possible that Hispanics use folk healers primarily for adult problems. The mothers rated a pediatric clinic as the second most preferred place to address concerns about their children.

In view of the Hispanic family's value of respect and deference to authority, their view of the school and teacher as in loco parentis, and the school's easy accessibility, it is understandable that the school is preferable to a traditional mental health service. Mental health clinics also pose the treat of stigma for the child and parent, which is minimized by using services within the school setting.

The above cited study offers empirical support for the full-service or community schools initiative that nationally emerged in the United States during the 1990s. Full-service schools describes a movement that has created an array of integrated supportive services within school settings (e.g., health, mental health, nutrition, parent-training, after-school programs) aimed at ameliorating and preventing the "new morbidities" found among youth: violence, depression and suicidal behavior, substance abuse, and teenage pregnancy (Dryfoos, 1994). Community or full-service schools may, in collaboration with community based health and social service agencies, respond to the biopsychosocial needs of vulnerable youth (children and adolescents) and their families while concomitantly affording every child with the opportunity of academically excelling. This school movement is consonant with the needs and realities of Hispanic immigrant children and families who often enter the United States with a compromised health and mental health status. One significant value of community schools is that it increases access to health and mental health care while minimizing the institutional barriers that often impede parents from securing life-enhancing services necessary for optimal health. Igoa (1995) has noted that schools must actively and concurrently respond to the cultural, academic and psychological needs of immigrant children if they are to succeed both socially and educationally in this country. Optimal acculturation of Hispanic immigrant children cannot occur if their learning/academic requirements are separated or fragmented from their need for psychological well-being, safety and socialization.

PROJECT MI TIERRA/MY COUNTRY: A SCHOOL-BASED MENTAL HEALTH APPROACH

School-based mental health practitioners must be prepared to assume diverse and non-traditional intervention roles when treating Hispanic immigrant children and their families. In particular, school-based clinicians must incorporate in their treatment of Hispanic immigrant children an understanding of how multiple socio-environmental factors (e.g., poverty, immigration status) interact with individual and family dynamics within a specific ethnic-cultural context. Clinicians, providing mental health care within school settings, should be skilled as resource locators, educators on normative and atypical child developmental issues, and providers of concrete services or information. Gibbs and Huang (1989) recommend that, in the mental health treatment of minority children (i.e., Hispanic immigrant children and adolescents), the therapeutic relationship between patient and clinician should be active, ego supportive and focused on person-environmental transactions. Canino and Spurlock (2000) note that, "clinicians need to juggle sociopolitical principles with their neurodevelopmental knowledge to become eclectic, ecologically minded systems brokers without losing sight of the fine, cultural, intrapsychic, and developmental dimensions of the assigned case" (p. 153).

Project Mi Tierra/My Country is an ongoing mental health program established in an elementary school in New York City, which seeks to help immigrant children with a multitude of concerns and stressors (for a full description of the program, please see Gonzáles-Ramos and Nester-Sanchez, 2001). This program is a collaborative partnership between an urban graduate school of social work and a local public school. The program has focused on Hispanic immigrant children, because they represent the largest immigrant population group in New York City and in its public school system (Citizens Committee for Children of New York, 1999). However, the principles on which the program is based are sufficiently generic that they can be replicated with other immigrant groups.

Designed as a program that can be replicated in different schools, and with different ethnic and age groups, the Project Mi Tierra/My Country addresses the need to help children connect to their new country and especially its educational system. This is particularly important because Hispanic children, far more than other ethnic groups, are often at greatest risk educationally, with many eventually becoming school dropouts.

The project celebrates culture and connection at the same time that it promotes hope through mentoring, educational opportunities, and awareness of and respect for cultural differences. Focused on new or recent immigrants of Hispanic origin, Project Mi Tierra/My Country's purpose is to enhance bicultural adjustment and to promote attachment to the host school as the children's mental health needs are being addressed. The project builds on a "biodimensional" model of acculturation in which both the host and ethnic culture are equally respected. In this model, the increase in identification with the new host culture does not imply a decrease in the identification with the homeland's culture (Pawliuk et al., 1996). Children of Hispanic origin who have been in this country fewer than five years are eligible to be part of the project.

The project's title reflects an acknowledgment and respect for the children's home and their language, *mi tierra*, as well as the gradual bicultural adjustment that may occur and thus allow the child to view the United States as "my country." For other children this bicultural transition may not happen for many years, if ever, and so they too can be respected for the need to have a sense of their identity tied to mi tierra. Project Mi Tierra/My Country has several components:

- short-term groups for immigrant children
- weekly mentoring program for immigrant children
- field trips to the university collaborating in this project
- workshops for immigrant parents

Short-Term Groups for Immigrant Children–The groups, which consist of 10 sessions, focus on the children's experiences in their country of origin, their transition to the host country, and their postmigration adjustment experiences. The groups are co-led by a Hispanic university professor of social work and a bilingual Hispanic social work intern. Groups are one hour long and meet on a weekly basis during the school day. The groups are activity-based using drawing material to facilitate discussion.

Weekly Mentoring Program–This aspect of the project consists of having undergraduate and graduate university students go to the school on a weekly basis to work with Hispanic immigrant children who are deemed to be at educational risk. The mentors work on a one-to-one basis with the children after school for two hours.

Field Trip to the University–Approximately twice a year all the children from a certain bilingual class, their teacher, and a group of volunteer parents are invited to spend a day at the university. This field trip exposes the children and their family to higher education in the United States and allows them to meet Hispanic and other professionals in various fields who can share with them their own immigrant stories and educational paths.

Workshop for Parents–Workshops for Hispanic immigrant parents are held during after-school hours or on Saturdays. The elementary public school is open on Saturdays (consonant with the community schools movement discussed earlier in this chapter) for various educational purposes, thus providing an easy location for interested parents to attend workshops. The workshops are tailored to meet the families' stated needs, and can include topics on child discipline issues, managing sibling rivalry, speaking to children about drugs and other dangerous behaviors, and negotiating the educational school system in New York City. The workshops offer parents support and mutual aid; thereby, decreasing the sense of social isolation that many immigrant parents feel while adjusting to life in the United States.

CONCLUSION

Hispanic immigrant children and their families are at times particularly vulnerable to stress because of a multiplicity of factors. School-based mental health programs, however, offer the opportunity to preventively assist immigrant children before severe mental health problems may develop. Despite the individual and collective traumas that Hispanic immigrant children have been exposed to, many continue to move toward health and mastery. In the midst of adversity and toxic socio-environmental conditions, resiliency is noted among many Hispanic immigrant children. School-based mental health programs are indeed instrumental in assisting immigrant children to achieve or sustain optimal psychosocial functioning while concomitantly contributing to the academic success of a population that must always balance the demands of two worlds: mi tierra and my country.

REFERENCES

Board of Education of the City of New York. (1996). *Annual pupil ethnic census city wide by school level.* New York: Author.

Bronfenbrenner, U. (1979). *The ecology of human development.* Cambridge, MA: Harvard University Press.

Canino, I. and Spurlock, J. (2000). *Culturally diverse children and adolescents: Assessment, diagnosis, and treatment.* 2nd Edition. New York: Guilford.

Center for Puerto Rican Studies. (2000). *New York City Latino Population: Census 2002.* http://www.sscnet.ucla.edu/soc/faculty/ayala/centro/Census2002/NYC/main. htm

Comer, J.P. (1980). *The school program: School power.* New York: The Free Press.

Citizens Committee for Children of New York. (1999). *Keeping track of New York City's Children.* New York: Author.

Dryfoos, J.G. (1994). *Full-service schools: A revolution in health and social services for children, youth, and families.* San Francisco, CA: Jossey-Bass.

Gibbs, J.T. and Huang, L.N. (Eds.). (1989). *Children of color: Psychological interventions with minority youth.* San Francisco: Jossey-Bass.

Gil, R.M. (1980). *Cultural attitudes toward mental illness among Puerto Rican migrant women and their relationship to the utilization of outpatient mental health services.* Unpublished dissertation, Adelphi University, New York.

Glenn, C. L. (1992). Educating the children of immigrants. *Phi Delta Kappan,* 73(5): 404-408.

Goldenberg, C. (1996). Latin American immigration and U.S. schools. *Society for Research in Child Development,* 10, 1-29.

González, M.J. (2002). Mental health intervention with Hispanic immigrants: Understanding the influence of the client's worldview, language, and religion. *Journal of Immigrant and Refugee Services,* 1(1): 81-92.

González-Ramos, G. (1990). Examining the myth of Hispanic families' resistance to treatment: Using the school as a site for service. *Social Work in Education,* 12(4): 261-274.

González-Ramos, G. and Nester-Sanchez, M. (2001). Responding to immigrant children's mental health needs in the schools: Project mi tierra/my country. *Children and Schools,* 23(1): 49-62.

González-Vucci (Ramos), G. (1985). Puerto Rican mothers' preferences for delivery of mental health services (Doctoral dissertation, New York University). *Dissertation Abstracts International*, 46, 2441.

Hutchinson, M.R. and Poole, D.L. (1998). Editorial: Adolescent health and school health: It's time to meet the challenge. *Health and Social Work*, 23, 3-7.

Igoa, C. (1995). *The inner world of the immigrant child*. Mahwah, NJ: Lawrence Erlbaum Associates.

Institute for Urban and Minority Education. (1999). *Latinos in School: Some facts and findings*. New York: ERIC Clearinghouse on Urban Education, Teachers College, Columbia University.

Jamieson, A., Curry, A. and Martinez, G. (2001). School enrollment in the United States–Social and economic characteristics of students. *Current Population Reports*. Washington, DC: U.S. Census Bureau.

Kao, G. (1999). Psychological well-being and educational achievement among immigrant youth. In D.J. Hernandez (Ed.), *Children of immigrants: Health adjustments and public assistance*. Washington, DC: Committee on the Health and Adjustment of Immigrant Children and Families, National Research Council.

Kopala, M., Esquivel, G. and Baptiste, L. (1994). Counseling approaches for immigrant children: Facilitating the acculturative process. *School Counselor*, 41, 352-359.

Lucas, T. (1996). *Promoting secondary school transitions for immigrant adolescents*. Washington, DC: ERIC Clearinghouse on Languages and Linguistics.

McDaniel, S. and Bielin, I.N. (1990). *Project self-esteem*. Newport Beach, CA: Enhancing Education.

McDonnell, L. and Hill, P. (1993). *New comers in American schools: Meeting the educational needs of immigrant youth*. Santa Monica, CA: Rand.

New York City Department of City Planning (1999). *The newest New Yorkers–1995 1996*. New York: Author.

Ogbu, J. (1991). Immigrant and involuntary minorities in comparative perspectives. In M. Gibson and J. Ogbu (Eds.), *Minority status and schooling: A comparative study of immigrant and involuntary minorities*. New York: Garland Press.

Pawliuk, N., Grizenko, N., Chan-Yip, A., Gantous, P., Matthew, J. and Nguyen, D. (1996). Acculturation style and psychological functioning in children of immigrants. *American Journal of Orthopsychiatry*, 66, 111-121.

Rogler, L., Cooney, R., Constantino, G., Earley, B., Grossman, B., Gurak, D., Malgady, R. and Rodriguez, O. (1984). *A conceptual framework for mental health research on Hispanic populations*. New York: Hispanic Research Center at Fordham University.

Rousseau, C., Drapeau, A. and Corin, E. (1996). School performance and emotional problems in refugee children. *American Journal of Orthopsychiatry*, 66, 239-351.

Short, K. and Johnson, C. (1997). Stress, maternal distress, and children's adjustment following immigration: The buffering role of social support. *Journal of Consulting and Clinical Psychology*, 65, 494-503.

Solomon, B. (1982). A theoretical perspective for delivery of mental health services to minority communities. In F.U. Munoz and R. Endo (Eds.), *Perspective on minority group mental health* (pp. 85-91). Washington, DC: University Press of America.

Spenser, M.B. and Dornbusch, S.M. (1990). Challenges in studying minority youth. In S.S. Feldman and G. Elliot (Eds.), *At the Threshold: The developing adolescent.* Cambridge, MA: Harvard University Press.

Suarez-Orozco, C. and Marcelo, C. (1995). *Transformation: Migration, family life, and achievement among Latino Adolescents.* Stanford, CA: Stanford University Press.

Suarez-Orozco, C. and Suarez-Orozco, M.M. (2001). *Children of immigration.* Cambridge, MA: Harvard University Press.

The White House Initiative on Educational Excellence for Hispanic Americans. (1999). *Latinos in education: Early childhood, elementary, secondary, undergraduate, graduate.* Washington, DC: Author.

Therrien, M. and Ramirez, R. (2000). *The Hispanic population in the United States: U.S. Census Bureau, current population report.* Washington, DC: U.S. Government Printing Office.

Thomas, T. (1992). Psychoeducational adjustment of English-speaking Caribbean and Central American immigrant children in the United States. *School Psychology Review,* 21, 566-576.

Urrabazo, R. (2000). Therapeutic sensitivity to the Latino spiritual soul. In M.T. Flores and G. Carey (Eds.), *Family therapy with Hispanics: Toward appreciating diversity* (pp. 205-227). Boston, MA: Allyn and Bacon.

U.S. Department of Education. (2002). *The educational progress of Hispanic students.* Washington DC: National Center for Education Statistics.

U.S. Department of Health and Human Services. (1999). *Mental health: A report of the surgeon general.* Rockville, MD: Author.

U.S. Department of Health and Human Services. (2001). *Mental Health: Culture, race, and ethnicity: A supplement to mental health: A report of the surgeon general.* Rockville, MD: Author.

Vernez, G. and Abrahamse, A. (1996). *How immigrants fare in U.S. education.* Santa Monica, CA: Rand.

Winters Glasgow, W. and Easton, F. (1983). *The practice of social work in schools: An ecological perspective.* New York: The Free Press.

Chapter 4

Concepts of Mental Health and Mental Illness in Older Hispanics

Cathy S. Berkman
Peter J. Guarnaccia
Naelys Diaz
Lee W. Badger
Gary J. Kennedy

SUMMARY. The effect of cultural context in symptom expression and interpretation among older Hispanics, and how they experience psychological distress are not well-understood. We use the illness representation model to learn about older Puerto Ricans' and Dominicans' conceptions and causes of positive mental health, the causes of emo-

Cathy S. Berkman, PhD, Naelys Diaz, MSW, and Lee W. Badger, PhD, are affiliated with the Center for Hispanic Mental Health Research, Fordham University Graduate School of Social Service, 113 West 60th Street, NY, NY 10023.

Peter J. Guarnaccia, PhD, is affiliated with the Institute for Health, Health Care Policy, and Aging Research, Rutgers University, New Brunswick, NJ 08901.

Gary J. Kennedy, MD, is affiliated with the Division of Geriatric Psychiatry, Albert Einstein College of Medicine, Montefiore Medical Center, Bronx, NY 10467.

The authors are grateful for the assistance and support of the following individuals, without whom this study would not have been possible: Cirilo Diaz, Kay Dundorf, Reverend Thomas B. Fenlon, Jose R. Ortiz Ortiz, and Carmen Reyes.

This work was supported by NIMH grant R24 MH60002.

[Haworth co-indexing entry note]: "Concepts of Mental Health and Mental Illness in Older Hispanics." Berkman, Cathy S. et al. Co-published simultaneously in *Journal of Immigrant & Refugee Services* (The Haworth Social Work Practice Press, an imprint of The Haworth Press, Inc.) Vol. 3, No. 1/2, 2005, pp. 59-85; and: *Mental Health Care for New Hispanic Immigrants: Innovative Approaches in Contemporary Clinical Practice* (ed: Manny J. González, and Gladys González-Ramos) The Haworth Social Work Practice Press, an imprint of The Haworth Press, Inc., 2005, pp. 59-85. Single or multiple copies of this article are available for a fee from The Haworth Document Delivery Service [1-800-HAWORTH, 9:00 a.m. - 5:00 p.m. (EST). E-mail address: docdelivery@haworthpress.com].

tional problems, the conceptions and causes of depression and anxiety, the distinction between depression and anxiety, and the relationship between age and depression. Greater understanding of the meaning of symptoms and syndromes of depression and anxiety might help to define more culturally-sensitive mental health treatments and service delivery systems. *[Article copies available for a fee from The Haworth Document Delivery Service: 1-800-HAWORTH. E-mail address: <docdelivery@haworthpress.com> Website: <http://www.HaworthPress.com> © 2005 by The Haworth Press, Inc. All rights reserved.]*

KEYWORDS. Mental health, mental illness, older Hispanics, symptom meaning

BACKGROUND

Older Hispanics have relatively high rates of depression and other types of psychiatric distress, yet are less likely to receive professional mental health treatment than younger persons [1-3] or non-Hispanics [4-14]. This is partially due to structural barriers, including access to services and the availability of Spanish-speaking professionals. However, it also appears that patient recognition and interpretation of psychiatric symptoms and preferences for treatment explain these lower rates of professional mental health services. One theory that might partially explain lower utilization of services by older persons is that older and younger persons react differently to psychiatric symptoms in relation to help-seeking [2, 15, 16]. Older persons are less likely to recognize their own depressive symptoms and prefer to use personally generated strategies such as self-help and behavioral changes in response to these symptoms [17].

The importance of cultural context in symptom expression and interpretation has been noted [18-20] but the effect this has on how Hispanics experience psychological distress is not well-understood. Research suggests that definition and interpretation of psychiatric distress is culturally influenced and affects help seeking. For example, Hispanics are more likely than other groups to define serious mental illness as *nervios* (nerves), a transitory, less serious condition not requiring mental health services [21-23].

Cultural conceptions of illness are thought to be critical antecedents of health-seeking behavior [24]. Cultural conceptions are defined as the culturally-patterned classification of symptoms into illness categories that both shape and constrain how patients perceive, express, explain, and evaluate health and illness [24, 25]. Cultural conceptions are the source of cognitive attributions that patients make about the meaning of a symptom; whether or not a symptom is perceived as a problem or as a condition requiring action; about the social acceptability or shamefulness of a symptom, and about the perceived cultural pathways for treatment. In sum, cultural conceptions provide the labels patients use to define and describe their pain and the explanations they give for their distress. There are indications, for example, that Hispanics are more likely to somatize psychological disorders or psychosocial distress [19, 26-28]. As noted by Angel and Thoits [25], the cognitive assessments of symptoms are likely to influence whether these symptoms are reported to professionals, the diagnoses made by professionals, the types of treatments that are chosen by patients and professionals, and adherence to treatment.

Little attention has been given to Hispanic patients' perspective on illness, including their health beliefs, expectations and preferences for care, and how these impact the course of mental disorder. Lopez stated that future research on psychopathology in Hispanic populations should incorporate measures of specific values and beliefs that are hypothesized to be related to the sign, the symptom, and the distress under study [29, 30]. Guarnaccia [19] emphasized the importance of understanding cultural expressions of psychiatric distress. Increased understanding of patient conceptions of illness, expectations and preferences, are needed to plan the delivery of mental health services that will better serve these patients, thus reducing health care disparities.

The cross-cultural validity of psychiatric disorders, typically defined using the DSM-IV classification system, has been questioned [19, 27, 31]. It is argued that disorders are several steps removed from the symptom, which is the basic unit of psychopathology as experienced by the patient [29]. Many researchers have also found that Hispanics' expressions of distress focus more on physical than psychological symptoms [32] and emphasize the importance of research that focuses on symptoms (both psychological and physical), rather than on disorders [19, 29, 33]. Understanding which symptoms define depression and anxiety for older Hispanics may help to understand ethnic differences in help-seeking preferences and adherence to treatment. The purpose of the research described in this chapter was to learn more about the attitudes and understandings of older Hispanics toward mental health and psychiatric distress.

The theoretical framework that guided the research described in this chapter is The Illness Self Regulation Model (ISRM) proposed by Leventhal and his colleagues [34-36]. This model of illness cognition and representations posits that the meaning of psychiatric symptoms and actions taken in response to these symptoms is due to the search for coherence between the experience of that symptom by the person and the social context in which that person is imbedded. Therefore, this interpretation is affected by physical, psychological, social, and cultural influences. The illness representation has five domains, which have been found to apply across different illnesses and in different cultures [36]. The five domains are: (1) the label or identity of the illness or condition; (2) the causes or precursors of the condition; (3) the timeline of the condition, including duration and chronicity; (4) the consequences of the condition; and (5) the conception of controllability, management and treatability of the condition. This explanatory model builds on work by Kleinman [37, 38], who emphasized the importance of examining culturally-specific models in order to understand patient's cognitions about their illness and how this affected their help-seeking behaviors, and Mechanic [39] with respect to illness behavior as a result of an interpretive evaluation process. Illness representation is predictive of strategies chosen for managing the condition, including help-seeking behaviors, and adherence to treatment [40-46], including treatment for depression [47].

The relationship between Hispanic elders' conceptualizations of psychiatric symptoms and syndromes and diagnostic criteria is not well understood. Studies of the illness representation in this population may help to understand previous findings of discrepancies between patient's definitions of psychological distress and diagnoses made by psychiatrists [48]. In order to understand more about the illness representations of older Hispanics, the specific aims of this study were to learn about older Puerto Ricans' and Dominicans' conceptions and causes of positive mental health, the causes of emotional problems, the conceptions and causes of depression and anxiety, the distinction between depression and anxiety, and the relationship between age and depression.

METHODS

Study Design

Three focus groups were conducted in different neighborhoods in New York City. A qualitative method was chosen due to the lack of prior information capturing the depth and range of views about symptoms and syndromes of depression and anxiety held by Hispanic elders. Focus groups were selected to encourage and capture the dialogue among Hispanic elders about their beliefs and experiences.

Sample

A purposive sampling plan was used to recruit focus group participants from three community sites in two boroughs in New York City. The three sites were:

Site #1, a senior center operated by a Hispanic senior services agency (n = 8); Site #2, a multipurpose senior service center (n = 4); and Site #3, a church in a predominantly Hispanic neighborhood (n = 10). Eligibility criteria were: age 65 or older, Puerto Rican or Dominican origin, Spanish speaking, and physically and cognitively able to participate in the focus group. These two groups have many cultural and language similarities to each other, and are relatively different from Central and South American Hispanics. In addition, these are the two largest Hispanic populations in New York City, and particularly in the neighborhoods in which the study was conducted. The first and third authors worked with staff at each of the study sites to select a sample that was heterogeneous with respect to age, gender, and representing both national origins. Participants were paid $35 for their time.

Measures

A semi-structured interview guide was followed, and included the following domains: (1) what is meant by the "good life"; (2) what factors are associated with positive mental health; (3) what causes emotional problems; (4) how would you describe depression and anxiety in older persons; (5) what are the causes of depression and anxiety in older persons; (6) what is the difference between depression and anxiety; and (7) how are age and depression related.

Data Collection

A focus group led by one of the authors (P. Guarnaccia) was conducted at each of the three sites. The focus groups lasted approximately 2 1/4 hours, not including a 15 minute break about halfway through. The focus groups were conducted in Spanish and were audiotaped. The tapes were transcribed and translated by one of the authors (N. Diaz) who is a native Spanish-speaker.

Data Analysis Plan. A grounded theory approach was used to analyze the data in order to allow the participants' beliefs and experiences to guide the analyses, rather than formulating a priori hypotheses [49]. Recurring, emergent themes were identified using constant comparison [50-52] of the transcripts. The coding scheme that emerged was developed to identify the salient and meaningful words and phrases [53].

There were three phases of coding. In phase one, codes to mark specific conceptions or experiences related to each of the domains of questions asked were marked in the word processing document. These were descriptive codes that described the content of the phrase, sentence or paragraph. There was no attempt to categorize or search for themes during this phase of coding. In the second phase of coding, broader categories of coding were created by identifying key words, phrases, or concepts in the descriptive codes created in phase one. These coding categories were not mutually exclusive, and a phrase or sentence could be tagged with several codes. The codes in the third phase were developed by examining the phase two codes for patterns, trends, commonalities, differences, and themes across the three focus groups [52, 54]. The words and phrases attached to the phase three codes were then aggregated and printed for each code. A final examination of the data included for each code was conducted, including comparing and contrasting with other phase three codes, to ensure the integrity of the category prior to writing the results.

The first author conducted the three phases of coding and then the second and third authors independently read the transcripts to verify these themes and key phenomena. A consensus approach was used to resolve differences.

RESULTS

Table 1 displays the distribution of gender, age, country of origin, and number of years in the United States of the study participants. Slightly more than two thirds of the participants were female, the mean age was in the early-to-mid-seventies, and half were Puerto Rican and the other half were Dominican. Participants had lived in the United States (entirely in the New York City area), for at least 25 years, on average, with over half the sample residing in the United States for approximately five decades.

Conception of the Good Life

The focus group began with a discussion of what the "good life" consisted of. Three main ingredients were consistently given as necessary for having a good

TABLE 1. Sample Characteristics

FOCUS GROUP	GENDER	AGE MEAN (S.D.)	ORIGIN	YEARS IN U.S. (= YRS IN NYC) MEAN (S.D)
Site #1	4 Female 4 Male	71.6 (9.5)	8 Puerto Rican	50.3 (6.7)
Site #2	4 Female	76.5 (8.4)	3 Puerto Rican 1 Dominican	49.0 (6.2)
Site #3	7 Female 3 Male	75.7 (1.2)	10 Dominican	25.0 (10.4)

life: (1) good relationships with friends and family; (2) faith in God and (3) good health. Maintaining good relationships within the home, with family, and with friends was an oft-cited component of the good life. Harmony and tranquility within the home and getting along with others were mentioned by many participants as necessary conditions for having the good life. Good relationships also include people who are not family or close friends. Providing assistance to friends and relatives, and even to the larger community, was an important part of having a good life. The following quotes emphasize these themes from the focus groups:

> To try to have love and harmony. There is a peace when there is love and faith, especially love.

> To me life is to keep friendships.

> A good life is to help one another.

> I think that if you are happy and someone else next to you is not, you cannot be happy because you have to share with others. We have to share in order to have the satisfaction to feel good because you did good to others.

> The most important thing for us right now is to help those in need, young people, and children.

These quotes emphasize the strong sociality of Hispanics in defining a good life. We will return to the centrality of social relationships in discussing how depression is understood.

Having faith in God was the second essential component of having a good life. This was expressed in several different ways, including having faith in God, expressing gratitude to God, and putting oneself in God's hands.

> . . . to have a good life, the first thing is to have faith in God.

> . . . to live according to God's principles.

> . . . first we have to put ourselves in God's hands.

This notion that people have a direct relationship to God and that God will help you if you have faith came through strongly in all the focus groups. The role of spirituality and faith in God has been an enduring theme in Hispanic mental health studies [55].

Good health was the third essential aspect of having a good life. A sentiment that was echoed by many of the participants was:

... the first thing is to have good health.

These three components of the good life are interrelated. In some ways, they reflect Hispanics' endorsement of a biopsychosocial model of mental health. Good health was viewed by some as a gift from God or something that one must ask God for. Good health was also seen as a necessary condition to having good relationships. Some participants mentioned economic well-being as necessary for having a good life, but there were others who downplayed its importance.

> First of all, we have to ask God for good health because without it we are nothing,
>
> We also have to seek God because if not, illness comes.
>
> Health, because everybody needs good health in order to share with others.
>
> ... to have the economic means to take care of oneself.
>
> I think I don't need money in order to be happy, because God has given me something wonderful.

Overall, these quotes emphasize the often mentioned themes of sociality and spirituality among Hispanics. Participants found it easy to discuss what a good life was like. For older Hispanics, there was unanimity in these perspectives on the "good life" which one might not find in younger generations, who have become more acculturated to American consumer society.

Conceptions and Causes of Good Health

Good health was defined as the absence of problems and having one's organs, blood, ambulation, and functioning well. In this sense, Hispanic elders' conceptions of good health fit with the attention in the health research field to assessments of physical and social functioning to complement symptom assessments. In addition to physical function, having a "good mind" was considered necessary to good health. This was important both in order to take care of oneself, but also to preserve the ability to maintain social relations and behave in a socially appropriate manner. The main determinants of good health were practicing healthy habits, refraining from bad health practices, and avoiding stressful situations. Alcohol and food high in sugar were frequently mentioned as things to be avoided. Adhering to doctors' orders, particularly with regard to medication, were viewed as necessary to maintaining good health.

> I have good health, good blood, my heart is fine, and I walk fine.

> Since the stroke . . . I suffer from dizziness, but still my mind can reason and I can be with people.

> . . . stay away from alcohol and things that are toxic to the body.

> . . . to avoid drinking, avoid sugar, avoid cake, avoid beer and all alcohol beverages.

> . . . to take care, to go to the doctor, and to take the medication.

> I think there are two types, mental health and physical health. Physical health is what affects your body. Mental health is whatever is around you, what you can perceive, what you can avoid, and I think both things are combined.

In discussing good health, there was clear integration of the physical and mental dimensions of health. While Hispanics often emphasize physical symptoms in medical encounters, they clearly have a strong awareness of the emotional dimensions of health as well. This comes out in their discussions of mental health problems in the next sections.

Conceptions of Emotional Health

Emotional health was viewed as essential to having a good life, possibly more so than having good physical health. Having patience, self-control, and trusting in God are pathways to emotional health. Positive thought and action, focusing on the future, and helping others are part of maintaining emotional health.

> . . . mental health is more essential than the physical because when someone is OK mentally, everything else becomes easier, and if you are not OK mentally and a nail hurts . . . then even the heart hurts, then you feel it double.

> And if we don't have the peace to control ourselves, that leads to desperation, and there is no health.

> We have to move forward always. We have to try to do things the right way in order to avoid feeling bad. If I start thinking about the past, what

am I going to do? Keep myself in a room and kill myself like a lot of people have done, or shoot myself, or do drugs and drink and the bad life. We have to think positively.

. . . elderly people think that they're too old and that they can't do anything, but age has nothing to do with what you can do or what you can do for your community because when you help others you help yourself. I believe there is a solution to every problem. . . . and years ago we did not have the opportunities we have now. They used to say if you are old you are old, but now I don't believe in age . . . The things we could not do when we were young we can do them now because there is always hope.

Just as social relationships and a relationship with God are pathways to physical health, they are also the keys to emotional health. In that sense, the elderly Hispanics in the three focus groups made little distinction between physical and emotional health; rather as these quotes make clear, the psyche and soma are integrally connected.

Causes of Emotional Problems

Many causes of emotional problems were discussed. One of the most important sets of causal factors was stress due to lost, disrupted, or problematic relationships. Other causes were physical illness and financial concerns. In addition to mounting debt or inability to provide for a family, another problem of poverty was the inability to provide a financial legacy for one's children. Dwelling on problems or bad relationships was seen as detrimental to emotional health. The distinction between physical symptoms and syndromes that can be observed and emotional problems that cannot be "seen" was discussed. Domestic violence was also mentioned as a cause of emotional distress.

Loneliness hurts. That is why we must share with other people because when we are alone in the house we feel sad.

. . . constant physical illness due to concerns brings mental illness and also mental illness weakens the organism resulting in physical illness . . . it is natural that a lot of stress you have with your job or because you don't have a job, or you don't have a house, or have problems with the neighbors, with family, those concerns bring anxiety and stress and can bring mental illness.

if your debts increase and you don't know how to go about it, and you don't have anywhere to go with a family, and you take in all of that. Everything is mental and affects the mind.

. . . that you don't have anything to give to your children . . . That is serious and brings a lot of problems . . . these are things that can affect people.

. . . there are many things and many mental illnesses that originate from those situations that for me was very difficult and I struggled a lot.

I wake up early in the morning because my hands get numb, my heart is palpitating too fast, I can't sleep at night, but sometimes I feel differently. Therefore, those are emotional moments due to stress . . . I had emotional diabetes and high blood pressure . . . And to me what I have is completely emotional because the doctors have done everything and they have told me that I am fine. And when they see something they tell you, but it is sad what I have because it is an illness that you would say I don't have.

Sometimes men abuse women . . . then you suffer all of those things . . . when I get upset I get headaches.

For elderly Hispanics emotional problems are very social in nature. They are social in terms of coming from disrupted social relationships with family and friends. And they are social in terms of coming from various social stresses such as job loss or neighborhood problems.

Conceptions of Depression

Depression was considered to be a very serious problem. Symptoms included sleep disorder, suicidal ideation, and impaired concentration. Anhedonia, lack of interest and pleasure in things, was mentioned often as part of depression. Inability to function was also mentioned as a symptom of depression. Finally, low self-esteem was considered to be a symptom of depression. In this sense, elderly Hispanics' descriptions of depression fit closely with clinical descriptions of the syndrome.

I would say that depression is the worst illness in the world.

Depression is one of the worst things there is because the person enters in a cycle of wanting to resolve the problem but you get more involved in the problem.

That you don't wish to live.

Desperation is part of the symptoms because you feel hopeless. When you feel desperate you are hopeless in regard to getting better.

> . . . Without desire to do anything, wash the dishes, nothing.

> You do what you can, but not because you want to. You force your body to do it.

> Depression is a person who does not have any interest in things . . . people are crying and one feels sick without being sick and stuff like that . . . you can say 'Look what a beautiful plant'. . . but there are times that you don't see the beauty of the plant. That I would say is depression.

> Sometimes we don't feel anything . . . The lack of happiness and socialization cause sadness and depression.

> I felt inferior to other people.

While elderly Hispanics' shared the clinical description of depressions, their descriptions of depression also often included symptoms of anxiety syndromes. The lines between depression and anxiety were often blurred, presenting more of a mixed anxiety-depression syndrome. In the following quotes, participants provided fairly comprehensive descriptions of depression and possible causal pathways. These participants described depressions accompanied by anxiety, with many common symptoms of depression in older age, including anhedonia.

> You have depression, you feel nervous, tearful, anxious, and this is taking control over people.

> I lost my husband, and that disturbed the nerves. I have always had the concern of my sons, and when I see my sons I feel better, because with the concern that something may happen I get nervous, and that is what happens to me, that I feel very depressed.

> Something that worries you, such as problems at work or family problems can make you feel bad . . . You think you are sick. Then you start thinking about it and that concern does not let you think freely, Then you don't have the ability to make decisions, to think, you don't know what to do. Then that brings nervousness, nervousness makes the heart pound . . . that does not let you sleep, you don't sleep throughout the night and some sleep too much, I could not sleep and eat, but others eat too much due to the anxiety. This brings a lot of anxiety, anguish, sadness, melancholia, you don't want to know anything. You don't want to watch TV, go to the movies, don't feel pleasure in anything, you don't want to talk; conversation bothers you. You don't want to participate; in other words, you isolate yourself. You prefer to isolate yourself than share with other peo-

ple. All these things make you feel worse and then you don't eat . . . I thought I was going to die.

Depression was conceptualized as a mental illness, but this did not mean that the person is crazy:

Depression is a level of mental illness. It is not craziness but it is a mental illness.

For elderly Hispanics, depression is a serious problem. The distinction above between mental illness and craziness is important because of the issues of stigma in the community. While elderly Hispanics recognize many of the classic features of depression, it is the isolation from others and lack of social-ization that are the hallmark features of the illness.

Causes of Depression

Isolation is seen as both a cause and a symptom of depression. Those who live alone are seen as particularly vulnerable to depression. Particularly trou-bling is when children grow up and move out of the family home. This loss of family relationships is particularly troubling to older Hispanics, many of whom are not used to the loss of contact with children and other close kin. In their home countries, family members tended to live closer together.

. . . sometimes depression comes from loneliness.

Depression is what I feel, that I feel that my daughters are not with me, that they ignore me, that I feel the house is too big, I feel small . . . some-times I feel ashamed because it bothers me too much, and then I cry . . .

Depression is what I have, for instance due to my age. I feel lonely and sometimes I feel like that and I think 'Why do I feel so lonely?' because af-ter I was married for 47 years, had 8 children and now everyone got mar-ried, and they left, and they have their own children. I say the day I die they will find me for the odor because no one comes to visit me; I am lonely. And that makes you think 'For what am I living?' Sometimes I say 'God forgive me but you should take me because I don't exist here'. . . sometimes we wish to die. It is loneliness. But loneliness hurts people; loneliness hurts.

There were many different causal pathways to depression. Stress due to problems, worries, and concerns were the common underlying factor pro-posed as the cause of depression. For some, personal vulnerability or lack of fortitude in the face of problems was a necessary concomitant condition to result in depression. Adopting a pessimistic view, failing to seek help from others, and dwelling on past events was seen as contributing to depression.

> If we don't have problems, there is no depression because depression comes with the problems.

> . . . unemployment or health problems, or friends, family, any circumstance. Those concerns accumulate stress and everyones mind is different. Some have a weak mind and those concerns increase and bring us depression.

> I think we are responsible for the depression because mentally, like I said before, we think in a negative way. Children have to get married and you have to think that is natural. Now you should look in your mind what you can do to live and what you like. You have to think about positive things because if you think about your kids, you find the pain (pena) and the depression.

> . . . why do I have to think about things that happened in the past, and in doing that I lose my sleep.

A commonly mentioned cause of depression is not talking with friends and family about your problems. Keeping problems to oneself or isolating oneself can lead to depression, while talking with others and sharing one's problems prevents or reduces feelings of depression:

> Depression sometimes causes problems with family or things you can't resolve, or sometimes you don't want to share it. That is when depression comes. When we have a problem and we share it, we feel better, but depression comes when you have mental things inside you that you cant get them out, then that depresses you because you have something inside you bothering you. But once you have a problem and you share it or you find a solution to the problem, depression decreases.

> . . . depression is when you don't share the problems with others and you don't tell how you feel. That is depression because that makes you tired.

There was a distinction made between feeling lonely and being isolated. The former was due to living alone or the loss or absence of loved ones, and the latter was a result of removing oneself from social interaction: Being isolated was mentioned as both a cause and a consequence of depression. Participants in the groups recognized that it was possible to feel lonely even when you were with other people. This was an important distinction in their social models of depression.

> I would say that if you feel lonely it is that you don't have family or friends. Isolated is that you separate yourself because you don't want to hear conversations

> . . . sometimes we can be in a group but feel lonely because your thoughts are not in what is around you.

There was no mention of a genetic component or of a chemical imbalance as a cause of depression. As already discussed, the emphasis was on the social origins of depression [56].

Conception and Causes of Anxiety

Anxiety was considered to be both an outcome of stress, and an intermediary condition on the pathway from stress to depression. In line with the social model of mental illness, loss of loved ones was a major cause of anxiety. Anxiety was also described as fear, having unrealized goals or the inability to express one's inner feelings. Finally, too much tranquility, in this case associated with loneliness, can also make one anxious.

> I had problems and there were nights that I could not sleep. I used to go to bed and I had numbness in my feet, a desperation, and shakiness . . . one night my heart was pounding very fast . . . I took medicine for the heart for about 7 months, but I knew I did not need to take it. It was not the heart. It was the nerves . . . thinking too much about my problems and my heart started pounding.

> I lost my husband, and that disturbed the nerves. I have always had the concern of my sons, and when I see my sons I feel better, because with the concern that something may happen I get nervous . . .

> Anxiety is a desperation, that you get desperate about anything.

> Anxiety is something that makes you desperate, something you want to accomplish and you can't . . .

> But sometimes I don't want tranquility, tranquility makes me anxious. When my daughters and their children come I feel better.

In response to a question about the difference between nerves or anxiety and nervous attacks (*ataques de nervios*), respondents felt that loss of self-control during an *ataque* was the distinguishing characteristic:

Sometimes you can control the nerves but when you lose control, personal balance, then you have a nervous attack.

Distinction Between Depression and Anxiety

There were a variety of ideas about the how depression and anxiety were related to each other. Some participants felt that anxiety and depression were the same thing and some felt that they were distinct entities. Among those who said they were different, the description of each syndrome often included symptoms from the other. Anxiety was considered to be less serious than depression, and not necessarily a disorder: nerves (*nervios*) were also frequently described as a cause of depression.

> The nerves, the anxiety, and the concerns are symptoms. The depression is the illness.

> Anxiety, desperation, and depression is the same thing.

> Depression, anxiety, and the nerves are the same thing.

> I don't know, to me they are the same thing.

> When I get nervous, I became moody and everything falls off.

> I believe that they are the same because the nerves give anxiety and depression comes from the nerves.

> . . . that is depression because the nerves are something else. The nerves is a fear. Because I know when I have the nerves and when I have depression. Sometimes I say, because of loneliness and I look but there is nothing that would interest me, and I know I am depressed. But the nerves are when you believe that you are going to die, or that you are going to have a heart attack. I have experienced it; I know what nerves are and I know when I have depression.

Relationship Between Age and Depression

Participants were asked whether depression was different for older persons as compared with younger age groups. While some felt that it was the same illness; others felt that there was more emotional distress in older age. Some expressed the view that younger persons have a more difficult time because they don't have the perspective of an older person.

It is the same thing because young and old people get it.

I think it is the same because there are young people who have a stronger depression than someone older, or . . . one believes that one is depressed because one is old.

Emotional problems come from a lot of years.

. . . when the young people have depression it is more difficult because they feel it more.

Young people get scared and see things bigger than what they are.

. . . everything affects young people more because I say I am already old. For them it is stronger.

DISCUSSION

In this study we attempted to learn about Hispanic elders' representations of emotional well-being and psychological distress by asking about the domains of the illness representation model. In this chapter, we report our findings on the first two domains: the identity of the condition, the causes of the condition, and to a lesser extent, the consequences of the condition. Participants in the three focus groups talked openly about their views and personal experiences of emotional health and depression and anxiety disorder. Great emphasis was placed on the importance of social relationships for maintaining emotional health; the core experiences of depression were isolation and loneliness. Having and nurturing harmonious friendships was seen as essential to emotional health. Poor mental health resulted when these relationships were disrupted. Emotional health was seen as equally, and by some, more important than physical health, because it was critical for having a happy and peaceful life. Having self-control and maintaining self-esteem were also seen as critical to having emotional well-being. Loss of either of these was viewed as very serious and could lead to desperation or becoming crazy. Keeping a positive outlook, not dwelling on past mistakes or losses, and accepting your situation in life were also seen as critical for maintaining emotional health.

Depression was considered to be a very serious problem. The symptoms of depression most commonly mentioned were anhedonia, difficulty concentrating, and physical symptoms, including fatigue and problems with sleep. Causes of depression were loneliness, isolation, and worries, particularly dwelling on negative circumstances. Keeping problems to oneself and not discussing them with loved ones was also identified as a cause of depression. Although depression was considered to be a mental illness, it was distinguished from being crazy. Anxiety was also viewed as an outcome of loss and stress. It was seen as a precursor to, a correlate of, and/or a component of depression. Biological explanations of depression and anxiety were not offered by participants. There were differing opinions about whether depression was more common in older persons, with some feeling that it was part of old age and others expressing the view that depression is seen at all ages, although older persons may be able to handle it better than younger persons.

The close connection between physical, mental, and spiritual health that was mentioned by participants was also found by Ailinger and Causey in their study of older Hispanics in the Washington, DC area [57]. We also replicated their finding that tranquility, spiritual peace, and good interpersonal relationships were components of mental health.

Our finding that expressions of distress focused more on physical rather than psychological symptoms was consistent with those of previous studies [16, 32]. Some of the symptoms were viewed as normal, or at least expected, for older persons, and others have written about the misattribution of pathological symptoms as a normal component of aging on the part of elders, relatives, and health care providers [58, 59].

Despite the possible lack of congruity between participants' views of depression and anxiety and DSM criteria, there was a high degree of recognition of symptoms of psychological distress. This is consistent with research that has shown that patients experiencing psychological symptoms recognize these as distressing [60-63].

The contribution of age, or cohort effect, must also be considered in addition to culture, in examining the illness representations of Hispanic elders. Age may affect how a symptom or syndrome is perceived and the coping strategies that are devised in response to this. As noted by Leventhal and Crouch [64], older persons may be exposed to different information currently and throughout their life span, as well as age-related increases in morbidity and mortality, and social and economic roles and status. There is concern that older persons have a tendency to attribute their illness symptoms to normal aging[58] and this may explain their decision to delay or not seek treatment [65], including underreporting depressive symptoms [66]. This phenomenon requires further investigation, particularly in light of evidence to the contrary. For example, a study of non-Hispanic white women did not support the hypothesis that psychopathological symptoms were viewed as part of normal aging by either women age 20 to 35 years or age 60 to 75 years [15]. However, researchers need more information on what older Hispanics learn about the aging process both in their home countries and when they come to the U.S. Ideas about aging are as culturally shaped as ideas about mental illness.

Issues of illness representation and symptom interpretation are likely to affect the measurement of psychiatric disorder, and account for apparent inconsistencies in epidemiologic studies of the prevalence of disorder in Hispanic populations in New York City and elsewhere. Variations in findings have been attributed to concerns about lack of attention to cultural issues [19] and difficulties in interpretation of findings [67], due to imprecise definitions of "Hispanic" [68], cultural variations in psychopathology or in response style [19], the effects of acculturation [19, 26, 29, 69-77] and the way in which symptoms and distress have been measured [19, 76, 77]. For example, in their review of epidemiology of Puerto Rican mental health, Guarnaccia and colleagues [19] found consistent reports that Puerto Ricans had higher numbers of psychiatric symptoms and higher levels of distress in comparison with other ethnic groups or Island Puerto Ricans. However, they were unable to determine whether these findings reflect cultural variations in the prevalence of certain forms of psychopathology; the severity of psychopathology, or were a matter of social and cultural differences in modes of expressing distress. Similarly, in the Puerto Rico Island Study, Canino and her associates [78] found that Puerto Rican prevalence rates for most psychiatric disorders no longer differed significantly from other ethnic and social class groups in the United States, once culturally-grounded changes were made in the assessment instrument. Both Potter and colleagues [79] in a study of Puerto Ricans in New York State and Vera and colleagues [80] in the New York City area, found high levels of unexplainable depression and concluded that it is important to capture the complexity of psychosocial and cultural processes relevant to psychological distress.

Despite the uncertain nature of psychiatric epidemiological findings in Hispanic populations [81], the inverse relationship that has been established between socioeconomic factors and some forms of mental illness [82] indicates that Hispanics are at higher risk for psychiatric disorder than other ethnic groups [83-85], and data from the National Comorbidity Survey (NCS) [82] revealed unexpectedly high rates of disorder among Hispanics as compared to non-Hispanic Whites and African Americans. This is compounded by the underutilization of mental health services by Hispanics as compared with white non-Hispanics [11], higher likelihood of delay in seeking care [26, 86], higher attrition rates from mental health care [87] and poorer treatment outcomes following psychotherapy [88, 89]. This is especially troubling in the face of evidence that depression and anxiety are both serious and disabling disorders [90-92] and that the treatments found to be highly effective for non-Hispanic patients work equally well for Hispanic patients [93].

In accordance with the view put forth by Rogler [94] that cultural sensitivity in mental health research requires examining the collective perceptions of members of ethnic groups about their own idiomatic expressions of distress, this study was conducted to understand how older Hispanics conceptualize depression and anxiety. Such research on the illness representations and idioms of distress of older Hispanics should contribute to understanding how to provide culturally-sensitive and culturally competent mental health services to this population. Anthropologists have long-understood how illness representations fit with treatment [37, 95, 96], but this has not been the focus of much research in mental health. Although the importance of understanding the illness representation of patients and the way culture shapes this [97], treatment is generally prescribed based on studies of efficacy that ignore the role of culture. Learning about Hispanic elders' illness representations of depression and anxiety may help to design and prescribe treatments that are acceptable to this population, thereby increasing the likelihood of adherence to and benefit from such treatments. In particular, focusing attention on the social nature of depression and anxiety and developing interventions to deal with the social problems which older Hispanics mentioned are key areas for mental health research.

Limitations and Strengths

This was an exploratory study with a small nonprobability sample, and our findings cannot be generalized to all Hispanic elders in New York City and beyond. Recruiting the focus group participants from sites in three different neighborhoods of New York City, and from very different types of agencies, assisted in making the sample more diverse. Differences that might be due to cultural variations among the different Hispanic groups in New York City were minimized by restricting the sample to Puerto Rican and Dominican elders.

Future Research

Future research should include both qualitative and quantitative approaches to understanding the illness representation of Hispanic elders with respect to the common psychiatric disorders seen in this population. Understanding how this population conceptualizes, experiences, and responds to psychological distress is necessary to develop and test interventions that will be acceptable and effective. The development of measures that can be used to assess illness representation of Hispanic elders using large probability samples is needed to advance research in this area. Studies with longitudinal design are needed to understand how illness representation is causally related to help-seeking behaviors and how these change over time. Studies that include other age groups and ethnic groups will allow us to examine the individual contributions of age and culture to the illness representations of Hispanic elders in relation to depression and anxiety.

CONCLUSION

The increasing racial and ethnic diversity of the United States presents formidable challenges to the delivery of effective, culturally respectful and relevant health and mental health care [98], and this is even more urgent with respect to older Hispanics, given the rate at which this segment of the population is growing. Currently, the reasons for low utilization of mental health services by Hispanics are still relatively unexplored. Little attention has been given to patients' perspectives on illness, including their conceptions of illness, expectations and preferences for care, and the impact of these factors on the course of mental disorder. All of these factors, if identified, might help to design more culturally-sensitive mental health treatments and service delivery systems.

REFERENCES

1. Burns, B., and D. Taube, *Mental health services in general medical care and in nursing homes*, in *Mental health policy for older Americans: Protecting minds at risk*, B. Fogel, A. Furino, and G. Gottlieb, Editors. 1990, American Psychiatric Press. p. 63-84.
2. Goldstrom, I. et al., *Mental health service use by elderly adults in a primary care setting*. Journal of Gerontology, 1987. 42(147-153).
3. Robins, L.N., B.Z. Locke, and D.A. Regier, *An overview of psychiatric disorders in America*, in *Psychiatric disorders in America: The Epidemiologic Catchment Area Study*, L.N. Robins and D.A. Regier, Editors. 1991, The Free Press: New York. p. 328-366.
4. Bachrach, L., *Utilization of state and county mental hospitals by Spanish Americans in 1972*. 1975, Washington, DC: U.S. Government Printing Office.
5. Barrera, M., *Mexican American mental health service utilization: A critical examination of some proposed variables*. Community Mental Health Journal, 1978. 14: p. 33-45.
6. Hough, R.L. et al., *Utilization of health and mental health services by Los Angeles Mexican Americans and Non-Hispanic White*. Archives of General Psychiatry, 1987. 44: p. 702-709.
7. Keefe, S.E., *Why Mexican Americans underutilize mental health clinics: Facts and fallacy*, in *Family and mental health in the Mexican American Community. Monograph No. 7*, J. Casas and S. Keefe, Editors. 1978, University of California Los Angeles. Spanish-Speaking Mental Health Research Center: Los Angeles. p. 91-108.

8. Keefe, S., and J. Casas, *Mexican Americans and mental health: A selected review and recommendations for mental health service delivery.* American Journal of Community Psychology, 1980. 8: p. 303-326.
9. National Institute of Mental, H., *Hispanic Americans and Mental Health Facilities: A Comparison of Hispanic, Black, and White Admissions to Selected Mental Health Facilities, 1975.* 1980, Washington, DC: U.S. Government Printing Office.
10. Padilla, A., M. Carlos, and S. Keefe, *Mental health service utilization by Mexican Americans,* in *Psychotherapy with the Spanish-speaking: Issues in Research and Service Delivery. Monograph No. 3,* M. Miranda, Editor. 1976, University of California Los Angeles. Spanish-Speaking Mental Health Research Center: Los Angeles. p. 9-20.
11. Rodriguez, O., *Hispanics and human services: Help-seeking in the inner city.* 1987, New York: Hispanic Research Center.
12. Wells, K.B. et al., *Which Mexican-Americans underutilize health services?* American Journal of Psychiatry, 1987. 144: p. 918-922.
13. Wells, K. et al., *Factors affecting the probability of use of general and medical health and social/community services for Mexican Americans and non-Hispanic whites.* Medical Care, 1988. 26: p. 441-452.
14. Berk, M.L. et al., *Health care use among undocumented latino immigrants.* Health Aff (Millwood), 2000. 19: p. 51-64.
15. Hochman, L.O.B., M. Storandt, and A.M. Rosenberg, *Age and its effect on perceptions of psychopathology.* Psychology and Aging, 1986. 4: p. 337-338.
16. Ray, D.C., M.A. Raciti, and W.E. MacLean, *Effects of perceived responsibility on help-seeking decisions among elderly persons.* Journal of Gerontology: Psychological Sciences, 1992. 47: p. 199-205.
17. Davies, R.M., K.O. Sieber, and S.L. Hunt, *Age-cohort differences in treating symptoms of mental illness: a process approach.* Psychol Aging, 1994. 9: p. 446-453.
18. Kirmayer, L.J., *Cultural variations in the response to psychiatric disorders and emotional distress.* Social Science & Medicine, 1989. 29: p. 327-339.
19. Guarnaccia, P.J., B.J. Good, and A. Kleinman, *A critical review of epidemiological studies of Puerto Rican mental health.* American Journal of Psychiatry, 1990. 147: p. 1449-1456.
20. Rogler, L.H., *Culturally sensitizing psychiatric diagnosis: A framework for research.* Journal of Nervous and Mental Disease, 1993. 181: p. 401-408.
21. Jenkins, J.H., *Conceptions of schizophrenia as a problem of nerves: A cross-cultural comparison of Mexican-Americans and Anglo-Americans.* Soc Sci Med, 1988. 26: p. 1233-1243.
22. Jenkins, J.H., *Ethnopsychiatric interpretations of schizophrenic illness: The problem of nervios within Mexican-American families.* Cult Med Psychiatry, 1988. 12: p. 301-329.
23. Guarnaccia, P.J., R. Lewis-Fernández, and M.R. Marano, *Toward a Puerto Rican Popular Nosology: "Nervios" and "Ataque de Nervios."* Culture, Medicine and Psychiatry, 2003. 27(3): p. 339-366.
24. Ell, K., and I. Castaneda, *Health care seeking behavior, in Handbook of Immigrant Health. New York,* S. Loue, Editor. 1998, Plenum Press: New York.

25. Angel, R., and P. Thoits, *The impact of culture on the cognitive structure of illness.* Culture, medicine, and psychiatry, 1987. 11: p. 465-494.
26. Hulme, P.A., *Somatization in Hispanics.* Journal of Psychosocial Nursing Mental Health Services, 1996. 34: p. 33-37.
27. Guarnaccia, P.J., *The role of culture in psychiatric epidemiology: An examination of research on Latin American mental health.* Sante Ment Que, 1991. 16: p. 27-43.
28. Guarnaccia, P.J., R. Angel, and J.L. Worobey, *The factor structure of the CES-D in the Hispanic Health and Nutrition Examination Survey: The influences of ethncity, gender, and language.* Social Science and Medicine, 1989. 29: p. 85-94.
29. Lopez, S.R., *Latinos and the expression of psychopathology: A call for the direct assessment of cultural influences,* in *Latino Mental Health: Current Research and Policy Perspectives,* C. Telles and M. Karno, Editors. 1994, National Institute of Mental Health: Washington, DC: p. 109-127.
30. Lopez, S., and P. Guarnaccia, *Cultural psychopathology: Uncovering the social world of mental illness.* Annu Rev Psychol, 2000. 51: p. 571-598.
31. Malgady, R.G., and L.H. Rogler, *Mental Health status among Puerto Ricans, Mexican Americans, and non-Hispanic whites: The case of the misbegotten hypothesis.* American Journal of Community Psychology, 1993. 21: p. 383-388.
32. Guarnaccia, P.J., R. Angel, and J.L. Worobey, *The factor structure of the CES-D in the Hispanic Health and Nutrition Examination Survey: The influences of ethnicity, gender, and language.* Social Science and Medicine, 1989. 29: p. 85-94.
33. Guarnaccia, P.J., M. Rubio-Stipec, and G. Canino, *Ataques de nervios in the Puerto Rico Diagnostic Interview Schedule: The impact of cultural categories on psychiatric epidemiology.* Cult Med Psychiatry, 1989. 13(3): p. 275-295.
34. Leventhal, H., D.R. Nerenz, and D.J. Steele, *Illness representations and coping with health threats,* in *Handbook of psychology and health,* A. Baum and J.A. Singer, Editors. 1984, Erlbaum: New Jersey. p. 219-252.
35. Leventhal, H., M. Diefenback, and E. Leventhal, *Illness cognition: Using common sense to understand treatment adherence and affect cognition interaction.* Cognitive Therapy Research, 1992. 16: p. 143-163.
36. Leventhal, H. et al., *Illness representations: Theoretical foundations,* in *Perceptions of health and illness: current research and applications,* K.J. Petrie and J.A. Weinman, Editors. 1997, Harwood Academic Publishers: Australia. p. 19-45.
37. Kleinman, A., *Patients and Healers in the Context of Culture.* 1980, Berkeley: University of California Press.
38. Kleinman, A., L. Eisenberg, and B. Good, *Culture, illness and care: Clinical lessons from anthropologic and cross-cultural research.* Annals of Internal Medicine, 1978. 88: p. 251-258.
39. Mechanic, D., *Medical Sociology, 2nd Edition.* 1978, New York: Free Press.
40. Strain, L.A., *Illness behavior in old age: from symptom awareness to resolution.* Journal of Aging Studies, 1989. 3: p. 325-340.
41. Meyer, D., H. Leventhal, and M. Gutmann, *Common-sense models of illness: The example of hypertension.* Health Psychol, 1985. 4(2): p. 115-135.
42. Cameron, L., E.A. Leventhal, and H. Leventhal, *Symptom representations and affect as determinants of care seeking in a community-dwelling, adult sample population.* Health Psychol, 1993. 12: p. 171-179.

43. Cameron, L., E.A. Leventhal, and H. Leventhal, *Seeking medical care in response to symptoms and life stress.* Psychosom Med, 1995. 57(1): p. 37-47.
44. Petrie, K.J. et al., *Role of patients' view of their illness in predicting return to work and functioning after myocardial infarction: Longitudinal study.* Bmj, 1996. 312: p. 1191-1194.
45. Moss-Morris, R., K.J. Petrie, and J. Weinman, *Functioning in chronic fatigue syndrome: Do illness perceptions play a regulatory role?* Br J Health Psychol, 1996. 1: p. 15-25.
46. Horne, R., *Representations of medication and treatments: Advances in theory and measurement,* in *Perceptions of health and illness: Current research and applications,* K.J. Petrie and J.A. Weinman, Editors. 1997, Harwood Academic Publishers: Australia. p. 155-188.
47. Brown, C. et al., *Primary care patients' personal illness models for depression: A preliminary investigation.* Family Practice, 2001. 18: p. 314-320.
48. Araya, R. et al., *"Patient knows best"–detection of common mental disorders in Santiago, Chile: Cross sectional study.* Bmj, 2001. 322(7278): p. 79-81.
49. Strauss, A.K., and J. Corbin, *Basics of qualitative research.* 1990, Newbury Park, CA: Sage.
50. Glaser, B.D., and A.K. Strauss, *The Discovery of Grounded Theory.* 1967, Chicago, IL: Aldine Publishers.
51. Strauss, A.K., and J. Corbin, *Basics of Qualitative Research: Grounded Theory Procedures and Techniques.* 1990, Newbury Park, CA: Sage.
52. Miles, M.B., and A.M. Huberman, *Qualitative data analysis (2nd Ed.).* 1994, Newbury Park, CA: Sage.
53. Marshall, C., and G.B. Rossman, *Designing Qualitative Research (2nd ed.).* 1995, Thousand Oaks, CA: Sage Publications.
54. Patton, M.Q., *Qualitative evaluation and research methods.* 1990, Newbury Park, CA: Sage.
55. Guarnaccia, P.J. et al., *Si dios quiere: Hispanic families' experiences of caring for a seriously mentally ill family member.* Culture, Medicine and Psychiatry, 1992. 16: p. 187-215.
56. Brown, G.W., and T.O. Harris, *Social origins of depression: A study of psychiatric disorder in women.* 1978, London: Tavistock.
57. Ailinger, R.L., and M.E. Causey, *Health concept of older Hispanic immigrants.* West J Nurs Res, 1995. 17(6): p. 605-13.
58. Kart, C., *Experiencing symptoms: Attribution and misattribution of illness among the aged,* in *Elderly Patients and Their Doctors,* M. Haug, Editor. 1981, Springer: New York. p. 70-78.
59. Morgan, R. et al., *Older people's perceptions about symptoms.* Br J Gen Pract, 1997. 47(420): p. 427-430.
60. Rao, A.V., *Indian and western psychiatry: A comparison,* in *Transcultural psychiatry,* J.L. Cox, Editor. 1986, Croom Helm: London. p. 291-305.
61. Bavington, J., and A. Masjid, *Psychiatric services for ethnic minority groups,* in *Transcultural Psychiatry,* J.L. Cox, Editor. 1986. p. 87-106.

62. Kirmayer, L.J., and J.M. Robbins, *Patients who somatize in primary care: A longitudinal study of cognitive and social characteristics.* Psychological Medicine, 1996. 26: p. 937-951.

63. Lloyd, K., *Ethnicity, primary care and non-psychotic disorders.* Epidemiology & General Practice, 2000: p. 257-265.

64. Leventhal, E.A., and M. Crouch, *Are there differences in perceptions of illness across the lifespan?* in *Perceptions of health and illness: Current research and applications,* K.J. Petrie and J.A. Weinman, Editors. 1997, Harwood Academic Publishers: Australia. p. 77-102.

65. Brody, E.M., and M.H. Kleban, *Physical and mental health symptoms of older people: Who do they tell?* J Am Geriatr Soc, 1981. 29: p. 442-449.

66. Lyness, J.M. et al., *Older age and the underreporting of depressive symptoms.* J Am Geriatr Soc, 1995. 43(3): p. 216-221.

67. Wacholder, S. et al., *Selection of Controls in Case-Control Studies: I. Principles.* Americal Journal of Epidemiology, 1992. 135(9): p. 1019-1028.

68. Thiel de Bocanegra, H., F. Gany, and R. Fruchter, *Available epidemiologic data on New York's Latino population: A critical review of the literature.* Ethn Dis, 1993. 3: p. 413-426.

69. Alderete, E. et al., *Lifetime prevalence of and risk factors for psychiatric disorders among Mexican migrant farmworkers in California.* American Journal of Public Health, 2000. 90: p. 608-614.

70. Alderete, E. et al., *Effects of time in the United States and Indian ethnicity on DSM-III-R psychiatric disorders among Mexican Americans in California.* Journal of Nervous and Mental Disorders, 2000. 90: p. 608-614.

71. Vega, W. et al., *Lifetime prevalence of DSM-III-R psychiatric disorders among urban and rural Mexican Americans in California.* Arch Gen Psychiatry, 1998. 55: p. 771-778.

72. Rogler, L.H., D.E. Cortes, and R.G. Malgady, *Acculturation and mental health status among Hispanics: Convergence and new directions for research.* American Psychologist, 1991. 46: p. 585-597.

73. Kaplan, M.S., and G. Marks, *Adverse effects of acculturation: Psychological distress among Mexican American young adults.* Soc Sci Med, 1990. 31: p. 1313-1319.

74. Escobar, J.L. et al., *Abridged somatization: a study in primary care.* Psychosomatic Medicine, 1998. 60: p. 466-472.

75. Escobar, J.I. et al., *Somatization in the community: Relationship to disability and use of services.* American Journal of Public Health, 1987. 77: p. 837-840.

76. Coelho, V.L., M.E. Strauss, and J.H. Jenkins, *Expression of symptomatic distress by Puerto Rican and Euro-American patients with depression and schizophrenia.* J Nerv Ment Dis, 1998. 186: p. 477-483.

77. Canino, I.A. et al., *Functional somatic symptoms: A cross-ethnic comparison.* American Journal of Orthopsychology, 1992. 62: p. 605-612.

78. Canino, G.J. et al., *The prevalence of specific psychiatric disorders in Puerto Rico.* Archives of General Psychiatry, 1987. 44: p. 727-735.

79. Potter, L.B., L.H. Rogler, and E.K. Moscicki, *Depression among Puerto Ricans in New York City: The Hispanic Health and Nutrition Examination Survey.* Soc Psychiatry Psychiatr Epidemiol, 1995. 30(4): p. 185-93.

80. Vera, M. et al., *Depressive symptoms among Puerto Ricans: Island poor compared with residents of the New York City area.* American Journal of Epidemiology, 1991. 134(5): p. 502-510.

81. U.S. Department of Health and Human Services, Substance Abuse and Mental Health Services Administration, Center for Mental Health Services, *Mental Health: Culture, Race, and Ethnicity–A Supplement to Mental Health: A Report of the Surgeon General.* 2001: Rockville, MD.

82. Kessler, R.C. et al., *Lifetime and 12-month prevalence of DSM-IIIR psychiatric disorders in the United States: Results from the National Comorbidity Survey.* Archives of General Psychiatry, 1994. 51: p. 8-19.

83. Moscicki, E.K. et al., *The Hispanic Health and Nutrition Examination Survey: Depression among Mexican-Americans, Cuban Americans, and Puerto Ricans,* in *Health and Behavior: Research Agenda for Hispanics,* M. Gaviria and J.D. Arana, Editors. 1987, University of Illinois at Chicago: Chicago, IL. p. 145-159.

84. Rogler, L.H., R.G. Malgady, and O. Rodriguez, *Hispanic mental health: A framework for research.* 1989, Malabar, FL: Krieger Publishing Co.

85. Kramer, M. *Population changes, schizophrenic and other mental disorders, 1990, 2000, and 2010: Their implications for mental health programs.* 1990. Baltimore, MD.

86. Greenley, J.R., D. Mechanic, and P.D. Cleary, *Seeking help for psychologic problems: A replication and extension.* Med Care, 1987. 25: p. 1113-1128.

87. Sue, S. et al., *Community mental health services for ethnic minority groups: A test of the cultural responsiveness hypothesis.* Journal of Consulting and Clinical Psychology, 1991. 59: p. 533-540.

88. Rogler, L.H. et al., *What do culturally sensitive mental health services mean?: The case of Hispanics.* American Psychologist, 1987. 42: p. 565-570.

89. Miranda, M., *Psychotherapy with the Spanish-speaking: Issues in research and service delivery.* 1976, Los Angeles: Spanish-Speaking Mental Health Research Center University of California.

90. Wells, K.B. et al., *The functioning and well-being of depressed patients: Results from the Medical Outcomes Study.* J Am Med Assoc, 1989. 262: p. 914-919.

91. Katon, W. et al., *Distressed high utilizers of medical care. DSM-III-R diagnoses and treatment needs.* Gen Hosp Psychiatry, 1990. 12: p. 355-362.

92. Katon, W., M. Von Korff, and E. Lin, *The predictors of chronicity of depression in primary care and the effects of adherence to antidepressant therapy.* 1993. Tyson's Corner, VA: Nimh.

93. Marcos, L.R., and R. Cancro, *Pharmacotherapy of Hispanic depressed patients: Clinical observations.* American Journal of Psychotherapy, 1982. 36: p. 505-512.

94. Rogler, L.H., D.E. Cortes, and R.G. Malgady, *The mental health relevance of idioms of distress: Anger and perceptions of injustice among New York Puerto Ricans.* Journal of Nervous and Mental Disease, 1994. 182: p. 327-330.

95. Janzen, J., *The Quest for Therapy in Lower Zaire.* 1978, Berkeley, CA: University of California Press.

96. Kirmayer, L.J., A. Young, and J.M. Robbins, *Symptom attribution in cultural perspective.* Canadian Journal of Psychiatry, 1994. 39.
97. Good, B.J., and M.-J.D. Good, *The meaning of symptoms,* in *The relevance of social science for medicine,* L. Eisenberg and A. Kleinman, Editors. 1980, University of California Press: Berkeley, CA. p. 165-196.
98. Kavanaugh, K., and P. Kennedy, *Promoting cultural diversity: Strategies for health care professionals.* 1992, Newbury Park, CA: Sage.

Chapter 5

Serious Mental Illness Among Mexican Immigrant Families: Implications for Culturally Relevant Practice

Concepcion Barrio
Ann Marie Yamada

SUMMARY. The importance of family involvement in psychosocial interventions for persons with serious mental illnesses continues to gain empirical support. However, even as ethnic minority cultures are known to be more family-centered in comparison to Euro-American cultures,

---

Concepcion Barrio, PhD, is Associate Professor, School of Social Work, San Diego State University.

Ann Marie Yamada, PhD, is Assistant Professor, School of Social Work, University of Southern California.

Address correspondence to: Concepcion Barrio, PhD, Associate Professor, San Diego State University, School of Social Work, 5500 Campanile Drive, San Diego, CA 92139.

The preparation of this manuscript was supported by the National Institute of Mental Health grants K01 MH-01954 awarded to the first author and a Supplement under R01 MH-59101 awarded to the second author.

[Haworth co-indexing entry note]: "Serious Mental Illness Among Mexican Immigrant Families: Implications for Culturally Relevant Practice." Barrio, Concepcion, and Ann Marie Yamada. Co-published simultaneously in *Journal of Immigrant & Refugee Services* (The Haworth Social Work Practice Press, an imprint of The Haworth Press, Inc.) Vol. 3, No. 1/2, 2005, pp. 87-106; and: *Mental Health Care for New Hispanic Immigrants: Innovative Approaches in Contemporary Clinical Practice* (ed: Manny J. González, and Gladys González-Ramos) The Haworth Social Work Practice Press, an imprint of The Haworth Press, Inc., 2005, pp. 87-106. Single or multiple copies of this article are available for a fee from The Haworth Document Delivery Service [1-800-HAWORTH, 9:00 a.m. - 5:00 p.m. (EST). E-mail address: docdelivery@haworth press.com].

only a few studies focus on family context or on family treatment approaches for Mexicans. The focus of this paper is on mental health practice with Mexican immigrant families dealing with serious mental illness. We review available research on treatment issues and the sociocultural context that has relevance to serious mental illness within the family. Practice implications for increasing the cultural relevance of community based mental health services for this population are addressed. Several treatment strategies are delineated for practitioners confronted with clinical, social, and ethnocultural complexities when serving Mexican immigrant families dealing with serious mental illnesses. *[Article copies available for a fee from The Haworth Document Delivery Service: 1-800-HAWORTH. E-mail address: <docdelivery@haworthpress.com> Website: <http://www.HaworthPress.com> © 2005 by The Haworth Press, Inc. All rights reserved.]*

KEYWORDS. Schizophrenia, Hispanic, cultural relevance, family caregiving, ethnic minority services

INTRODUCTION

Recent cross-cultural literature recognizes the cultural resources and resilience that ethnic minority families exhibit in coping with health and mental health problems affecting the family system (Lefley & Johnson, 2002; Parra & Guarnaccia, 1998; Taylor, 1994). Among ethnic minority households, a web of relationships extends across relatives, fictive kin, and even across generations to provide a support network. This broad network is sustained by affiliative emotional traditions and rules of mutual obligation (Moore-Hines, Garcia-Preto, McGoldrick, Almeida, & Weltman, 1999). An extended family and multigenerational structure, under-girded by collectivistic cultural values and traditions, create conditions for the care and support of family members in times of need.

In the mental health field, the importance of family involvement in psychosocial interventions for persons with severe mental illnesses is gaining increased empirical support (Lefley & Johnson, 2002; Montero et al., 2001). However, even as ethnic minority cultures are known to be more family-centered in comparison to Euro-American cultures (Barrio, 2000; Lin & Kleinman, 1988), only a few studies have focused on the family context or on family treatment approaches for ethnic minority groups.

This paper focuses on Mexican origin Hispanics,[1] the largest ethnic minority group in the United States. Specifically, we are concerned with the sociocultural issues that impact the service needs of Mexican immigrant families of adults with a severe psychiatric condition (i.e., schizophrenia or other psychotic disorders) that often requires ongoing mental health treatment and the participation of family members. Findings from pertinent research and practice literature are reviewed to offer conceptual and practice strategies in working with this population. We will also draw on our own experience as practitioners and researchers in the field of serious mental illness in discussing the cultural and practice implications in working with recent Mexican immigrant families in community mental health settings.

DEMOGRAPHIC PROFILE

According to the findings from the 2000 U.S. Census, Hispanics of Mexican origin are the largest and most diverse Hispanic group in the United States. Mexican immigrants account for more than one quarter of the foreign born population, and more than half of the foreign born originating from Latin America. The Mexican immigrant population is nearly six times as large as the immigrant population from the next highest country, China (U.S. Bureau of the Census, 2002). From 1990 to 2000, the Hispanic population increased by more than fifty percent. Mexicans, who comprise 58.5 % of all Hispanics, increased by 52.9% from 13.5 million to 20.6 million (U.S. Bureau of the Census, 2001; 2002).

Persons of Mexican origin reside in different regions throughout the country. The break-down by region is as follows: 55.3% in the West, 31.7% in the South, 10.7% in the Midwest and 2.3% in the Northeast. The largest Mexican populations of more than a million reside in California, Texas, Illinois and Arizona. Combined, the population of Mexican immigrants residing in Texas and in the Los Angeles basin account for almost half of the Mexican immigrant population (3.6 million).

Based on the 2000 Census, the median age of Mexican immigrants is thirty-three years. Regarding educational attainment, only twenty percent of Mexican immigrants graduate from high school in either the USA or Mexico. Approximately fourteen percent achieve more than a high school education. These immigrants take an important role in the U.S. labor force. Eighty-three percent of Mexican immigrants report employment as service or skilled workers, farm or manual laborers. Only six percent of Mexican immigrant workers are employed in professional occupations. Among those between the ages of 25-54 approximately 55 percent of Mexican women have paid employment.

Earnings are low. In all, the poverty rate in 1999 was 26% for Mexican immigrants. The 1999 median earnings of full time, year-round Mexican immigrant male workers was only $19,200. The median earnings for Mexican born female workers was $15,100. Forty-seven percent of the Mexican born had some kind of health insurance for all or part of the year for 1999. In California alone, almost twenty-six percent of the Mexican immigrant population speak only Spanish (U.S. Bureau of the Census, 2001; 2002).

MENTAL HEALTH SERVICE UTILIZATION

Research has consistently shown ethnic disparities in the use of mental health services (Cheung & Snowden, 1990; Maynard et al., 1997). Generally, studies indicate underutilization of services among Latinos (primarily of Mexican origin) even when they have a serious psychiatric disorder (Barrio, Yamada, Hough, Hawthorne, Garcia, & Jeste, 2003a; Gallo et al., 1995; Hough et al., 1987; Peifer, Hu, & Vega, 2000; Wells et al., 1989). Moreover, disproportionate under-usage among low acculturated Spanish-speaking Mexican immigrants is even more dramatic (Flaskerud, 1986; Sue et al., 1991; U.S. Surgeon General Report, 2001; Vega et al., 1999; Wells, Hough, Golding, Burnam, & Karno, 1987). This pattern corresponds to a shortage of bilingual bicultural clinicians. While there are approximately 173 non-Hispanic white mental health providers per 100,000 persons, there are only 29 Hispanic professionals per 100,000 people (U.S. Surgeon General Report, 2001).

Specific to California, a recent large scale study documented that Mexican immigrants have significantly lower rates of psychiatric disorders than Mexican Americans or the national population of the United States (Vega, Kolody, Aguilar-Gaxiola, Alderete, Catalano, & Caraveo-Anduaga, 1998). The literature suggests that new immigrants to the United States bring with them certain culturally protective factors from their culture of origin. These protective factors serve to shield them from high risk health behaviors (Escobar, 1998; Neff & Hoppe, 1993; Vega & Alegria, 2001). Studies have shown that acculturation to American values and behaviors has a negative effect on the mental health of Mexican immigrants and their families and that the retention of Mexican traditional culture has a positive effect (Vega et al., 1998).

Studies that address treatment of patients with serious mental disorders have uncovered several disparities in service use. For example, in our own research we found a significant disparity in use of case management services by Latinos (Barrio et al., 2003a). Among a large sample of over 4,000 adults diagnosed with schizophrenia receiving mental health services in San Diego County, Latinos (primarily of Mexican origin) were less likely to use case management services compared to Euro-Americans. Similar to other studies that have examined mental health use among low acculturated Spanish-speaking Mexican Americans (Hough, Landsverk, & Karno, 1987; Vega et al., 1999), the results from our study indicated lower use of case management services among Spanish-speaking Latinos as compared to English-speaking Latinos (Barrio et al., 2003a). With respect to the use of public mental health services, researchers have found that ethnic disparities in service use among the serious mentally ill were related to variations in how mental health service systems responded to the sociocultural needs of ethnic minority clients (Snowden & Hu, 1997).

RESEARCH ON SYMPTOM EXPRESSION AND ETHNOCULTURAL FACTORS

Serious mental illness refers to the presence of any *DSM* mental disorder, substance use, or developmental disorder that substantially interferes with a person's life activities and ability to function (Wang, Demler, & Kessler, 2002). In this paper, the term serious mental illness will refer to the most severe mental disorders, schizophrenia spectrum disorders. Such disorders are often characterized by an illness course that is debilitating, persistent, and overwhelming for family and others involved.

The influential role of ethnocultural factors in the symptomatic expression of psychopathology has been widely recognized (Castillo, 1997; Coelho et al., 1998; Hopper & Wanderling, 2000; Lin, 1996; Lin & Kleinman, 1988; Tseng & Streltzer, 1997). Specific to schizophrenia, several studies on symptomatic differences between Latino (primarily of Mexican origin) and Euro-American psychiatric samples have found higher somatic symptoms among Latino patients (Escobar et al., 1986; Weisman et al., 2000). In a recent study, we found that Latinos report higher somatic concerns than both Euro-American and African American patients diagnosed with schizophrenia (Barrio et al., 2003b). Somatic symptoms are manifestations of emotional distress often attributed as culturally sanctioned expressions for accessing and receiving care (Castillo, 1998; Chaplin, 1997; Escobar, 1995).

There are a small but growing number of studies that have begun to advance our understanding of the cultural mechanisms that underlie the expression of psychopathology. Lin and Kleinman (1988) postulated that the sociocentric nature of collectivistic societies might serve as a buffering mechanism that accounts for the more favorable course and outcome of the illness in non-Western developing nations and among ethnic immigrant groups. Latino families come from collectivistic, sociocentric societies in contrast to

Western European cultures that are characterized as more individualistic. One study (Brekke & Barrio, 1997) that included a Latino sample (primarily of Mexican origin) found that higher levels of sociocentric cultural mechanisms among ethnic minority groups mediated more benign symptom profiles when compared with the non minority group. Similarly, cross-cultural studies on the construct of Expressed Emotion have shown that levels of Expressed Emotion vary by culture, with Euro-American families showing higher rates of Expressed Emotion than Mexican American families (Jenkins, 1991; 1992; Karno et al., 1987). The Expressed Emotion construct captures attitudes and feelings, namely criticism, hostility, and emotional overinvolvement, expressed by family members toward the patient. Lopez and colleagues (2000) report that for Euro-American families criticism was the key predictor of relapse, whereas for Mexican American families the lack of family warmth was the significant predictor of relapse. Additionally, Weisman and colleagues have found that Mexican Americans tend to make greater religious attributions than do Euro-Americans and that these attributions play an influential role in shaping family members' reactions to schizophrenia (Weisman, 2000; Weisman et al., 2000; Weisman & Lopez, 1996). Taken together, the findings on symptomatic expression, the sociocentric and Expressed Emotion constructs, family warmth, and religious attributions among Mexican Americans and Mexican immigrants appear to reflect cultural relational styles and behaviors. Such styles and behaviors can facilitate improved functioning or attenuate risk for relapse for persons with schizophrenia (Barrio, 2001; Karno & Jenkins, 1993). Cross-cultural variation in interpersonal and familial factors also offers some explanation for the cross-ethnic differences in manifestations of the illness. These differences have implications for understanding serious mental disorders and for approaching the involvement of family members in the treatment of patients.

RESEARCH ON MENTAL HEALTH PRACTICE WITH ETHNIC MINORITIES

Numerous studies have been conducted on characteristics related to cultural relevance or cultural competence of services, such as ethnic matching, help-seeking pathways, service underutilization, and the racial and ethnic disparities in treatment outcomes (Brach & Fraser, 2000; Sue, 1998). However, as Sue (1998) has asserted, there are only a few rigorous studies that examine the efficacy of treatment for members of ethnic minority groups. In fact, there are less than a handful of controlled studies that relate more directly to psychosocial interventions for persons with serious mental illness (Baker et al.,

1999; Jerrell & Wilson, 1997; Telles et al., 1995). Only one study included a Mexican immigrant sample (Telles et al., 1995). A few ethnic specific descriptive studies of programs serving the serious mentally ill address methods for culturally adapting services (Lefley & Bestman, 1991; Rivera, 1988; Rodriguez, 1986). Although these studies included Latino patients, most have not focused on Mexican Americans or Mexican immigrants.

Rehabilitative and psychosocial treatment interventions range from supportive, behavioral approaches, vocational and independent-living programs, to family-centered psychoeducational models (Anderson et al., 1980; Falloon et al., 1982a, 1982b; Kavanagh, 1992; McFarlane, 1983; Santos et al., 1995). Family-based approaches specific to serious mental illness have been considered particularly relevant for ethnic minority groups in the United States (Karno & Jenkins, 1993; Lefley, 1990). International studies conducted in developing (Shankar & Menon, 1991; 1993; Xiong et al., 1994) and in developed countries (Arevalo Ferrera, 1990; Brown et al., 1972; Dixon & Lehman, 1995), have also shown the importance of family issues and their implications for treatment effectiveness.

Studies on culturally-specific treatment programs for persons with severe mental illness describe the flexibility and appropriateness of a culturally adapted psychoeducational framework for ethnic minority patients and their families (Jordan, Lewellen, & Vandiver, 1995; Lefley, 1987; Lefley & Bestman, 1991; Rivera, 1988; Rodriguez, 1986). Lefley and Bestman (1991) highlight the use of culture brokers for meeting the mental health needs of multicultural immigrant communities. Culture brokers can occupy integral roles within the service delivery system by providing bridging, interpretive, collaborative, and teaching services between stakeholders and systems of care.

Researchers who have reviewed demonstration services for patients with comorbid serious mental illness and substance use disorders reported on culturally sensitive programming for specific ethnic minority groups (Mercer-McFadden et al., 1997). Culturally-specific interventions consisted of a multi-purpose cultural group that incorporated personal and social components designed to correspond with cultural themes, needs, and values of Latino patients. Bilingual and bicultural service providers were available for Latino patients as needed. Findings indicated a degree of success in engagement and involvement in long-term dual-disorder services, attributed in part to the emphasis on culturally tailored services. These types of strategies may also have applicability in working with Mexican immigrant families dealing with comorbid conditions.

In a project known as Community Organization for Patient Access (COPA), Rodriguez (1986) describes a framework that incorporates several program objectives and treatment approaches. The program's main purpose was to enhance clinical services for an inner city population of seriously mentally ill Latinos. Project designers set out to increase utilization of mental health services, implement culturally sensitive services, and evaluate the overall effectiveness of the project. Staff were trained in the psychoeducational approach, behavior modification, structural family therapy, problem-solving group therapies, recreational therapies, and in providing active community outreach. Psychosocial treatments primarily combined a psychoeducational approach with behavior modification. Several features of the model contributed to its success. Staff were bilingual and bicultural. They were also well-trained in diverse and comprehensive therapeutic approaches, illness education, and the use of adjunctive and community resources. Acculturation levels of clients and families were assessed to individualize treatment and outreach services. Extended kin and social networks were involved in therapeutic and educational services. Utilization levels increased, attendance rates improved, and measures of psychosocial adjustment showed favorable client outcomes. Further controlled studies are needed in this area.

A family intervention study conducted by Telles and colleagues (1995) compared the effectiveness and cross-cultural applicability of behavioral family treatment (BFT) versus case management among low-income Mexican immigrant patients diagnosed with schizophrenia. BFT was described as a highly structured, active program of interventions, which involves communication exercises and directives. Although, the results showed that the two treatments did not differ significantly, BFT was associated with greater risk of exacerbation of symptoms and at one year follow-up, the less acculturated patients treated by BFT had poorer outcomes on all the measures. In addition several families shifted from low Expressed Emotion to high Expressed Emotion. Based on these unexpected findings, the authors suggested that a highly structured program of interventions and directives may have been experienced as intrusive and stressful by the less acculturated Mexican immigrant patients and families. These findings were surprising particularly because the intervention was translated and aspects of the BFT approach had been culturally modified for the Mexican immigrant sample. However, the results of the study call into question whether the BFT was sufficiently adapted for the low-acculturated participants (Lopez, Kopelowicz, & Cañive, 2000). Since Mexican immigrants have been so rarely studied in the research on community based treatments, it is important to investigate the outcomes from effective intervention models that deal specifically with serious mental illness among this cultural group.

FAMILY CAREGIVING AND PARTICIPATION IN SERVICES

International perspectives from the literature indicate that the family represents a vital but underutilized resource in the care of persons with long-term mental illness (Karno & Jenkins, 1993; Shankar & Menon, 1991). According to DiNicola (1985), the portability of a family approach across cultures is supported by two findings: (1) the contribution of the extended family as reported in studies showing better outcomes for several psychiatric conditions in Third World cultures; and (2) the development of culturally-appropriate approaches, stressing family and community as treatment contexts. Family, extended kin as well as informal and formal community networks help ensure the applicability of family approaches in working with recent Mexican immigrants whose culture is characterized as sociocentric or collectivistic (Karno & Jenkins, 1993; Lefley, 1990).

There is great variation across families in practices, conceptions of mental illness, stigma attributed to mental illness, and expectations of the provider system. Mexican immigrant culture like other ethnic minority cultures is typically centered on the family and supported by extended networks which generate emotional and instrumental supports for family members in need (Karno & Jenkins, 1993).

A multicultural study that specifically addressed family caregiving of serious mental illness found that 75 percent of Latino patients and 60 percent of African-American patients lived with their families, compared with 30 percent of Euro-American patients (Guarnaccia, 1998). These findings exemplify the caregiving ideology of ethnic culture that reflects adaptive attributions and expectations regarding the family member's illness and social adjustment (Guarnaccia, 1998; Pickett, Cook, & Heller, 1998). Latino families expressed greater hope, optimism and faith regarding long-term outcomes of their family member's mental illness (Guarnaccia, 1998).

The following case illustrates cultural influences operating within the client-family system that correspond with several important issues raised by studies on family caregiving among Latino families dealing with a severe mental illness. The description is based on actual case material, although names and other identifying information have been changed.

Josie Mora, a 35-year-old woman, was diagnosed with schizophrenia (disorganized type) at the age of 22. Despite large doses of psychotropic medication, Josie exhibited disruptive and bizarre behavior, disorganized speech, inappropriate affect, and daily auditory hallucinations. For example, she called out to people using derogatory language, often falsely accusing them of trying to harm her. At home, she required constant limit setting as she would drink continuous pots of coffee and large amounts of soft drinks unless stopped. During the night she would get up several times to pace and clang pots and pans in the kitchen. As a result, she required ongoing supervision and was unable to participate in any psychiatric rehabilitation program activities offered at the mental health center.

The Mora family lived in the same community since they emigrated from Mexico over thirty years ago. The parents preferred to speak in Spanish, although they understood and spoke limited English. Josie preferred English, although Spanish was her first language. Josie lived at home and her parents were her primary caretakers. Several adult siblings and other extended family members lived in the same city and participated in Josie's care. Mrs. Mora had not worked outside the home since the onset of Josie's illness. During the day while Mr. Mora was at work, Mrs. Mora relied on a network of family and friends to help her with Josie, particularly whenever Mrs. Mora had her own medical appointments or needed to run certain errands. Eventually, Mr. Mora opted for early retirement from his factory job because he wanted to help his wife with Josie's care.

Both parents always accompanied Josie to her medication management appointments and monthly meetings with a social worker. The Moras took turns sharing the highlights of the month regarding Josie's behavioral outbursts involving family members, friends, and neighbors. Often they shared certain successful outcomes, like going to the park for a family gathering where Josie was able to tolerate being around many people without causing much disruption. Because of her severe impairment and her extensive need for supervision, on several occasions the social worker gently raised the option of board and care or other supervised residential care for Josie. The Moras considered the various options presented, but always expressed their willingness to accept their parental responsibility for Josie's caregiving, and their great "hope" that Josie would get better. The Mora family wanted to raise enough money for a trip to Mexico City. They hoped to take Josie to a special church to receive a holy blessing that would lead to healing and possibly a miracle. Several years later Josie was prescribed a new atypical anti-psychotic medication and with additional rehabilitation she made a substantial improvement in her social functioning. The Moras expressed that this progress was more than they had "hoped" Josie would achieve.

This case illustrates several cultural resources available while working with Mexican immigrant families dealing with serious mental illness. These include: a high degree of collectivism and interdependence represented by the degree of family involvement in the caregiving and in the treatment process; the resilience of the family in coping with a severely impaired family member; and the importance of faith and of hope regarding the future of the mentally ill family member. A culturally responsive approach in this case requires that the practitioner work from the perspective of the cultural orientation of the client-family system, to genuinely support values of interdependence, validate collectivistic behaviors, and to sustain the family's sense of hope. Services and interventions need to be coordinated to foster and cultivate cultural resources while also incorporating a psychoeducational approach that increases illness education and facilitates linkages to service programs and family support groups.

FAMILY PARTICIPATION IN SUPPORT SERVICES

Several barriers have affected the participation of Latinos and other ethnic minority families in services. Lower socioeconomic status, and in particular lower educational attainment, has been shown to relate to inadequate illness education and lack of familiarity with formal support groups (Cook & Knox, 1993; Guarnaccia, 1998; Medvene et al., 1995). The stigma attached to mental illness, coupled with minority status, can contribute to family members' reluctance to ask for help outside the immediate family (Cook & Knox, 1993). Additionally, families' attitudes toward the provider system vary from distrust of professionals, and reluctance to access services, to great deference by some Latinos (Guarnaccia, 1998; Pickett, Cook, & Heller, 1998). Collectively, these issues highlight the role of poverty, education, stigma, and attitudes that shape the interface between Latino culture and the culture of interventions within the provider system (Solomon, 1998). Although most of the findings discussed here focused on Latino and other disadvantaged ethnic minority groups, they were not specific to Mexicans. However, the characteristics found among ethnic minority families dealing with mental illness provide useful insights about cultural influences and resources that may also apply to Mexican immigrants.

In a recent study that examined family participation in support and self-help groups, we found several ethnic differences in the origin and nature of the groups (Barrio, Garcia, & Atuel, 2000). Most of these groups began in response to a great need for culturally relevant and linguistically accessible psychoeducational and supportive services for families. The Spanish-speaking Mexican immigrant support groups were all initiated and carried out by mental health professionals, whereas the African American and Native American groups were started and facilitated by family members or consumer advocates. The mental health professionals serving as facilitators of the Mexican immigrant groups emphasized the importance of ethnic matching and the cultural relevance of a psychoeducational approach in meeting the needs of Spanish-speaking families. In addition to psychoeducational topics regarding serious mental illness, other common topics were: spirituality, faith, hope, and meaning-making. Other issues included addressing causal attributions and cultural beliefs about mental illness, and dealing with stigma-related issues.

Successful groups emphasized an aggressive and continued outreach beyond mailings or posting of group meetings initiated by mental health providers in predominately Mexican immigrant communities. Outreach strategies consisted of identifying and engaging families at the first contact with the provider system. Several groups employed a family-to-family outreach strategy that worked well, particularly with parents of newly diagnosed patients. Several group facilitators identified economic barriers to ongoing participation in groups (e.g., work schedules, transportation, and the burden of sole caregiving). Among the Mexican origin support groups, providers indicated that families lacked an awareness of advocacy and activism roles, and stressed that these roles should not be expected outcomes of group participation.

In sum, few published studies have examined the family context or family treatment approaches for ethnic minority groups dealing with serious mental illness. The available findings from the literature on sociocultural context and treatment issues were reviewed for their relevance to Mexican immigrant families dealing with serious mental illness in a family member. There appears to be strong support for greater involvement of families in the rehabilitative process. Based on this research, there are practice implications for increasing the cultural relevance of community based mental health services for this population. Several of these include more specific treatment strategies for practitioners confronted with clinical, social, and ethnocultural complexities when serving recent Mexican immigrant families dealing with serious mental illnesses.

IMPLICATIONS FOR PRACTICE

When designing programs, providers need to start by taking the client's and family's perspective. By doing so they can recognize the unique ethnocultural qualities, service needs and expectations of family members. A culturally relevant approach combines such a perspective with the ability to balance culturally-specific values of families with those of the treatment culture. Invariably, this approach tests cultural and alternative hypotheses (Lopez, 1994; 1997).

Assessment should include an understanding of the extended family network, formal and informal natural supports, the family's history with multigenerational family living and caregiving, generational strengths, and sociocentric patterns of interdependence. Such knowledge increases the ability to forge collaborations that incorporate cultural roles and relationships. A careful cultural assessment process can draw from a provider's knowledge about sociocentric versus individualistic cultural orientations (see Markus & Kitayama, 1991). Cultural orientations are best assessed along a continuum rather than a dichotomy to assist in approaching Mexican immigrant families who may have family cultural traditions that differ from those of the provider. Based on what is learned, providers should endeavor to involve key family members in services from the initial engagement and throughout the process of treatment.

In addition, an assessment of interpersonal and prosocial orientation reflected in the sociocentric characteristics of empathy and social competence can be useful in cultivating and fostering these qualities in social skills training and family-centered modalities (Brekke & Barrio, 1997). Cultural domains can be incorporated into psychosocial assessments. Also, qualitative explorations should be conducted by practitioners knowledgeable and respectful of cultural differences in symptom expression and the family environment. For example, a careful assessment of somatic symptoms may signal high levels of emotional distress to be discerned by culturally respectful evaluation strategies. In addition, culturally sanctioned expressions imply that there are familial and social contextual forces operating that need to be appraised in the assessment and treatment process with Mexican immigrant patients and their families.

The design of rehabilitative services and individualization of treatment planning for Mexican origin patients and their families necessitates a comprehensive cultural assessment of the family system and an appraisal of the fit with the provider culture. A cultural assessment encompasses: the family's cultural perceptions and beliefs about mental illness; values, and expectations of social adjustment; family practices and supportive social networks; and attitudes and expected relationships toward the provider system (Higginbotham, 1984).

Regarding family support groups, it is important to recognize the impact of sociocultural, linguistic, and economic issues that may interface with participation in such services. Particularly for low income Spanish-speaking Mexican immigrant families, support groups should be linguistically and geographically accessible as well as tailored to the cultural needs and expectations. Providers and program designers need to recognize the cultural preference for professional leadership and a psychoeducational approach. Professionals have an instrumental role in developing, organizing and facilitating family support groups and effective outreach strategies.

Recent research shows that some approaches based on Western behavioral models may produce iatrogenic effects on clinical and functional outcomes for Mexican Americans (Telles et al., 1995; Barrio, 2001). Western cultures highly value independent action (Lefley, 1990). However, sociocentric-collectivistic ethnic cultures typically reflect attributes such as interdependence, sociability, familism, and concern for others (Lin & Kleinman, 1988; Marin & Triandis, 1985). The attempt to promote independence and self-sufficiency may be in conflict with cultural norms and be counter-therapeutic. Applying Euro American values of independence, self-reliance, rationalism, competitiveness, mastery over one's destiny, autonomous action, and emotional detachment to persons from sociocentric cultures may not be culturally syntonic.

Providers trained in Western behavioral models may tend unwittingly to pathologize ethnic minority cultural practices and sociocentric family relations. Family practices need to be viewed within the given cultural context, without imposing labels such as enmeshed, dependent and codependent to describe the various relationships and networks. Clinicians should approach familial traditions and practices as cultural hypotheses (Lopez, 1997). These can be explored and appraised for their therapeutic value and the benefit they bring the family member with the serious mental illness, as well as the family as a whole.

NOTE

1. The term Hispanic or Latino will be used consistent with the term in the source cited.

REFERENCES

Anderson, C. M., Hogarty, G. & Reiss, D. (1980). Family treatment of adult schizophrenic patients: A psycho-educational approach. *Schizophrenia Bulletin*, 6(3), 490-505.

Arevalo Ferrera, J. (1990). Intervenciones familiares en el tratamiento de los pacientes con esquizofrenia: Aproximaciones recientes. *Estudios de Psicologia*, 43-44, 169-193.

Baker, F. M.., Stokes-Thompson, J., Davis, O. et al. (1999). Two-year outcomes of psychosocial rehabilitation of Black patients with chronic mental illness. *Psychiatric Services*, 50(4), 535-539.

Barrio, C. (2000). The cultural relevance of community support programs. *Psychiatric Services*, 51(7), 879-884.

Barrio, C. (2001). Culture and schizophrenia: A cross-ethnic growth curve analysis. *Journal of Nervous and Mental Disease*, 189(10), 676-684.

Barrio, C., Garcia, P. & Atuel, H. (2000). Ethnic Minority Participation in Support & Self-help Groups for Families of the Mentally Ill, Presented at the Annual Meeting of the National Alliance for the Mentally Ill, San Diego, CA. June 16.

Barrio, C., Yamada, A.M., Atuel, H., Hough, R.L., Yee S., Berthot, B. & Russo, P. (2003a). A tri-ethnic examination of symptom expression on the positive and negative syndrome scale in schizophrenia spectrum disorders. *Schizophrenia Research*, 60(2-3), 259-269.

Barrio, C., Yamada, A. M., Barrio, C., Hough, R., Hawthorne, W. & Jeste, D.V. (2003b). Ethnic disparities in use of public mental health case management services among patients with schizophrenia. *Psychiatric Services*, 54, 1264-1270.

Brach, C. & Fraser, I. (2000). Can cultural competence reduce racial and ethnic health disparities? A review and conceptual model. *Medical Care Research and Review*, 57, 181-217.

Brekke, J. & Barrio, C. (1997). Cross-ethnic symptom differences in schizophrenia: The influence of culture and minority status. *Schizophrenia Bulletin*, 23(2), 305-316.

Brown, G. W., Birely, J. L. T. & Wing, J. K. (1972). Influence of family life on the course of schizophrenia disorders: Replication. *British Journal of Psychiatry*, 121, 241-258.

Castillo, R. (1997). *Culture and mental illness: A client-centered approach*. Pacific Grove, CA: Brooks/Cole.

Chaplin, S. L. (1997). Somatization, In W. S. Tseng and J. Streltzer. (Eds.). *Culture and Psychopathology: A guide to clinical assessment*. (pp. 67-86). New York: Brunner/Mazel.

Cheung, F. K. & Snowden, L. R. (1990). Community mental health and ethnic minority populations. *Community Mental Health Journal*, 26(3), 277-291.

Coelho, V. L. D., Strauss, M. E. & Jenkins, J. H. (1998). Expression of symptomatic distress by Puerto Rican and Euro-American patients with depression and schizophrenia. *Journal of Nervous & Mental Disease*, 186, 177-483.

Cook, J. & Knox, J. (1993). NAMI outreach strategies to African-American and Hispanic families: Results of a national telephone survey. *Innovations & Research*, 2(3), 35-42.

Cook, J., Wessell, M. E. & Dincin, J. (1987). Predicting educational achievement levels of the severely mentally ill: Implications for the psychosocial program administrator. *Psychosocial Rehabilitation Journal*, 9(1), 23-37.

DiNicola, V. F. (1985). Family therapy and transcultural psychiatry: An emerging synthesis, Part II: Portability and culture change. *Transcultural Psychiatric Research Review*, 22(3), 151-180.

Dixon, L. B. & Lehman, A. F. (1995). Family interventions for schizophrenia. *Schizophrenia Bulletin*, 21, 631-643.

Escobar, J. I. (1998). Immigration and mental health: Why are immigrants better off? *Archives of General Psychiatry*, 55, 781-782.

Escobar, J. I. (1995). Transcultural aspects of dissociative and somatoform disorders. *Psychiatric Clinics of North America*, 18, 555-569.

Escobar, J. I., Randolph, E. T. & Hill, M. (1986). Symptoms of schizophrenia in Hispanic and Euro-American veterans. *Cultural Medicine & Psychiatry*, 10, 259-276.

Falloon, I. R., Boyd, J. L., McGill, C. W., Razani, J., Moss, H. & Gilderman, A. M. (1982a). Family management in the prevention of exacerbations of schizophrenia: A controlled study. *The New England Journal of Medicine*, 306(24), 1437-1140.

Falloon, I. R., Boyd, J. L., McGill, C. W., Williamson, M., Razani, J., Moss, H., Gilderman, A. M. & Simpson, G. M. (1982b). Family management in the prevention of morbidity of schizophrenia. *Archives of General Psychiatry*, 42, 887-896.

Flaskerud, J. H. (1986). The effects of culture-compatible intervention on the utilization of mental health services by minority clients. *Community Mental Health Journal*, 22(2), 127-141.

Gallo, J. J., Marino, S., Ford, D. & Anthony, J. C. (1995). Filters on the pathway to mental health care, II. Sociodemographic factors. *Psychological Medicine*, 25, 1149-1160.

Guarnaccia, P. J. (1998). Multicultural experiences of family caregiving: A study of African American, European American, and Hispanic American families. *New Directions for Mental Health Services*, 77, 63-73

Higginbotham, H. N. (1984). *Third World challenge to psychiatry: Culture accommodation and mental health care*. Honolulu: University of Hawaii Press.

Hopper, K. & Wanderling, J. (2000). Revisiting the developed versus developing country distinction in course and outcome in schizophrenia: Results from ISoS, the WHO collaborative follow up project. *Schizophrenia Bulletin*, 26, 835-846.

Hough, R. L., Landsverk, J. A. & Karno, M. (1987). Utilization of health and mental health services by Los Angeles Mexican Americans and non-Hispanic Whites. *Archives of General Psychiatry*, 44, 702-709.

Jenkins, J. H. (1991). Anthropology, expressed emotion, and schizophrenia. *Ethos*, 19, 387-431.

Jenkins, J. H. (1992). Too close for comfort: Schizophrenia and emotional overinvolvement among Mexicano families. In A. D. Gaines (Ed.), *Ethnopsychiatry: The cultural construction of professional and folk psychiatries* (pp. 203-221). Albany: State University of New York Press.

Jerrell, J. M. & Wilson, J. L. (1997). Ethnic differences in the treatment of dual mental and substance disorders: A preliminary analysis. *Journal of Substance Abuse Treatment*, 14(2), 133-140.

Jordan, C., Lewellen, A. & Vandiver, V. (1995). Psychoeducation for minority families: A social work perspective. *International Journal of Mental Health*, 23(4), 27-43.

Karno, M. (1996). Cultural comments on organic and psychotic disorders, In J. E. Mezzich, A. Kleinman, H. Fabrega, & D. L Parron. (Eds.), *Culture & Psychiatric Diagnosis: A DSM-IV perspective* (pp. 71-73). Washington, DC: American Psychiatric Press, Inc.

Karno, M. & Jenkins, J. H. (1993). Cross-cultural issues in the course and treatment of schizophrenia. *Psychiatric Clinics of North America*, 16(2), 339-350.

Karno, M., Jenkins, J. H., de la Selva, A., Santana, F., Telles, C., Lopez, S. & Mintz, J. (1987). Expressed emotion and schizophrenic outcome among Mexican-American families. *Journal of Nervous Mental Disorders*, 175, 143-151.

Kavanagh, D. J. (1992). Family interventions for schizophrenia. In D. J. Kavanagh, (Ed.), *Schizophrenia: An overview and practical handbook* (pp. 407-423). London: Chapman & Hall.

Lefley, H. P. (1990). Culture and chronic mental illness. *Hospital and Community Psychiatry*, 41(3), 277-286.

Lefley, H. P. & Bestman, E. W. (1991). Public-academic linkages for culturally sensitive community mental health. *Community Mental Health Journal*, 27(6), 473-488.

Lefley, H. P. & Johnson, D. L. (Eds.). (2002). *Family interventions in mental illness international perspectives*. West Port, CT: Praeger.

Lin, K. M. (1996). Cultural influences on the diagnosis of psychotic and organic disorders, In Mezzich, A., Kleinman, H., Fabrega, H. and Parron, D. L. (Eds.). *Culture & Psychiatric Diagnosis: A DSM-IV Perspective*. American Psychiatric Press, Inc., Washington, DC. pp. 49-62.

Lin, K. M. & Kleinman, A. M. (1988). Psychopathology and clinical course of schizophrenia: A cross-cultural perspective. *Schizophrenia Bulletin*, 14(4), 555-567.

Lopez, S. R. (1994). Latinos and the Expression of Psychopathology: A call for the Direct Assessment of Cultural Influences. In C. A. Telles & M. Karno. (Eds.), *Mental disorders in Hispanic populations* (pp. 109-127). Los Angeles: Neuropsychiatric Institute, UCLA Press Mental Health.

Lopez, S. R. (1997). Cultural competence in psychotherapy: A guide for clinicians and their supervisors. In C. Z. Watkins, Jr. (Ed.), *Handbook of psychotherapy supervision*, (pp. 570-588). New York: John Wiley & Sons, Inc.

Lopez, S. R., Kopelowicz, & Cañive, J. M. (2002). Strategies in developing culturally congruent family interventions for schizophrenia: The case of Hispanics. In H.P. Lefley & D.L. Johnson (Eds.), *Family interventions in mental illness: International perspectives* (pp. 61-90). West Port, CT: Praeger.

Marin, G. & Triandis, H. C. (1985). Allocentrism as an important characteristic of the behavior of Latin Americans and Hispanics. In R. Diaz Guerrero (Ed.), *Cross-Cultural and national studies in social psychology* (pp. 85-104). North Holland: Elsevier Science Publishers.

Markus, H. R. & Kitayama, S. (1991). Culture and the self: Implications for cognition, emotion, and motivation. Psychological Review, 98, 224-253.

Maynard, C., Ehreth, J., Cox, G. B., Peterson, P. D. & McGann, M.E. (1997). Racial differences in the utilization of public mental health services in Washington State. *Administration and Policy in Mental Health*, 24(5), 411-424.

McFarlane, W. R. (Ed.). (1983). *Family Therapy in Schizophrenia*. New York: Guilford Press.

Medvene, L. J., Mendoza, R., Lin, K. M., Harris, N. & Miller, M. (1995). Increasing Mexican American attendance of support groups for parents of the mentally ill: Organizational and psychological factors. *Journal of Community Psychology*, 23, 307-325.

Mercer-McFadden, C., Drake, R. E., Brown, N. B. & Fox, R. S. (1997). The Community Support Program demonstrations of services for young adults with severe mental illness and substance use disorders, 1987-1991. *Psychosocial Rehabilitation Journal*, 20(3), 13-24.

Montero, I., Asencio, A., Hernandez, I., Masanet, M. J., Lacruz, M., Bellver, F., Iborra, M. & Ruiz, I. (2001). Two strategies for family intervention in schizophrenia: A randomized trial in a Mediterranean environment. *Schizophrenia Bulletin*, 27(4), 661-70.

Moore-Hines, P., Garcia-Preto, N., McGoldrick, M., Almeida, R., & Weltman, S. (1999). Culture and the family cycle. In B. Carter & M. McGoldrick (Eds.), *The expanded family life cycle: Individual, family, and social perspectives* (pp. 69-87). Boston: Allyn & Bacon.

Neff, J. A. & Hoppe, S. K. (1993). Race/ethnicity, acculturation, and psychological distress: Fatalism and religiosity as cultural resources. *Journal of Community Psychology*, 21, 3-20.

Parra, P. A. & Guarnaccia, P. (1998). Ethnicity, culture, and resiliency in caregivers of a seriously mentally ill family member. In H. I. McCubbin, E. A. Thompson et al., (Eds.), *Resiliency in Native American and immigrant families* (pp. 431-450). Thousand Oaks, CA: Sage.

Peifer, K. L., Hu, T-W. & Vega, W. A. (2000). Help-seeking by persons of Mexican origin with functional impairments. *Psychiatric Services*, 51(10), 1293-1298.

Pickett, S., Cook, J. & Heller, T. (1998). Support group satisfaction: A comparison of minority and white families. In H. P. Lefley (Ed.), Families coping with mental illness: The cultural context. *New Directions for Mental Health*, 77 (63-73). San Francisco CA:

Rivera, C. (1988). Culturally sensitive aftercare services for chronically mentally ill Hispanics: The case of the psychoeducational treatment model. Fordham University Hispanic Research Center Research Bulletin, vol. 11.

Rodriguez, O. (1986). Overcoming barriers to clinical services among chronically mentally ill Hispanics: Lessons from the evaluation of Project COPA. Fordham University Hispanic Research Center Research Bulletin, vol. 9.

Santos, A. B., Henggeler, S. W., Burns, B. J., Arana, G. W. & Meisler, N. (1995). Research on field-based services: Models for reform in the delivery of mental health care to populations with complex clinical problems. *American Journal of Psychiatry*, 152(8), 1111-1123.

Shankar, R. & Menon, R. S. (1991). Interventions with families of people with schizophrenia: The issues facing a community-based rehabilitation center in India. *Psychosocial Rehabilitation Journal*, 15(1), 85-90.

Shankar, R. & Menon, R. S. (1993). Development of a framework of interventions with families in the management of schizophrenia. *Psychosocial Rehabilitation Journal*, 16(3), 75-91.

Snowden, L., Hu, T-W. & Jerrell, J. (1995). Emergency care avoidance: Ethnic matching and participation in minority-serving programs. *Community Mental Health Journal*, 31(5), 463-473.

Snowden, L. & Hu, T-W. (1997). Ethnic differences in mental health services use among the severely mentally ill. *Journal of Community Psychology*, 25, 235-247.

Solomon, P. (1998). The cultural context of interventions for family members with a seriously mentally ill relative. In H. P. Lefley (Ed.), Families coping with mental illness: The cultural context. *New Directions for Mental Health*, 77 (5-16). San Francisco CA: Jossey-Bass Inc.

Sue, S. (1998). In search of cultural competence in psychotherapy and counseling. *American Psychologist*, 53, 440-448.

Sue, S., Fujino, D. C., Hu, L., Takeuchi, D. T. & Zane, N. W. S. (1991). Community mental health services for ethnic minority groups: A test of the cultural responsiveness hypothesis. *Journal of Consulting & Clinical Psychology*, 59(4) 533-540.

Taylor, R. L. (1994). Minority families and social change. In R. L. Taylor (Ed.), *Minority families in the United States: A multicultural perspective* (pp. 204-248). NJ: Prentice Hall.

Telles, C., Karno, M., Mintz, J., Paz, G. et al. (1995). Immigrant families coping with schizophrenia: Behavioural family intervention v. case management with a low-income Spanish-speaking population. *British Journal of Psychiatry*, 167, 473-479.

Tseng, W-S., & Streltzer, J. (1997). *Culture and Psychopathology: A guide to clinical assessment*. Brunner/Mazel, New York.

U.S. Bureau of the Census. (2001). The Hispanic Population: 2000 (Census Brief C2KBR/01-3) Washington, DC: U.S. Government Printing Office.

U.S. Bureau of the Census. (2002). Coming from the Americas: A profile of the nation's foreign-born population from Latin America: 2000 (Census Brief: Current Population Survey CENBR/01-2) Washington, DC: U.S. Government Printing Office.

U.S. Surgeon General. (2001). *Mental Health: Culture, Race, and Ethnicity–A Supplement to Mental Health: A Report of the Surgeon General*. U.S. Department of Health and Human Services. Rockville, MD: U.S. Department of Health and Human Services, Substance Abuse and Mental Health Services Administration, Center for Mental Health Services.

Vandiver, V. L. & Keopraseuth, K-O. (1998). In H. P. Lefley (Ed.), Families coping with mental illness: The cultural context. *New Directions for Mental Health*, 77 (75-88). San Francisco CA: Jossey-Bass Inc.

Vega, W. A. & Alegria, M. (2001). Latino mental health and treatment in the United States. In M. Aguirre-Molina, C. W. Molina & R. E. Zambrana (Eds.), *Health issues in the Latino Community* (pp. 179-208). San Francisco: Jossey-Bass.

Vega, W. A., Kolody, B., Aguilar-Gaxiola, S. et al. (1998). Lifetime prevalence of DSMII-R psychiatric disorders among urban and rural Mexican Americans in California. *Archives of General Psychiatry*, 55, 771-778.

Vega, W., Kolody, B., Aguilar-Gaxiola, S. & Catalano, R. (1999). Gaps in service utilization by Mexican Americans with mental health problems. *American Journal of Psychiatry*, 156(6), 928-934.

Wang, P. S., Demler, O. & Kessler, R. C. (2002). Adequacy of treatment for serious mental illness in the United States. *American Journal of Public Health*, 92, 92-98.

Weisman, A. G. (2000). Religion: A mediator of Anglo-American and Mexican attributional differences toward symptoms of schizophrenia. *Journal of Nervous Mental Disorders*, 188, 616-621.

Weisman, A. G., Lopez, S. R., Nuechterlein, K. H., Goldstein, M. J. & Hwang, S. (2000). A comparison of psychiatric symptoms between Euro-American-Americans and Mexican-Americans with schizophrenia. *Schizophrenia Bulletin*, 26, 817-824.

Weisman, A. G. & Lopez, S.R. (1996). Family values, religiosity, and emotional reactions to schizophrenia in Mexican and Anglo-American cultures. *Family Process*, 35, 227-237.

Wells, K. B., Golding, J. M., Hough, R. L., Burnam, A.M. & Karno, M. (1989). Acculturation and the probability of use of health services by Mexican Americans. *Health Services Research*, 24(2), 237-257.

Xiong, W., Phillips, M. R., Hu, X. et al. (1994). Family based intervention for schizophrenia patients in China: A randomized controlled trial. *British Journal of Psychiatry*, 165, 239-257.

Chapter 6

Psychosocial Stressors, Psychiatric Diagnoses and Utilization of Mental Health Services Among Undocumented Immigrant Latinos

M. Carmela Pérez
Lisa Fortuna

SUMMARY. The combined effects of minority status, specific ethnic group experiences (political, economic, trauma and immigration history), poverty, and illegal status pose a set of unique psychiatric risks for undocumented Latinos in the United States. Restrictive legislation and policy measures have limited access to health care, and other basic human services to undocumented immigrants and their children through-

M. Carmela Pérez, PhD, is affiliated with St. Vincent's Medical Health Centers of New York, and is Program Director, Adult and Latino Ambulatory Services, Behavioral Health Services, 203 West 12th Street, Suite 2061, New York, NY 10011 (E-mail: cperez@svcmcny.org).

Lisa Fortuna, MD, MPH, is affiliated with the Center for Child and Adolescent Health Policy, Massachusetts General Hospital, 50 Staniford Street, Suite 901, Boston, MA 02114 (E-mail: lfortuna@partners.org).

[Haworth co-indexing entry note]: "Psychosocial Stressors, Psychiatric Diagnoses and Utilization of Mental Health Services Among Undocumented Immigrant Latinos." Pérez, M. Carmela, and Lisa Fortuna. Co-published simultaneously in *Journal of Immigrant & Refugee Services* (The Haworth Social Work Practice Press, an imprint of The Haworth Press, Inc.) Vol. 3, No. 1/2, 2005, pp. 107-123; and: *Mental Health Care for New Hispanic Immigrants: Innovative Approaches in Contemporary Clinical Practice* (ed: Manny J. González, and Gladys González-Ramos) The Haworth Social Work Practice Press, an imprint of The Haworth Press, Inc., 2005, pp. 107-123. Single or multiple copies of this article are available for a fee from The Haworth Document Delivery Service [1-800-HAWORTH, 9:00 a.m. - 5:00 p.m. (EST). E-mail address: docdelivery@haworthpress.com].

out the nation. However, little is known about the patterns of mental health care use, psychiatric diagnoses and psychosocial problems prevalent among the undocumented who do succeed in presenting to clinical settings and to the mental health sector. To begin to address the need for further understanding in this area, we completed a clinical chart review of 197 outpatient adult psychiatric charts in a Latino mental health outpatient treatment program located in an urban hospital system.

We compared the diagnoses and mental health care use of undocumented Latino immigrants (15%) with that of documented (73%) and US born Latinos (12%) treated in this clinical setting. The undocumented Latinos in our study were more likely to have a diagnosis of anxiety, adjustment and alcohol abuse disorders. The undocumented also had a significantly greater mean number of concurrent psychosocial stressors (mean number = 5, $p < .001$) as compared to documented immigrants and US born groups, which both had a mean number of 3 stressors identified at evaluation. The undocumented were more likely to have psychosocial problems related to occupation, access to healthcare and the legal system. However, the undocumented had a lower mean number of total mental health appointments attended (mean visits = 4.3, $p < .001$) in which to address these stressors as compared to documented immigrants (mean visits = 7.9) and US born (mean visits = 13.3). In terms of other previous mental health service use, the undocumented group had lower rates of lifetime inpatient and outpatient treatment use.

The results of this study suggest the importance of early assessment of psychosocial stressors, substance use and barriers to care when treating undocumented immigrants. Although all Latino groups included in this investigation demonstrated numerable concurrent stressors, our investigation highlights the particular importance of accessible social services and supports for addressing psychosocial stressors in the lives of undocumented patients. Our results stress the importance of reexamining policies, that restrict access to social services and healthcare for the undocumented. Our results also suggest the importance of culturally appropriate evaluation and treatment of substance abuse disorders as well as addressing other psychological and behavioral responses to multiple stressors among undocumented individuals. *[Article copies available for a fee from The Haworth Document Delivery Service: 1-800-HAWORTH. E-mail address: <docdelivery@haworthpress.com> Website: <http://www.HaworthPress.com> © 2005 by The Haworth Press, Inc. All rights reserved.]*

KEYWORDS. Undocumented immigrants, Latino mental health, immigrant health, health and social disparities

INTRODUCTION

In the last 10 years, the population of Latinos in New York City and throughout the United States has shown a growing number of illegal or undocumented immigrants. In stark contrast to Latinos who are born in the United States, or immigrants who reside legally in the US, undocumented immigrant Latinos are unable to qualify for most governmental aid or healthcare. Migration, poverty, prejudice, illegal status, lack of access to healthcare, lack of supports, and the inability to speak English, are compounded problems which undocumented, immigrant Latinos face. These issues augment any mental health problems, which arise in this population. Although, the field of Latino mental health has continued to expand during the past decades to include issues of immigration and stress, there is still much that we do not know about the diverse emotional experiences and circumstances of Latinos in the United States; specifically, undocumented Latino immigrants are among those most underrepresented in the mental heath treatment literature.

DEMOGRAPHICS

The number of Latinos in the United States grew by almost 13 million people between 1990 and 2000 (US Census Bureau, 2000). The percentage difference for the total population between 1990 and 2000 was 13.2 while the percentage difference for Hispanics was 57.9 during the same period (US Census Bureau, 2000). Among the growing number of Latinos are a significant proportion of unnaturalized, non-citizen and undocumented immigrants. In 1997, only 24% of the foreign-born populations from Latin America currently living in the United States were naturalized citizens (US Census Bureau, 2000). In addition, while Latin-American immigrants reside all across the United States, many concentrate in or near metropolitan areas. The traditional settlement areas include California, Texas, New York, Florida, Illinois and New Jersey. Foreign-born newcomers also migrated in the 1990s to "new destination states" such as Utah, Nevada and the South (US Census Bureau, 2000). Over 40 percent (1.4 million) of all undocumented immigrants live in California and almost five percent of Californian residents are illegal immigrants–three times the national average. Prior to the Immigration Reform and Control Act (which offered citizenship to illegal aliens who entered before 1982), California's illegal immigrant count reached 2.4 million, which represented over half the undocumented resident population of the U.S. at the time (Undocumented Immigration to California, 1980-1993).

A recent study, which was conducted by the People-To-People Health Foundation (commonly known as The Project HOPE Center for Health Affairs), completed in-depth interviews of households having undocumented immigrants in order to better understand the characteristics of this population. Household members were interviewed in El Paso and Houston, Texas. Key findings of this study concluded that the population of undocumented Latino immigrants was relatively young (in Houston, 59% were between the ages of 18 and 34 and in El Paso, 39% were in this age group), and that the majority of undocumented Latinos (99% in El Paso and 86% in Houston) emigrated from Mexico. None of the respondents at either site reported coming to the United States for health or social services. However, even though the use ambulatory care services were very low compared to that of the overall US population, the rates of hospitalization for undocumented Latinos were similar to the overall Latino and US populations. In terms of family income, this study concluded that almost 50% of the undocumented Latinos in both cities reported annual family incomes of less than $5,000, and more than 90% reporting incomes under $20,000 (Berk & Shur, 2000).

Foreign Latino workers who lack documentation usually obtain jobs that are toward the bottom of the social ladder. According to Hondagneu-Sotelo (1997), undocumented women have few employment options in the local economy and often work in the informal sector of the economy in industries such as street vending and paid domestic work. Undocumented workers commonly satisfy most requirements for inclusion in the lower segment of the population (Papademetriou & DiMarzio, 1986). Based on supply and demand conditions, these jobs tend to involve low wages, long-term instability, lack of mobility, and poor working conditions that are usually harsh, unpleasant, and often unsafe (de Lourdes Villar, 1990; Djajíc, 1997).

PSYCHOSOCIAL RISKS

The undocumented are particularly vulnerable to being poor and exploited, most do not receive mental health care services regardless of need and the emotional consequences of severe disenfranchisement. Mental health needs remain unaddressed resulting in an increased risk for chronic psychological symptoms and morbidity (Vega et al., 1985). Ethnic and racial minorities in the United States face a social and economic environment of inequality that includes greater exposure to racism and discrimination, violence and poverty, all of which take a toll on mental health (USDHHS, 2001). A legal status that limits access to social and health services for addressing these problems further hinders undocumented immigrants–especially for individuals with minimal family contacts and other protective social supports.

The general immigrant population has a similar rate of some mental health disorders as the general population, but has much lower rates of mental health care use (Chelminsky, 1991; Jimenez et al., 1997; Neighbors et al., 1992). The Epidemiologic Catchment Area (ECA) study has been one of the most important psychiatric epidemiological surveys that included Latinos (Regier et al., 1984). The Los Angeles ECA site was the only one where significant numbers of Latinos were interviewed and assessed, and most of these Latinos were Mexican-American. The prevalence of major depression among Latinos in the ECA was similar to that of non-Latino whites (Burnam et al., 1987). However, high rates of alcohol abuse and dependence were found among Latinos. The ECA also showed higher lifetime prevalence of dysthymia, panic disorder, and phobias among Mexican-American women older than 40 years than among all other groups. Less is known about the psychiatric diagnoses and mental health needs of undocumented Latinos even among those who do seek care. In primary care settings, alcohol abuse and dependence have been found to be quite common among Latinos (Borges et al., 2001; Nielson, 2000, 2001; Randolph et al., 1998; Treno et al., 1999). Community research and clinical practice have shown that alcohol and drug use and depression are highly interrelated among Latinos. Between immigrant and undocumented Latinos, acculturation, immigration stresses and undetected and untreated mental illness may play a role in higher rates of alcohol use disorders (Lipton, 1997; Wells et al., 2001; Zayas, 1998).

The ECA study also found that Latinos were less likely to seek outpatient psychiatric care or visit a mental health professional for their problems than were non-Latino whites (Karno et al., 1987). The literature shows that low income, unemployment, and lack of health insurance are major financial constraints that contribute to lower utilization of mental health services by recent immigrants (Alvidez, 1999; Leslie & Leitch, 1989; Trevino et al., 1991). Cultural beliefs and other non-financial barriers also hinder access to mental health care (Keefe, 1997; Woodward et al., 1992). Some of these other obstacles include: language barriers; unfamiliarity with health service resources; a cultural heritage which stigmatizes psychiatric illness; lack of transportation to health care services located outside the community; lack of provider sensitivity manifested by systemic prejudices in treatment; and lack of culturally relevant mental health services (Briones et al., 1990; Estrada & Trevino, 1990; Takeuchi et al., 1995; Sue et al., 1994; Sue & Yeh, 1995; Vega & Miranda, 1985).

General rates of all medical service use by undocumented Latinos are even lower than that of the rest of the U.S. population including other Latinos

(Hough et al., 1987; Hu et al., 1990). In one community-based study, rates of annual physician visits were much lower for undocumented Latino immigrants in California and Texas than for all other Latinos and all persons in the United States (Berk & Shur, 2000). They found that the proportion of undocumented immigrants who had a physician visit in 1999 ranged from 27% to 50% (vs. 75% of all other Americans and 60% of all other Latinos). Further, these researchers found that for those undocumented immigrants who did obtain access, intensity of use was much lower (average = 3-4 visits per year) as compared to other Latinos or the nation overall (average = 6 visits per year). There are no comparable studies examining patterns of mental health service use or substance abuse treatment by undocumented Latinos.

CLINICAL ASSESSMENT FACTORS
AMONG UNDOCUMENTED LATINOS

The most important challenge to the clinical assessment of undocumented Latinos is the lack of access to mental health services. However, a relatively small percentage of undocumented Latinos do enter to the mental health care sector. We designed a clinical chart review study with the objective of examining psychiatric diagnoses and patterns of mental health services use among undocumented Latinos at our Latino Mental Health Program at Saint Vincent Catholic Medical Centers in Manhattan, New York. We aimed to look at how the undocumented compare to other immigrants and to the more acculturated United States born Latinos, in regards to psychiatric diagnoses, including alcohol and substance abuse disorders, psychosocial problems and presenting illness severity. We were also interested in delineating patterns of mental health care use and examining number and percentage of clinical appointments used as well as lifetime history of inpatient and outpatient services. Our long-term objective was to assess what specific services may be needed for improving access and retention of patients who are of undocumented status.

Study Setting

The Latino Mental Health Program (LMHP) is an outpatient psychiatric service of Saint Vincent Catholic Medical Centers-Manhattan, Behavioral Health Program. The LMHP was founded in 2000 with a mission to provide culturally sensitive bilingual and bicultural mental health treatment to Latino individuals and families, who are experiencing mental health and substance abuse problems. Located in the West Village area of Manhattan, the LMHP provides services to Latinos from the five boroughs of New York City. The multidisciplinary team of LMHP clinicians includes psychiatrists, psychologists, and clinical social workers, is bilingual and bicultural. The patient population served by the LMHP is an underserved population of monolingual Spanish speaking and bilingual Latinos, some of whom are uninsured or on public assistance and others who are nonresidents or undocumented.

Sample

We reviewed the psychiatric record of 197 Latino patients who presented for services in the LMHP at least one time, during a 15-month period (July, 2000-September, 2001). We specifically reviewed diagnoses at initial psychiatric assessment and mental health use in our clinic after initial assessment. The total sample (N = 230) was divided into three groups: 15% (N = 29) undocumented immigrant Latinos, 73% (N = 144) documented immigrant Latinos and 12% (N = 24) Latinos born in the United States. Because the total sample included a group of patients who had only presented for one visit, a subsample of (N = 188) was used when analyzing patterns of care after initial assessment in our clinic. *Legal status:* We determined the patient's immigration/legal status based on written documentation in the chart of such by the evaluating clinician at the time. However, this data was not always readily available in the chart and we questioned the reliability of this method of identifying the undocumented. In cases where this information was not available, we determined undocumented status by consensus, and by asking the treating provider for the patient to verify each case. In addition, a dual status of having no health insurance and no social security number was also used for tagging cases for verification. The United States born group was composed of Latinos born and raised in the United States mainland, and did not include those born in Puerto Rico which were categorized as legal immigrants. This separated the groups into three: 29 undocumented immigrant Latinos (15%), 144 documented immigrant Latinos (73%), and 24 Latinos born in the United States (12%).

Inclusion and Exclusion Criteria

We screened all of the patients who were newly admitted to the LMHP between July, 2000 and September, 2001 (N = 197). We excluded those individuals already previously admitted to our affiliate hospital in order to restrict our analyses to the cohort beginning care during the opening of the LMHP and therefore to those receiving comparable bilingual services.

Study Variables

Demographic background variables: Included age, gender, country-of-origin, primary language, and health insurance status. *Suicidality*: Was assessed in terms of documentation of both presence of past suicidal attempts, and current suicidal ideation. *Substance abuse*: Prevalence of substance abuse was determined only by whether the patient had been given a substance abuse disorder diagnosis by the clinician initially assessing the patient. *Psychiatric diagnoses and severity of illness*: Psychiatric diagnoses were assigned using DSM-IV nomenclature and as assessed and documented by the evaluating clinician. Severity of illness was taken from the clinicians' reported Global Assessment of Functioning (GAF) score. The GAF is a clinician reported rating used regularly in our clinic's initial assessments. GAF scores range from 0 to 100, where 100 indicates excellent life adjustment with completely intact social, personal, and occupational functioning, and no symptoms; scores under 20 represent very poor functioning in all areas, and severe mental illness with multiple symptoms, and/or danger to self or others secondary to suicidal and/or homicidal ideation. *Psychosocial stressors*: We examined both the type and number of stressors reported. Psychosocial stressors were categorized by clinicians at the time of evaluation and included: problems with family/primary supports, social environment, educational, occupational, housing, economic, access to health care, and legal system/crime. We also totaled the number of psychosocial stressors for each patient. *Current and past mental health service utilization*: Data was extracted in terms of mental health service use including both historical and present utilization. Past mental health service use was determined based on whether the patient had *any* prior inpatient or outpatient psychiatric service use either for mental health or substance abuse reasons. In addition, the ratio of appointments kept was calculated (appointments kept/appointments given) for each patient. The time period for calculating this ratio included appointments given and attended between July, 2000 and April, 2001. This was done in order to keep the 10-month time frame as a consistent and fixed period of examination.

STATISTIC ANALYSIS

Analyses compared the total sample, N = 197, of three groups of Latinos (undocumented immigrant Latinos, documented immigrant Latinos, and US born Latinos) on demographic variables, legal status, suicidality, substance abuse, and DSM-IV diagnoses. Continuous data variables were entered into a statistical program for T-test and ANOVA (analyses of variance) analyses. Only those variables, which were uniformly available in the subject medical record, were utilized in the data analyses. Data were analyzed using T-tests for two group comparisons and ANOVAs for three group comparisons. Statistical significance was set at p = 0.05. The chi square statistic was used to determine significant group differences on categorical measures (e.g., history of outpatient mental health service use, yes or no).

RESULTS

Demographics and Characteristics of the Study Population

The undocumented in our clinic are a relatively young group. Table 1 shows that the documented immigrant group is significantly older (mean age = 52 yrs.) than the undocumented group (mean age = 33 yrs.), and the United States-born group (mean age = 34 yrs.) (p < .05). The documented and United States-born groups had a high percentage of females relative to the undocumented group, which was almost entirely male. As expected, the undocumented group was found to be entirely uninsured. Both immigrant groups, documented and undocumented were found to be primarily Spanish speaking; the documented group originated predominantly from the Caribbean (Puerto Rico), and the undocumented group was primarily from South America and Mexico.

Distribution of Diagnoses

Table 2 shows the distribution of diagnoses by group, the frequency of current suicidal ideation, frequency of stressors by type, and the mean global assessment of functioning. All three groups were found to have major depression as the most frequently assigned diagnosis. There were similar rates of suicidal ideation, though a trend towards lower prevalence of suicidal ideation existed among the documented.

Mean Number of Stressors

The difference in mean number of stressors among the three study groups was also found to be significant (p < .01). The undocumented group was found to have a significantly greater number of stressors than the documented and US-born groups. All three groups were found to have problems most frequently in the area of family/primary support, and social environment. The undocumented were more likely to have occupational problems, legal difficulties, and impeded access to health care when compared to the other two groups, how-

TABLE 1. Demographics and Characteristics

	Undocumented Group 1 N = 29 (15%)	Documented Group 2 N = 144 (73%)	US Born Group 3 N = 24 (12%)
Sociodemographic			
Mean Age	34	52	34
Female*	6 (21%)	104 (72%)	18 (75%)
Uninsured**	29 (100%)	8 (5%)	2 (8%)
Language Spoken			
Spanish	20 (69%)	103 (72%)	0 (0%)
English**	0 (0%)	7 (5%)	16 (67%)
Bilingual	9 (31%)	34 (23%)	8 (33%)
Region of Origin			
Caribbean*	2 (7%)	113 (79%)	0 (0%)
North America			
Mexico*	10 (34%)	3 (2%)	0 (0%)
USA**	0 (0%)	0 (0%)	24 (100%)
South America*	13 (46%)	19 (13%)	0 (0%)
Central America	3 (10%)	9 (6.3%)	0 (0%)
Other**	1 (3%)	0 (0%)	0 (0%)

* Significant difference between undocumented and combined other two Latino groups (Group 2 and 3) at p < .001
** Significant difference between undocumented and combined other two Latino groups (Group 2 and 3) at p < .05

ever the differences in mean current GAF were not found to be statistically significant or clinically meaningful between study groups.

Past and Current Mental Health Services

Table 3 shows the rates of past and current mental health services. The undocumented group was found to have much lower rates of prior outpatient and inpatient services when compared to the documented and US-born groups. The undocumented group was also found to have a significantly lower number of appointments in our clinic when compared to the other two groups (p < .01). However, despite having fewer number of appointments, the undocumented group was found to have a similar percentage of appointments kept (74%) as did the documented group (77%) and the US born group (69%).

TABLE 2. Frequency of Psychiatric Diagnoses, Suicidal Ideation, Type of Stressors, and Global Assessment of Functioning

	Undocumented Group 1 N = 29	Documented Group 2 N = 144	US Born Group 3 N = 24
Axis I Diagnosis			
Major Depression	21 (72%)	86 (60%)	13 (54%)
Depression with Psychosis	1 (3%)	16 (11%)	1 (4%)
Bipolar	2 (7%)	8 (5%)	1 (4%)
Psychosis	3 (10%)	17 (12%)	3 (13%)
Anxiety	6 (14%)	16 (11%)	4 (17%)
Substance Abuse**	6 (21%)	9 (6%)	4 (17%)
Adjustment Disorder	4 (14%)	7 (5%)	1 (4%)
Dementia	0 (0%)	4 (3%)	0 (0%)
Other	1 (3%)	4 (3%)	1 (4%)
Suicidal Ideation	3 (10%)	18 (13%)	4 (17%)
Type of Stressors			
Family/Primary	23 (79%)	117 (81%)	22 (92%)
Social Environment	22 (76%)	90 (63%)	20 (83%)
Educational	5 (17%)	32 (22%)	6 (25%)
Occupational*	18 (62%)	68 (47%)	11 (46%)
Housing	7 (24%)	30 (21%)	3 (13%)
Economic	12 (41%)	49 (34%)	9 (36%)
Access to Healthcare*	8 (28%)	14 (10%)	3 (13%)
Legal System/Crime*	29 (100%)	6 (4%)	1 (4%)
Other	2 (7%)	4 (3%)	0 (0%)
Mean Number of Stressors *	4.45	2.90	3.08
Mean Current GAF	59	54	58

* Significant difference between undocumented and combined other two Latino groups (Group 2 and 3) at p < .001
** Significant difference between undocumented and combined other two Latino groups (Group 2 and 3) at p < .05

DISCUSSION

Treatment Needs and Approaches

This study confirmed our clinical impression that undocumented patients are seen for less frequent visits and for shorter courses of treatment as compared to our other two Latino groups. This finding is consistent with the litera-

TABLE 3. Utilization of Services: Prior and Current Use

	Undocumented Group 1 N = 29	Documented Group 2 N = 144	US Born Group 3 N = 24
Prior Outpatient*	11 (40%)	102 (71%)	17 (71%)
Prior Inpatient*	4 (14%)	59 (41%)	10 (42%)
Current Utilization of Services	Undocumented Group 1- Partial Sample N = 20	Documented Group 2 N =144	US Born Group 3 N = 24
Mean number of appts.*	4.4	7.9	13.3
% of appt. kept	74%	77%	69%

* Significant difference between undocumented and combined other two Latino groups (Group 2 and 3) at p < .001

ture on general health services utilization patterns among undocumented Latinos, which shows less frequent use of medical care by this group as compared to the general United States population and other Latino groups. It seems important to point out, however, that even though our undocumented sample attended fewer appointments, the percentage of appointments that this group kept (roughly 75%) was not significantly different when compared to our documented and US born samples. The finding that undocumented Latino patients keep appointments at a similar rate than other Latino groups may help to clarify biases regarding undocumented patients' lack of adherence to treatment. It does not seem to be the case that undocumented Latino patients do not follow up with their treatment, but rather that they attend to fewer visits. In our clinic, we have found that undocumented patients are uninsured (our study sample was entirely uninsured), have not had much experience with US mental health systems, and often have limited resources to pay for treatment. As treatment providers, knowing this can be helpful information in outlining a brief and effective course of treatment. Spending the first couple of sessions educating the patient about US mental health systems is extremely important as many undocumented patients may not be familiar with issues of confidentiality, patient rights, and more recently, with Health Insurance Portability and Accountability Act (HIPAA) regulations. In addition, we have found that our undocumented patients respond to a direct, problem-solving, supportive and informative approach. It is our belief that providing education and resources should be central to the treatment.

The undocumented Latinos in our study were more likely to have diagnoses of depression, anxiety, alcohol abuse and adjustment disorders when compared to the other studied groups. In addition, the undocumented group in this study had a greater number of psychosocial stressors including no access to health care benefits, lack of family supports, grim living conditions, occupational and economic hardships, which can all be expected of populations with illegal status. Without legal status, it is difficult for immigrants to obtain jobs, health care benefits, and advance economically. Clinicians often find serving this group of immigrants particularly challenging since they are often "stuck" in dire economic need without an apparent escape. In our clinic, we have learned that addressing specific psychosocial issues in a proactive way is usually the primary focus of the treatment. We have found that often times, it is the compounding of mounting stressors that trigger the initial visit to the clinic, even though the patient has been suffering with psychiatric symptoms for some time. The complexity of multiple concurrent and overlapping psychosocial stressors warrants well-developed and culturally relevant acute care, assessment and psychosocial support.

The undocumented in our sample were found to have higher rates of substance abuse disorders as compared to the other two groups, which warrants close examination of this issue not only in our clinical assessments and treatment, but also in program evaluation and research. Our projections of the prevalence of substance abuse disorders in clinic populations may actually be an underestimation as this is an area of frequent under-diagnosis. The treatment of substance abuse disorders in the undocumented Latino population can be a challenge not only because of these patients' limited resources, but also because of the scarcity of affordable services available. In our undocumented clinic sample, a typical substance-abusing patient was a 25-35-year-old Mexican male, living in an overcrowded situation, with no family or supports in the US, doing low level manual labor (i.e., dishwashing), and abusing alcohol. We have found that these patients are not necessarily interested in stopping their substance abuse, and may not even see their excessive drinking as problematic, but rather as a way of coping with the stress in their lives. In our clinic, we have learned that engaging these patients and gaining the their trust is of utmost importance to obtaining accurate information about substance use and abuse. Following a thorough assessment, we recommend a focus on education and information as central to the treatment.

In summary, clinicians involved in assessing and treating undocumented Latinos must consider a complex set of environmental and systemic cultural factors that have a direct impact on their problem and potential their healing.

Ideally, working with undocumented immigrants requires providing general education (i.e., about mental health systems, psychiatric disorders and treatments); information on prevention; treatment and support services related to mental health, substance abuse and domestic violence; as well as vocational rehabilitation and employment services. However, as we know, the undocumented are not eligible for many needed services. As a result, agencies, clinics and hospitals working with this population will need to be creative in identifying appropriate and viable treatment and referral options (i.e., provide brief free care treatment, looking for additional sources of funding for the undocumented, and collaborating with other agencies who provide treatment for the undocumented).

Directions for Future Research

Undocumented Latinos are poorly studied in the literature. This project was a pilot study intended to be a guide for more in depth, future investigation and program evaluation. Due to the retrospective nature of the study, we were limited in our ability to describe the psychosocial factors that contribute to the differences we have found in our sample or to assess risk factors for underutilization. In addition, immigrant populations have not been sufficiently studied regarding the accuracy of diagnostic categories or appropriate identification of symptoms in clinical settings. Because of this, we feel strongly that our findings should be viewed as tentative.

The undocumented group in our sample was younger (33 yrs.) as compared to the documented immigrant group (52 yrs.), but was similar to the United States-born Latinos group (34 yrs.). In addition, the undocumented were more frequently male (80%) and were predominantly of Mexican nationality. It must be considered that these demographic differences between groups may contribute to the observed differences in utilization patterns and clinical diagnoses between groups. Future studies with larger sample sizes may lend the opportunity for stratified analysis of clinical differences and utilization patterns between the groups.

The population in this investigation may not be representative of Latinos in need of mental health services in the community, as they have all made at least an initial attempt at seeking care. However, this study is a first step in understanding patterns of utilization and treatment needs for these different Latino groups who present to clinics and mental health care programs.

We have come to the conclusion that anticipating barriers to care and proactive evaluation of psychosocial stressors for crisis intervention and support are essential when working with the undocumented Latino population. This is a population with significant psychosocial needs, which can lead to both worsening mental health and loss to follow-up simultaneously. Mental health treatment programs working with the undocumented population need to provide concrete, social work services to their clients in addition to culturally responsive clinical care. In addition, the clinician/provider and community need to be involved at the level of health policy and social service legislation, promoting access to mental health and preventative services.

REFERENCES

Alvidrez, J. (1999). Ethnic Variations in mental health attitudes and service use among low-income African American, Latina, and European American young women. *Community Mental Health Journal, 35(6)*, 515-519.

Berk, M. L., & Shur, C. L. (2000). Health care use among undocumented Latino immigrants. *Health Affairs, 19(40)*, 51-64.

Borges, G., & Cherpitel, C. J. (2001). Selection of screening items for alcohol abuse and alcohol dependence among Mexicans and Mexican Americans in the emergency department. *Journal of Studies on Alcohol, 62(3)*, 277-285.

Burnam, M. A., Hough, R. L., & Escobar, J. I. (1987). Six month prevalence of specific psychiatric disorders among Mexican-Americans and Non-Hispanic Whites in Los Angeles. Archives of General Psychiatry, 44, 687-694.

Briones, D. E., Heller, F. L., & Chalfant, H. P. (1990). Socioeconomic status, ethnicity, psychological distress, and readiness to utilize a mental health facility. *American Journal of Psychiatry, 10*, 1333-1340.

Chelminsky, E. (1991). Hispanic Access to Health Care: Significant Gaps Exist. Washington DC: US General Accounting Office.

De Lourdes Villar, M. (1990). Rethinking settlement processes: The experience of Mexican undocumented migrants in Chicago. *Urban Anthropology, 19(1/2)*, 63-79.

Djajíc, S. (1997). Illegal immigration and resource allocation. *International Economic Review, 38(1)*, 97-117.

Estrada, A. L., Trevino, F. M., & Ray, L.A. (1990). Health care utilization barrier among Mexican Americans: Evidence from HHANES 1982-1984. *American Journal of Public Health, 80(supplement)*, 27-31.

Healthy People 2010. Chapter 18: Mental Health and Mental Disorders. National Institutes of Health, Substance Abuse and Mental Health Services Administration, 18-3-1828.

Hondagneu-Sotelo, P. (1997). Working 'without papers' in the United States: Toward the integration of legal status in frameworks of race, class, and gender. In E. Higginbotham & M. Romero (Eds.), *Women and Work: Exploring Race, Ethnicity, and Class.*

Hough, R. L., Landsverk, J. A., Karno, M., Burnam, M. A., Timbers, D. M., Escobar, J. I., & Regier, D. A. (1987). Utilization of health and mental health services by Los Angeles Mexican Americans and non-Hispanic whites. *Archives of General Psychiatry, 44*, 702-709.

Hu, T. W, Snowden L. R., & Jerrel, J. M. (1991). Ethnic populations in public mental health: Services choice and level of use. *American Journal of Public Health, 81,* 1429-1434.

Jimenez, A. L., Alegria, M., Pena, M., & Vera, M. (1997). Mental health utilization in depression. *Women & Health, 25(2),* 1-21.

Karno, M., Hough, R. L., & Burnam, M. A. (1987). Lifetime prevalence of specific psychiatric disorders specific psychiatric disorders among Mexican-Americans and Non-Hispanic Whites in Los Angeles. *Archives of General Psychiatry, 44,* 695-701.

Keefe, S. E. (1997). Mexican Americans' underutilization of mental health clinics: An evaluation of suggested explanations. *Hispanic Journal of Behavioral Sciences; 1,* 93-115.

Leslie, L. A., & Leitch, M. L. (1989). A demographic profile of recent Central American immigrants: Clinical and service implications. *Hispanic Journal of Behavioral sciences, 11,* 315-329.

Lipton, R. (1997). The relationship between alcohol, stress and depression in Mexican-Americans and Non-Hispanic Whites. *Behavioral Medicine, 23(3),* 101-111.

Neighbors, H. W., Bashshur, R., Price, R., Donavedian, A., Selig, S., & Shannon, G. (1992). Ethnic minority health service delivery: A review of the literature. *Research in Community and Mental Health, 7,* 55-71.

Nielson, A. (2000). Examining drinking patterns and problems among Hispanic groups: Results from a national survey. *Journal of Studies in Alcohol, 61(2),* 301-310.

Nielson, A., & Ford, J. (2001). Drinking patterns among Hispanic adolescents; Results from a national household survey. *Journal of Studies on Alcohol, 62(4),* 448-456.

Papademetriou, D. G., & DiMarzio, N. (1986). Undocumented Aliens in the New York Metropolitan Area: An Exploration into their Social and Labor Market Incorporation. *The New York labor market.* New York: Center for Migration Studies.

Randolph, W., Stroup-Benham, C., Black, S. A., & Markides, K. S. (1998). Alcohol use among Cuban-Americans, Mexican Americans, and Puerto Ricans. *Alcohol Health and Research, 22(4),* 256-269.

Regier, D. A., Myers, J. K., & Kramer, M. (1984). The NIMH Catchment Area Program, *Archives of General Psychiatry, 41,* 934-948.

Sue, S., Zane, N., & Young, K. (1994). Research on psychotherapy with culturally diverse populations. In A. E. Bergin & S. L. Garfield (Eds.), *Handbook of psychotherapy and behavior change* (4th ed). New York: Wiley, pp. 783-817.

Sue, S., & Yeh, M. (1995). Return rates and outcomes from ethnicity-specific mental health programs in Los Angeles. *American Journal of Public Health, 85,* 638-643.

Takeuchi, D., Snowden, L. R., Hu, T. W., & Jerrell, J. M. (1995). Emergency care avoidance: Ethnic matching and participation in minority-serving programs. *Community Mental Health Journal, 31,* 463-473.

Treno, A. J., Alaniz, M. L., & Gruenewald, P. J. (1999). Drinking patterns among US Hispanics: A Multivariate analysis of alcohol consumption patterns. *Hispanic Journal of Behavioral Sciences, 21(4),* 405-419.

Trevino, F. M., Moyer, E., & Valdez, R. B. (1991). Health insurance coverage and utilization of health services by Mexican Americans, mainland Puerto Ricans and Cuban Americans. *The Journal of the American Medical Association, 265,* 233-237.

Undocumented Immigration to California: 1980-1993, *The Statistical Yearbook of the Immigration and Naturalization Service*, The California Department of Finance and the U.S. Census Bureau, Hans Johnson, Public Policy Institute of California.

United States Department of Health and Human Services. (2001). *Mental Health: Culture, Race, and Ethnicity–A Supplement to Mental Health: A Report of the Surgeon General*. Rockville, MD: U.S. DHHS and CMHS, SAMHSA.

United States Bureau of the Census. (2000, September). *Census Brief: Coming from the Americas: A profile of the nation's Latin-American foreign born.*

Vega, W., & Miranda, M. (1985). *Stress and Hispanic mental health: Relating research to service delivery.* DHHS Publication No. (ADM) 85-1410, Rockville MD: National Institute of Mental Health.

Wells, K., Klap, R., Koike, A., & Sherbourne, C. (2001). Ethnic disparities in unmet need for alcoholism, drug abuse, and mental health care. *American Journal of Psychiatry, 158(12)*, 2027-2032.

Woodward, A. M., Dwinell, A. D., & Arons, B. S. (1992). Barriers to mental health care for Hispanic Americans: A literature review and discussion. *Journal of Mental Health, 19(3)*, 224-236.

Zayas, L. H., Rojas, M., & Malgady, R. G. (1998). Alcohol and drug use, and depression among Hispanic men in early adulthood. *American Journal of Community Psychology, 26(3)*, 425-438.

Chapter 7

Mental Health Intervention with Dominican Immigrants: A Psychosocial Perspective

Annecy Baez

SUMMARY. Dominicans are a significant force in the changing composition of Hispanic immigration in the United States, and all indications are that they will continue to be in the years to come. A framework has been applied in which Dominican culture, psychosocial strengths and risks, and treatment implications are explored in the context of how Dominicans appear to be similar to and different from other Hispanic groups in the U.S. Much more needs to be done in terms of elaborating this combination of homogeneity and heterogeneity. Mental health practitioners who are open to such inquiry, and to keeping an open mind regarding the possibilities of modifications in therapeutic techniques and modality choices, will find Dominicans to be a clinically responsive, and an enjoyable population to work with. *[Article copies available for a fee from The Haworth Document Delivery Service: 1-800-HAWORTH. E-mail address: <docdelivery@haworthpress.com> Website: <http://www.HaworthPress.com> © 2005 by The Haworth Press, Inc. All rights reserved.]*

KEYWORDS. Clinical practice, Dominican immigrants, mental health, treatment

Annecy Baez, CSW, PhD, is Assistant Professor of Social Work, New York University School of Social Work, 1 Washington Square North, New York, NY 10003 (E-mail: annecy.baez@nyu.edu).

[Haworth co-indexing entry note]: "Mental Health Intervention with Dominican Immigrants: A Psychosocial Perspective." Baez, Annecy. Co-published simultaneously in *Journal of Immigrant & Refugee Services* (The Haworth Social Work Practice Press, an imprint of The Haworth Press, Inc.) Vol. 3, No. 1/2, 2005, pp. 125-139; and: *Mental Health Care for New Hispanic Immigrants: Innovative Approaches in Contemporary Clinical Practice* (ed: Manny J. González, and Gladys González-Ramos) The Haworth Social Work Practice Press, an imprint of The Haworth Press, Inc., 2005, pp. 125-139. Single or multiple copies of this article are available for a fee from The Haworth Document Delivery Service [1-800-HAWORTH, 9:00 a.m. - 5:00 p.m. (EST). E-mail address: docdelivery@haworthpress.com].

Digital Object Identifier: 10.1300/J191v3n01_07

INTRODUCTION

The fastest rate of growth in the Hispanic population of the United States in recent years is not in the traditionally largest Hispanic groups (Mexicans, Puerto Ricans, or Cubans), but among Dominicans (now the 4th largest group), Salvadorans, Columbians and other peoples from a diverse set of countries in Central and South America (Logan 2001). The Dominican Diaspora occupies a prominent place in the discussion of new Hispanic immigrants in the United States because of its size, growth rate, and its relatively recent tenure.

The Dominican Republic, with its 8.1 million inhabitants, covers the Eastern two-thirds of Hispaniola, the island it shares with Haiti. Dominican culture consists of three major influences, Indian, African and Spanish. Their racial diversity begins with the Taino Indians whose influence remains today in the names of foods, towns and the Taino name for the island, still commonly used, *Quisqueya*, which means "the mother of all lands." The African influence in Dominican culture has been felt in agriculture, religion and spiritual practices. The Spanish influence is prominent in the national language and in many customs, as it is in Cuba and Puerto Rico. Dominican cultural diversity reaches still further, to include Italians, Germans, Sephardic Jews from Curacao, Jewish refugees from Europe, Puerto Ricans, Cubans, West Indians, Chinese, Japanese and Lebanese. All of these diverse ethnic groups have intermingled to create modern Dominican culture. (Alcantara, Aquino et al. 1995; Chapman 1997; Torres Saillant and Hernandez 1998).

The Census 2000 tally of 764,495 Dominicans[1] is considered significantly undercounted by some researchers. Accounting for misclassification (i.e., Dominicans who were listed as "other Hispanics") but not for undercounting (i.e., undocumented immigrants and others who did not respond to the census) Castro and Boswell (2002) estimate the number of Dominicans at 1,014,879, while (Logan 2001) estimates the number to be 1,121,257. Castro and Boswell assert that ". . . it is quite possible that the Dominican population could exceed even the higher figure of 1.12 million estimated by Logan" (p. 5).

Among Dominicans in the U.S. who were born in the Dominican Republic, 37.5% immigrated between 1990 and 2000, and an additional 33.6% immigrated from 1980 to 1990. Compared to the other leading Hispanic groups, the total of 71.1% of all native Dominicans in the U.S. immigrating from 1980 to 2000 is rivaled only by the Mexican total of 70.9%, but far exceeds the Puerto Rican and Cuban figures of 44.2% and 43.1%, respectively (Castro and Boswell 2002).

Dominicans are thus clearly prominent among the newer immigrant populations in the United States (Logan 2001). Dominicans in the United States are also a markedly youthful population. Castro and Boswell (2002) indicate that 22.9% of the Dominican population in the U.S. are ten years of age or younger, 44.2% under twenty, and 59% under thirty.

The large scale migration from the Dominican Republic has its roots in the end of the dictatorship of Rafael Trujillo in 1961, and its totalitarian controls over all aspects of Dominican life. Emigration was liberalized under the next lengthy governmental regime, that of Joaquin Balaguer, which lasted from 1966 to 1978. Despite considerable economic growth, high unemployment, continuous economic crises and political unrest combined to make emigration to the United States an attractive prospect (Moya Pons 1993). Dominican immigrants from the 1960s and 70s are generally more likely to be politically motivated and of professional background (as is the case with the authors' parents), whereas immigrants from the 1980s and forward are more likely to be from working class backgrounds (Graham 1998).

The Dominican population in the U.S. is highly concentrated in several urban areas, with 85% residing in the vicinity of just six major metropolitan areas: New York/Northern New Jersey (67%), Miami/Fort Lauderdale (7.7%), Boston/Worchester (4.1%), Los Angeles/Riverside (3.5%), Philadelphia/Wilmington (1.7%) and Houston/Galveston (1.2%). New York City is the epicenter of the Dominican presence in the U.S., and Dominicans are the city's largest and fastest growing immigrant population. A startling 49% of New York's Dominican households are headed by women (Hernandez and Torres Saillant 1997; Ojito 1997).

Educational attainment figures for Dominicans in this country reflect an improving, but still woefully inadequate situation. In the U.S. as a whole, 24.8% of the population has a BA degree or higher. Among the four largest Latino groups, rates for attainment of a BA or higher are as follows: Mexicans (6.2%), Puerto Ricans (13.1%), Cubans (24.6%), and Dominicans (9.6%). Among U.S. born Dominicans, the BA attainment rate of 21.7% is twice that of post-1990 immigrants (10.7%), and three times that of pre-1990 immigrants (7.2%, Castro and Boswell 2002). The probability of a Dominican youth achieving a college degree is decreased by the fact that in many of the U.S. urban areas where Dominicans reside, they often receive an inferior education (Anyon 1997) in public primary and secondary schools plagued by shortages of teachers, high teacher turnover, lack of adequate supplies, overcrowded classes and poor building maintenance. It is not uncommon for Dominican students in these settings to have taken five or six years to complete high school (Lopez 2002) while Dominican students at a community college in New York City, 65% of whom are women, generally start college an average age of 27, very frequently drop out before completing their associate degree, or exceed the school average of three years to associate degree completion (Rodriguez 2003).

Dominicans primarily work in service occupations (33.2%), as operators, fabricators and handlers (30.4%), or as technical, sales and administrative support workers (25.4%). Managers and professionals account for 10.9% of occupations held by Dominicans. Among the new Hispanics, Dominicans stand out for their very low income. Many earn below $8,000 (Logan 2001) and 45.7% live below the poverty line (Hernandez and Torres Saillant 1997). New arrivals from the Dominican Republic have a higher average rate of unemployment and they are very likely to receive public assistance (Logan 2001). On the average, Dominican women earn approximately 25% less than their male counterparts (Castro and Boswell 2002). Duany (1994) pointed to the frequent struggles of New York City based Dominicans, even by the standards of recent immigrants, for fair wages and decent housing.

Dominicans thus share with their other Hispanic immigrant counterparts conditions that put them and their children at greater psychosocial risk for negative social, health, and developmental outcomes compared to non-Hispanic Whites: poor education, employment at lower paying jobs, and high rates of poverty (Zayas 1992).

CULTURAL CHARACTERISTICS AND FAMILY LIFE

Dominicans share with other Hispanic groups adherence to important customs which serve as guides for conduct (Iltis 2002): the centrality of family life as a concern and an area of obligation, adherence to traditional gender roles, showing respect, and the importance of both Christian and complementary (i.e., Espiritismo and Santeria) spiritual beliefs (Baez and Hernandez 2001). Observance of life cycle markers and appropriate rituals are a similarly central feature: birthday celebrations, religious rituals, wedding anniversaries, even Sunday picnic traditions, are all treated with reverence and call for almost obligatory attendance (Falicov 1999). Very often, Dominicans of very modest means absorb the expenses of participation on these occasions, even when it represents a financial hardship.

Certain nuances of Dominican family life merit further explanation because they differ dramatically from American family life, and to a lesser extent from family life in other Hispanic cultures. Dominican families are intensely loyal and interdependent. It is important to bear in mind that family parameters include non-blood relatives, most significantly the *hijo de crianza* (a "child of upbringing" or informally adopted child) and the *compadre* (a godparent or co-parent). These members participate in family life and are subject to the same expectations and privileges as blood relatives, so much so that a sexual liaison between a *compadre* and his godchild is virtually unheard of, and is considered tantamount to incest. Three marriage forms are generally viewed as acceptable, civil, religious, and free union. While some free unions last a lifetime, their potential disadvantage becomes more apparent in situations where men leave the household due to affairs or economic pressures, leaving the women without legal recourse and to fend for themselves (Hernandez 1997). Given the centrality of family life for Dominicans, it is not commonly frowned upon as much to have children from different relationships, but a man's failure to maintain those children is viewed as dishonorable. In Dominican culture, the man is viewed as the head of the household. This places great pressures on a man to meet the needs of his family despite the limited economic opportunities, high cost of living, and sometimes unemployment that often confront him in this country. Leaving the family often becomes a preferable alternative to living with them under these dishonorable circumstances, and also places these men at increased risk for depression and alcoholism (Kail, Zayas et al. 2000).

Among the other features that to some degree distinguish Dominicans from other Hispanics, are Dominican determination to preserve their culture and identity, and the high frequency of travel between the United States and the Dominican Republic (Iltis 2001). This is convergent with Grasmauck and Pessar's (1991) observation that Dominican rates of U.S. naturalization are historically low. Duany (1994) and (Georges 1989) also highlighted the *transnational* nature of the Dominican community; the ambivalent attachment that Dominicans have with the U.S. and the Dominican Republic ("One foot here and the other one there," is how one therapist in the Iltis study put it (p. 82)), as well as their frequent travel between the countries, and their commitment to sending money and material goods back to their homeland. Dominican immigrants send approximately 500 million dollars a year to the Dominican Republic (Sontag and Dugger 1998) with Mother's Day remittances exceeding even those of Christmas Day.

Numerous studies of inner-city youth indicate that exposure to traumatic life events and neighborhood disadvantage significantly predicts antisocial behavior and drug use among youth (D'Imperio, Dubow et al. 2000; Dubow et al. 1997). This is a reality that appears to be intuitively understood by Dominican parents. In a 1998 *New York Times* article, educators and government officials in the Dominican Republic estimated that as many as 10,000 students from the United States are enrolled in Dominican schools, sent there by parents fearful of the dangers of urban street life in the U.S. In one school highlighted in the article, one in every five students was an American-born Dominican (Rohter 1998). The country's former President Leonel Fernandez

Reyna, is also an example of the Dominican American transnational educational experience, having come to New York City with his immigrant mother, a seamstress and nurses aide, at age eight.

Cosgrove (1992) points to another noteworthy aspect of the relatedness many Dominicans have with the two countries; the phenomenon of *remigration*, wherein significant numbers of Dominicans emigrate to the U.S., then after a period of years, they remigrate from the U.S. to the Dominican Republic. Some of these *retornos* or "returners" may even repeat this pattern more than once. Cosgrove believes that Dominicans are perhaps "the most outstanding example" of this practice, and as a Dominican American woman, this writers' experience is that this practice occurs much more frequently with Dominicans than with other Hispanic group in the New York City area.

Among the effects of this transnational Dominican style may be a slowing of acculturation and assimilation. Substantial numbers of Dominicans live in the U.S. for many years and learn just a handful of English words during that time. Between the frequent travel, the abundance of money transfer companies and phone parlors in Hispanic neighborhoods, modems, fax machines, discount phone cards and long distance plans, the effect is such that families and cultural values remain intact; "to a certain extent, personal conduct can even be monitored and violations of traditional norms reported, almost as if this had just taken place around the corner" (Cosgrove, p. 106, paraphrasing Georges 1989).

This encapsulation of Dominican identity and cultural values, while strong, is not airtight, and tensions related to bicultural exposure sometimes make themselves apparent with Dominicans as they do with other Hispanic groups. This can be a good thing, an enriching experience that gives persons and families a wider set of adaptive resources, or it can be a source of difficulty and frustration as contradictory cultural views collide (Falicov 1999). When children enter adolescence, for example, Dominican parents, like other Hispanic parents who often speak little English and have little understanding of American culture, may manifest overprotectiveness as they struggle to understand their children's interest in hip-hop fashion, numerous piercing for jewelry, and rap music.

Dominican women enter the U.S. workforce in substantial numbers (Cosgrove 1992) but often suffer under the strain of working full time while also being primarily responsible for child rearing, domestic chores and maintaining an attractive feminine appearance while doing it all.

PROTECTIVE FACTORS

Despite the substantive psychosocial risks that confront Dominicans in the U.S., some researchers have found evidence of the presence of protective factors that mediate between psychosocial risks and their consequences.

In a noteworthy study on depression in Hispanics, Das et al. (2000) screened 533 Dominicans and 202 non-Dominican Hispanic adult primary care patients for depression, and found the prevalence to be similar in the two groups (22.0% versus 22.8%, respectively). Among the Dominicans, women were at higher risk than men (25.6% vs. 10.7%), those with lower household incomes at greater risk than those with higher incomes (27.0% vs. 17.6%) and persons in poor physical health at greater risk than those in fair health or better (28.5% vs. 6.3%). Among the non-Dominican Hispanic group, only poor physical health yielded a similar association with depression.

The fact that depression levels were not significantly higher among Dominicans in comparison to non-Dominican Hispanics in the Das study is noteworthy, given that some researchers have suggested that the prevalence of depression might be higher among Hispanics because of the socioeconomic deprivations experienced (Vega, Kolody et al. 1986; La Roche and Turner 1997). Since Dominicans are one of the most socioeconomically strained Hispanic groups (Morales 2000), manifestation of higher rates of depression would have seemed likely. The results of the Das study may be reflective of the presence of protective factors at work among Dominicans, but as La Roche (1999) notes, very few studies have explored the variables that reduce or increase the risk of depression among Dominicans.

La Roche's (1999) own research study in this area with 82 Dominican subjects was inconclusive with regard to depression rates among Dominicans, but did find higher levels of social support to be correlated with lower levels of depression, and that the family was the context in which Dominicans obtained the vast majority of their supportive interactions. La Roche concluded that Dominicans manifest high rates of *familismo*, or familism. *Familismo* is defined by Marin and Marin (1991) as a cultural value that involves an individual's strong attachment to their nuclear and extended families; feelings of loyalty, reciprocity, and solidarity among family members; and a tendency to devalue potential supports that fall outside of the family. Comas-Diaz (1995) is prominent among those who emphasize that strong family bonds help Hispanics cope with adverse and difficult situations.

Castro and Boswell (2002) point to a number of other psychosocial strengths among Dominicans in the United States. These include ". . . emerging political clout, the small business sector, the voluntary associations . . . the solidarity of other Latino groups . . . and the large number of sports and entertainment celebrities whose success are a source of pride and philanthropy to Dominicans" (p. 13).

TREATMENT APPROACHES

As a clinician, professor, and Dominican American woman, the author believes that a range of skills are essential for effective practice with Dominican families:

1. Dominicans have many needs, including employment, vocational training, child care, transportation, English language training, health services, life skills, substance abuse or mental health counseling, and legal assistance. The clinician may be required to provide different services at different times, including education, advocacy, counseling, and linkages with other services. Clinicians need to manifest openness to these roles if they expect to engage Dominican families. (Cockcroft 1995) notes that increased access to higher education is essential, as well as public policies that support the educational efforts of students from low socioeconomic background.

2. Be aware of level of immigration-related stress and how it may be impacting on the individual. Dominicans experience many stressors and challenges including: language barriers that impact on their ability to find employment, financial difficulties and social discrimination. Studies show that immigration can be traumatic (Foster 2001) and several studies show a higher rate of mental health problems such as depression, alcohol abuse and panic disorders associated with the stress of immigration (Golding and Bunam 1990; Escobar 1998; Vega et al. 1998).

3. Be aware of the individuals' strengths. Many Dominicans maintain cultural practices and traditional values that mediate and "buffer" against health and mental health problems. Escobar (1998) highlighted how Hispanics rely on family for emotional, social and financial support.

4. Educate the client about the therapeutic process. Be honest. Do not promise what you or your agency cannot provide. Educate them about your role and theirs. Explain the limits or your role and/or your agency.

5. Be present oriented, directive and solution focused. Szapocznik et al. (1994) suggest that a modality that uses this kind of approach is more suitable to Hispanic families. Cognitive-behavioral therapy, which utilizes concrete assignments has been recommended as culturally relevant (Ho 1987; Paniagua 1998). Sue and Sue (1990) note that the day to day challenges, the cultural emphasis on the present, and the pressures of day to day life result in a desire to solve problems without necessarily uncovering their origins. Be patient if Dominican clients do not adhere to therapeutic recommendations. Remember that many have overwhelming life demands and relatively few resources and supports.

6. Avoid framing Hispanic clients as a homogeneous population (Kail, Zayas, and Malgady 2000); what Fontes (2002) refers to as "ethnic lump-

ing." The features that distinguish Dominicans from other Hispanic groups become apparent with experience, as is the diversity within them as a group.

Some research findings on the efficacy of individual, family and group modalities with Hispanics appear to be applicable for Dominicans as well. In Rosenthal (1999), fifteen clinicians self-described as bilingual, bicultural and employing psychodynamic approaches with Latino clients were interviewed in depth regarding their treatment experience with Hispanics. The clinicians underscored the need to be considerate of each client as an individual, understanding of external reality and its impact on treatment, and increasing flexibility around self-disclosure (Rosenthal 1999).

Tiago De Melo (1998) studied the factors relating to Hispanics and non-Hispanic White Americans' willingness to seek psychotherapy for five discrete problems: anxiety, depression, speech anxiety, financial concerns, and ethnic and racial discrimination and found Hispanics order of preference for treatment was cognitive-behavioral, psychodynamic, group, and pharmacotherapy treatment. Significant differences were found among Hispanics from different countries of origin on their level of acculturation, income, overall severity of concerns, and depression.

In Iltis (2002), psychotherapists who work with Dominican clients highlighted several other features of the therapeutic process that therapists unfamiliar with Dominican culture might encounter:

1. Discontinuities in psychotherapeutic or psychopharmacologic treatment may arise because of the propensity for frequent travel to the Dominican Republic.

2. The willingness of clients to disclose some aspects of their selves may be inhibited by the position of the therapist outside of the immediate or extended family, by fearfulness of judgment by a professional, or by reluctance to discuss alternative, yet traditional spiritual beliefs and practices.

3. There are practices in Dominican culture which might seem unusual to some clinicians with Western training, but are considered proper demonstrations of appreciation and respect in Dominican culture. Two examples in particular were cited. The first was the desire of clients to give token gifts (including such things as food, or an herbal tea as a cold remedy). The second was the tendency to have occasional minor types of physical contact, such as the client touching the therapist on the arm, or an occasional desire to hug. The therapists' refusal to participate or expressed concern about either behavior, might be viewed by the client as offensive.

Philippe (2002) also studied the perceptions of therapists towards their Dominican clients. He reported that Dominicans present very differently in therapy depending socioeconomic status, social class, level of education, accult-uration, area of origin in the Dominican Republic, stage of migration, genera-tion in the US, immigration status, psychopathology, source of referral, and socialization to therapy. The reluctance to share nontraditional beliefs was common among Dominican clients.

Canino (1994) and Baez and Hernandez (2001) are among those who assert that theoretical frames used by clinicians in working with Hispanics should be matched to the specific characteristics of the Hispanic group in question. La Roche and Turner (1997) found Dominicans in a depression study group to be highly *allocentric*, that they define themselves in terms of social commonali-ties and bonds to the group, an assertion also made by Comas-Diaz (1995). La Roche and Turner concluded that relational and interpersonal theories of de-pression and treatments for depression are better matched with this high de-gree of allocentrism in Dominicans as opposed to theories and treatments for depression that emphasize individual etiology, such as cognitive behavioral therapy.

The need to foster greater congruence between clinicians and Dominican patients was similarly highlighted by Bearison, Minian et al. (2002), who in-terviewed Dominican mothers of children with asthma. The beliefs of the mothers about the nature and preventive management of the asthma were of-ten divergent with Western medical beliefs, and the mothers were often non-compliant or partially compliant with Western medical advice while co-vertly resorting to indigenous Dominican treatments and remedies. The re-searchers concluded that the most promising approach to improving outcomes for Dominican children is not the standard, patronizing approach of increased parental education on Western medical approaches to asthma management. Instead they recommend that clinicians initiate a dialogue with Dominican parents that acknowledges the reliance on indigenous healing methods. This serves to break the taboo on discussing differing belief systems about asthma management, and can lead to eventual reconciliation of contradictory prac-tices that may impede optimal treatment for the child.

Dominican reliance on indigenous healing methods goes well beyond asthma management. Ososki et al. (2001) have been conducting an on-going study in New York City investigating Dominican and Chinese healing system and the herbal treatments used for health problems affecting women such as uterine fibroids, menorrhagia, endometriosis, and hot flashes. A total of 87 plants species were reported in the Dominican literature for these and other conditions and symptoms. Allen et al. (2000) found that nearly half of Domin-ican patients presenting at a New York City emergency room had used indige-nous medicine, usually in the form of medicinal plants and herbal teas, for their presenting complaints.

There is a wide spectrum of belief and adherence (Baez and Hernandez 2001) to traditional healing among Dominicans, beliefs that extend into diagnosis and treatment not only of physical ailments, but of most psychological and interpersonal problems as well. Mental health clinicians should not be surprised or manifest opposition if patients bring up such practices; they represent culturally accepted attempts at problem solving. An example that might be encountered in work with Dominican patients would be the use of candles and incense to cleanse the home of negative energies, or to obtain money, marital stability, or health. Another would be the presence in the home of statues of saints or African deities, for whom small offerings are left, including water, flowers, and favorite foods.

Family therapy as a preferred method of working with Hispanics has been supported for use with Hispanics of different origins (Soto-Fulp and Delcampo 1994; Arredondo, Orjuela, and Moore 1989; Szapocznik et al. 1989) and may be a viable modality for Dominicans given their reliance on family. Family therapy interventions, many based on structural family therapy (SFT; Minuchin 1974), have been found to be effective in treating antisocial behavior and drug use in Hispanic youth compared with group therapy and/or control groups (Santisteban et al. 1997; Szapocznik et al. 1994).

Dominicans, although group focused and family focused, may be reluctant to participate in group psychotherapy because they feel shame and do not feel it is respectful to share private matters with a group of individuals. Group leaders who work with Dominicans should be willing to be an active participant and provide some information about themselves. When the author conducted groups with Dominican women, it was very important for the women who were going to share their lives with me to know about me. An appropriate amount of transparency and self disclosure was important. The women wanted to know my ethnic background, if I came from the Dominican Republic what part of the country my family was from, how long had I lived in New York City, and how did I, at such young age, achieve the level of education I had achieved. If I had stopped the flow of inquiry, I would never had learned that they felt proud that a Dominican young woman had achieved what they hoped to achieve themselves and for their children. Appropriate self disclosure is important, this does not mean that one cannot explore the meaning of the inquiry in light of the therapeutic relationship, one can still do this and then self disclose information that may be useful to the therapeutic process.

Health and human service providers need to work closely with Dominican voluntary agencies that have virtually unrestricted access to the close-knit Dominican community because of their reliance on indigenous peer counselors, home visitation strategies, and their willingness to go wherever their clientele are, be it beauty salons, church services, retail stores, grocery stores or *botanicas*. Because the Dominican Diaspora is a relatively new and a continuing migration, traditional mores and values remain strong and are continually reinvigorated by new arrivals. Providers therefore also need to develop creative strategies for engaging the Dominican community in way which are viewed by Dominicans as culturally congruent and affirming, such as offering traditional crafts classes or serving an occasional *sancocho* (a hearty typical stew) in an agency waiting room.

CONCLUSION

Dominicans are the fourth largest Hispanic group in the United States; therapists need to get familiar with risk and protective factors. Dominicans are a significant force in the changing composition of Hispanic immigration in the United States, and all indications are that they will continue to be in the years to come. A framework has been applied in which Dominican culture, pyschosocial strengths and risks, and treatment implications were explored in the context of how Dominicans appear to be similar to and different from other Hispanic groups in the U.S. Much more needs to be done in terms of elaborating this combination of homogeneity and heterogeneity. Mental health practitioners who are open to such inquiry, and to keeping an open mind regarding the possibilities of modifications in therapeutic techniques and modality choices, will find Dominicans to be a clinically responsive, and an enjoyable population to work with.

NOTE

1. Unless otherwise clear in the context of a sentence, the term Dominican is defined herein as a U.S. resident either born in the Dominican Republic, or born in the United States from one or two native Dominican parents.

REFERENCES

Alcantara, A., J. Aquino et al. (1995). *From Quisqueya: In Search of New Horizons. Dominican Cultural Heritage Resource Guide.*

Allen, R., Cushman, L.F., Morris et al. (2000). Use of complementary and alternative medicine among Dominican emergency department patients. *American Journal of Emergency Medicine* 18(1): 51-54.

Kronenberg, F. and Anyon, J. (1997). *Ghetto Schooling: A Political Economy of Urban Educational Reform.* New York, Teacher's College.

Baez, A. and D. Hernandez (2001). "Complementary spiritual beliefs in the Latino community: The interface with psychotherapy." *American Journal of Orthopsychiatry* 71(4): 408-415.

Bearison, D. J., N. Minian et al. (2002). "Medical management of asthma and folk medicine in a Hispanic community." *Journal of Pediatric Psychology* 27(4): 385-392.

Castro, M. J. and T. D. Boswell (2002). "The Dominican Diaspora Revisited: Dominicans and Dominican-American in a New Century." *A North-South Agenda Paper.*

Chapman, F. (1997). "The Dominican Racial Setting: Frame of Reference for the Understanding of Cultural Diversity in the Dominican Republic. Occasional Paper No. 38."

Cockcroft, J. D. (1995). *Latinos in the Making of the United States. The Hispanic Experience in the Americas.*

Cosgrove, J. (1992). "Remigration: the Dominican experience." *Social Development Issues* 14(2/3): 101-20.

D'Imperio, R. L., E. F. Dubow et al. (2000). "Resilient and stress-affected adolescents in an urban setting." *Journal of Clinical Child Psychology* 29(1): 129-142.

Duany, J. (1994). *Quisqueya on the hudson: The transnational identity of Dominicans in Washington Heights.* New York, CUNY Dominican Studies Institute.

Escobar, J. I. (1998). "Immigration and mental health: Why are immigrants better off?" *General Psychiatry* 55: 781-782.

Falicov, C. J. (1999). "Religion and spiritual folk traditions in immigrant families: Therapeutic resources with Latinos." In B. Carter and M. McGoldrick (Eds.), The expanded family life cycle (141-167). Boston: Allyn & Bacon.

Fontes, L. A. (2002). "Child discipline and physical abuse in immigrant Latino families: reducing violence and misunderstandings." *Journal of Counseling and Development* 80(1): 31-40.

Foster, R. P. (2001). "When immigration is trauma: Guidelines for the individual and family clinician." *American Journal of Orthopsychiatry* 71(2): 153-170.

Georges, E. (1989). *The making of a transnational community: Migration, development and cultural changes in the Dominican Republic.* New York, Columbia University Press.

Golding, J. M. and M. A. Bunam (1990). "Immigration, stress, and depressive symptoms in a Mexican-American community." *Journal of Nervous and Mental Disease* 178: 161-171.

Graham, P. M. (1998). "The politics of incorporation: Dominican in New York City." *Latino Studies Journal* 9: 39-64.

Grasmauck, S. and P. R. Pessar (1991). *Between two islands: Dominican International Migration.* Berkeley, CA, University of California Press.

Harris Reid, M. A. (1999). "Coming to America: Immigration, stress, and mental health." *Dissertation Abstracts International Section A: Humanities and Social Sciences* 59(10-A): 3975.

Hernandez, R. & Torres-Saillant, S. (1997). "Constructing the New York Area Hispanic Mosaic: A Demographic Portrait of Colombians and Dominican in New York Minorities, Education, Empowerment."

Ho, M. K. (1987). *Family therapy with ethnic minorities.* Newbury Park, CA, Sage.

Iltis, C. E. (2002). "Adult Dominicans in therapy: Psychotherapists' perceptions of cultural treatment issues." *Dissertation Abstracts International: Section B: The Sciences and Engineering* 62(11-B): 5377.

Kail, B., L. H. Zayas et al. (2000). "Depression, acculturation, and motivations for alcohol use among young Colombian, Dominican, and Puerto Rican men." *Hispanic Journal of Behavioral Sciences* 22(1): 64-77.

La Roche, M. J. (1999). "The association of social relations and depression levels among Dominicans in the United States." Hispanic Journal of Behavioral Sciences 21(4): 420-430.

La Roche, M. J. (1999). "Culture, transference, and counter-transference among Latinos." *Psychotherapy: Theory, Research, Practice, Training* 36(4): 389-397.

La Roche, M. J. and C. Turner (1997). "Self-orientation and depression level among Dominicans in the United States." *Hispanic Journal of Behavioral Sciences* 19(4): 479-488.

Logan, J. R. (2001). "The New Latinos: Who They Are, Where They Are." *Lewis Mumford Center for Comparative Urban and Regional Research.*

Lopez, N. (2002). "Rewriting race and gender high school lessons: Second-generation Dominicans in New York City." *Teachers College Record* 104(6): 1187-1203.

Marin, G. and B. V. O. Marin (1991). *Research with Hispanic population.* Newbury Park, CA, Sage.

Mendoza F.S., F.-A. E. (1999). "Latino children's health and the family-community health promotion model." *West J Med.* 170: 85-92.

Morales, E. E. (2000). "A Contextual Understanding of the Process of Educational Resilience: High Achieving Dominican American Students and the "Resilience Cycle." *Innovative Higher Education* 25(1): 7-22.

Ojito, M. (1997). Dominicans, scrabbling for hope: As poverty rises more women head the households. *New York Times*: 1.

Olarte, S. W. and R. Masnik (1093). "Benefits of long-term group therapy for disadvantaged Hispanic outpatients." *Hospital and Community Psychiatry* 36(10): 1093-97.

Ososki, A. L., Lohr, P. et al. (2000). "Ethnobotanical literature survey of medicinal plants in the Dominican Republic used for women's health conditions." *Journal of Ethnopharmacology* 79, 285-298.

Paniagua, F. A. (1998). *Assessing and treating culturally diverse clients.* Thousand Oaks, CA, Sage.

Peeks, A. L. (1999). "Conducting a social skills group with Latina adolescents." *Journal of Child and Adolescent Group Therapy* 9(3): 139-156.

Perez, G. (2000). "Factors that influence motivation to pursue higher education among Dominicans." *Dissertation Abstracts International: Section B: The Sciences and Engineering* 60(9-B): 4902.

Philippe, J. (2002). "The relations between emotion socialization, attachment style and acculturative stress in a sample of Haitian and Dominican immigrants." *Dissertation Abstracts International: Section B: The Sciences and Engineering* 62(9-B): 4231.

Robert J. Ledogar, A. P., C. Cecilia Iglesias Garden, and Luis Garden Acosta (2000). "Asthma and Latino Cultures: Different Prevalence Reported Among Groups Sharing the Same Environment." *American Journal of Public Health* 90(6): 929-35.

Rodriguez, V. (2003). Dominican population in Bronx community college. P. communication. Bronx, New York.

Rohther, L. (1998). Island life not idyllic for youths from U.S. *New York Times*: 4.

Rosenthal, C. S. (1999). "Toward a better understanding of the use of psycho-dynamically-informed treatment with Latinos: Findings from clinician experience." *Dissertation Abstracts International Section A: Humanities and Social Sciences* 59(8-A): 3212.

Santisteban, D. A., J. D. Coatsworth et al. (2003). "Efficacy of brief strategic family therapy in modifying Hispanic adolescent behavior problems and substance use." *Journal of Family Psychology* 17(1): 121-133.

Shedlin, M. G. and S. Deren (2002). "Cultural factors influencing HIV risk behavior among Dominicans in New York City." *Journal of Ethnicity in Substance Abuse* 1(1): 71-95.

Sontag, D. and C. W. Dugger (1998). The new immigrant tide: A shuttle between worlds. *New York Times*: 1.

Sue, D. W. and D. Sue (1990). *Counseling the culturally different: Theory and practice*. New York, Wiley.

Tiago De Melo, J. A. (1998). "Factors relating to Hispanic and non-Hispanic white Americans' willingness to seek psychotherapy." *Dissertation Abstracts International: Section B: The Sciences and Engineering* 59(5-B): 2440.

Torres Saillant, S. and R. Hernandez (1998). *The Dominican Americans. The New Americans Series*.

Vega, W., B. Kolody et al. (1986). "The relationship of marital status, confidant support, and depression among Mexican-American woman." *Journal of Marriage and Family*: 48: 597-605.

Zayas, L. H. (1992). "Childrearing, social stress, and child abuse: Clinical considerations with Hispanic families." *Journal of Social Distress and the Homeless* 1: 291-309.

Vega, W. A., Kolody, B., Aguilar-Gaxiola, S., Alderete, E., Catalano, R. and Caraveo-Anduagg, J. (1998). Lifetime prevalence of DSM-III-R psychiatric disorders among urban and rural Mexican Americans in California. *American Archives of General Psychiatry* 55: 771-778.

Chapter 8

The Mariel and Balsero Cuban Immigrant Experience: Family Reunification Issues and Treatment Recommendations

Manny J. González
José J. Lopez
Eunjeong Ko

SUMMARY. This chapter focuses on the differential family reunification issues experienced by Cuban Marielitos and balseros upon entrance into the United States. Treatment recommendations, aimed at ameliorating the emotionally laden reunification issues, are presented within a family systems and ecological context. The overall intent of this chapter/article is to assist mental health practitioners in their therapeutic

Manny J. González, DSW, is Associate Professor of Social Work, Fordham University, Graduate School of Social Service.

José J. Lopez, DCSW, is a Private Practitioner, Garden City, New York, and Adjunct Professor, Adelphi University School of Social Work.

Eunjeong Ko, MSW, is a Doctoral Student, Fordham University, Graduate School of Social Service.

[Haworth co-indexing entry note]: "The Mariel and Balsero Cuban Immigrant Experience: Family Reunification Issues and Treatment Recommendations." González, Manny J., José J. Lopez, and Eunjeong Ko. Co-published simultaneously in *Journal of Immigrant & Refugee Services* (The Haworth Social Work Practice Press, an imprint of The Haworth Press, Inc.) Vol. 3, No. 1/2, 2005, pp. 141-153; and: *Mental Health Care for New Hispanic Immigrants: Innovative Approaches in Contemporary Clinical Practice* (ed: Manny J. González, and Gladys González-Ramos) The Haworth Social Work Practice Press, an imprint of The Haworth Press, Inc., 2005, pp. 141-153. Single or multiple copies of this article are available for a fee from The Haworth Document Delivery Service [1-800-HAWORTH, 9:00 a.m. - 5:00 p.m. (EST). E-mail address: docdelivery@haworthpress.com].

work with members of a relatively small but distinct Hispanic ethnic group. Two case vignettes are presented as a means of illustrating the key family reunifications issues that have impacted–and continue to affect–Cuban Marielitos and balseros. *[Article copies available for a fee from The Haworth Document Delivery Service: 1-800-HAWORTH. E-mail address: <docdelivery@haworthpress.com> Website: <http://www.HaworthPress.com>* © 2005 by The Haworth Press, Inc. All rights reserved.]*

KEYWORDS. Cuban balseros, Cuban Marielitos, family reunification, treatment

INTRODUCTION

The culmination of the Cuban revolution in 1959 resulted in the exodus of over one million Cubans from their homeland into the United States. Cubans have entered the United States through four major waves of political migration. Each of these migration waves has been marked by distinct socio-demographic characteristics such as social class, race and levels of education (Pedraza, 1995). The first migration wave (1960-1964), identified as the "Golden Exile," brought to the United States 174,275 of Cuba's elite (Bach, 1980). This group of Cubans consisted primarily of upper-middle class professionals who were forced to exit the island for political reasons. The second migration wave (1965-1974), referred to as the "petite bourgeoisie," allowed for the exiting and relocation of Cuba's working class labor force (e.g., skilled and semi-skilled employees). This second migration wave was uniquely prompted by the need for economic survival (Bernal & Shapiro, 1996; Pedraza, 1995). It is important to note, however, that the history of the exodus and exile of Cubans both in the United States and throughout other countries cannot be separated from the oppressive political aftermath following Fidel Castro's revolution. The "Mariel boatlifts" or the "Marielitos" (1980-1981) represented the third migration wave of Cuban immigrants. This third migration wave ushered into the United States more than 125,000 Cubans. The exodus of this group has at times been depicted as chaotic because of the many overcrowded boats that in a brief span of time arrived in the state of Florida (Miami), bringing thousands of individuals and families in need of political asylum and freedom (Gonzalez, 2000). The majority of the Marielitos consisted of young single males. In contrast to previous Cuban immigrants, the Marielitos were classified as "socially undesirable" because of the prevalence of individuals (within this group) with a history of incarceration and mental illness. The "social undesirability" of this

group was compounded further by the fact that–racially–many of the Marielitos represented Cuba's black population (Bernal & Guiterrez, 1988; Gonzalez, 2000). Cuba's persistent economic crisis and its political deterioration set
the stage for the fourth wave of migration (1989-present): Cuban "balseros."
Balsero is the Spanish term that describes an individual who has left Cuba on a
raft or small boat. From 1989 to 1994, over 37,000 Cuban balseros have successfully reached Miami, Florida by dangerously traveling on small boats and
rafts. Since the onset of this fourth migration wave more than 30,000 Cubans
have been intercepted by the United States Coast Guard and sent to
Guantanamo, a United States military base in Cuba. Intercepted Cuban immigrants who are taken to Guantanamo remain there as refugees for an average
of about nine months before entrance into the United States is granted
(Pederaza, 1995). As a result of the migration waves of Cuban immigrant/refu-
gees, it is important to both view and understand the Cuban exile community
residing in the United States as a socially and psychologically diverse Hispanic group.

As refugees, Cubans are differentiated from other types of immigrants by
the nature of the forced exiting from their country of origin (Cuba). The refugee process is composed of three phases: preflight, flight and resettlement.
During this process, the impact of socio-cultural shock and psychological distress is highly stressful and traumatic for refugees (Gonsalves, 1992). The type
of psychological symptoms and corresponding effects experienced by refugees differ by age and the degree of exposure to traumatic events (Rothe,
Castilo-Matos & Busquets, 2002a). Stressful experiences in the ocean and refugee camps have left chronic symptoms of trauma in many Cubans including
children and adolescents. Many Cuban immigrants/refugees have suffered
moderate to severe post traumatic stress disorder symptoms related to the witnessing of people dying in the ocean, hunger, thirst and violence in refugee
camps (Rothe et al., 2002a). Despite the massive hardship and trauma, Cuban
immigrants have successfully adapted to the mainstream culture of the United
States. Because of this successful adaptation, Cuban immigrants have been
identified as a "model minority group" (Bernal, 1982; Bernal & Shapiro,
1996; Wenk, 1968). Inevitably, however, as noted earlier not all Cubans have
succeeded in navigating psychologically unharmed through the acculturation
maze. Acculturation stress has resulted in intergenerational conflict, marital
conflict and other social problems for many Cuban immigrants. Delivering of
effective culturally sensitive mental health services to this population should
be an area of significant concern for mental health professionals.

This chapter focuses on the differential family reunification issues experienced by both the Marielitos and balseros upon entrance into the United
States. Treatment recommendations, aimed at ameliorating the emotionally

laden reunification issues, are presented within a family systems and ecological context. The overall intent of this chapter is to assist mental health practitioners in their therapeutic work with members of a relatively small but distinct Hispanic ethnic group. Two case vignettes are presented as a means of illustrating the key family reunifications issues that have impacted–and continue to affect–Cuban Marielitos and balseros.

DEMOGRAPHIC PROFILE

The current United States Cuban population is 1.2 million, constituting 3.5% of the total Hispanic population (35.3 million) (U.S. Census Bureau, 2000). Of the 952,000 Cuban born immigrant population, over 51% (552,000) are U.S. naturalized citizens. The U.S. Census Bureau (2000), however, estimates that there are currently 216,297 Cubans living as undocumented immigrants in the United States.

The geographic region where Hispanics reside is different depending on each ethnic group. For example, 43.5% of total Hispanic population lives in the West region of the United States; however, 74.2% of Cubans are concentrated in the South, 13.6% in the North East, 8.5% in the West and 3.6% in the Midwest (U.S. Census Bureau, 2000). The states where most Cubans reside include Florida, New Jersey, California and New York, with the majority of Cubans (70%) living in Florida (Altarriba & Bauer, 1998).

On an academic level, twenty-seven percent of the Hispanic population has less than a ninth grade level of education (Gonzalez, 2000). Compared to other Hispanic groups, Cubans have the highest level of education. According to the U.S. Census Bureau (2000), seventy-three percent of Cubans completed at least a high school education, as compared to 64.3% of Puerto Ricans, 51.0% of Mexicans, and 64.3% of Central and South Americans. As for college and post-college academic attainment, twenty-three percent of Cubans have completed a college education or higher, as compared to 13.0% of Puerto Ricans, and 6.9% of Mexicans. The association of Cuban immigrants' high level of education and economic success in the United States should be understood within the socio-cultural context of the Cuban migration. The Cuban immigrants of the 1960s were mostly white, highly educated, and professionals from upper or upper-middle class. Bernal (1982) and Bernal and Gutierrez (1988) have suggested that these socio-cultural variables assisted Cubans to adjust to the mainstream culture without experiencing significant economic and racial barriers.

In terms of full-time employment and annual median income levels, 51.6% of Cubans earn $35,000 or more annually as compared to 44.5% of Mexicans,

43.3% of Puerto Ricans, and 47.0% of central and South Americans. A significant percentage of employed Cuban Americans (39.5%) have an annual income of $50,000 or more (U.S. Bureau of Labor Statistics, Employment and Earnings, 2001). Among Hispanic groups, 8.1% of Puerto Ricans, 7.0% of Mexicans, 5.8% of Cubans and 5.1% of Central and South Americans are unemployed. In terms of poverty level, 17.3% of Cubans as compared with 24.1% of Mexicans, 25.8% of Puerto Ricans, and 16.7% of Central and South Americans live in poverty (U.S. Bureau of Labor Statistics, Employment and Earnings, 2001).

THE MARIEL EXODUS

In April of 1980, over a seven month period, facing no possibility of leaving Cuba by normal means and recognizing no prospect of the Castro regime changing or their families' human rights and financial future improving, over 125,000 Cubans left the island on boats headed for Miami, Florida. Bevin (2001) has noted that, "the Mariel exodus of 1980 was a critical event for many Cubans, whether they were Marielitos themselves, relatives, or simply witnesses of the boatlift" (p. 186). Hope and desperation are the two main constructs that characterized the cargo of Cuban refugees that arrived in Southern Florida throughout the Mariel exodus.

The Marielitos, however, were a significantly different group of Cuban refugees as compared to Cuban exiles who had entered the United States twenty years earlier. As noted earlier in this chapter, many of the Marielitos were Afro-Cubans and, therefore, racially different from the predominantly white Cuban community that was well established in southern Florida. In addition, Boswell and Curtis (1983) have noted that approximately 4-6 percent of the Marielitos included individuals suffering from mental illness, persons with criminal records, hard-core criminals and those with physical aliments such as leprosy. The Marielito worldview was juxtaposed to the life experience of earlier Cuban émigrés. Pedraza (1995) and Navarro (1999) have observed that the Marielitos represented a different political generation. The Marielitos were identified as a generation of Cubans immersed in the tenets and philosophy of Castro's Revolutionary Communist Party. Many of the Marielitos–including children and adolescents–had been raised in a sociopolitical system completely remote from the United States American way of life. As a generational cohort, the Marielitos arrived to the United States void from any understanding of the American mainstream culture. Identified as "children of communism" (Pedraza, 1995), Marielitos often struggled in their adaptation to United States life as a result of cognitive dissonance with comprehending the political-economic principles of capitalism and the structure of a democratic government.

Case Vignette: Ricardo

Ricardo is a 35-year-old unemployed SSI recipient who lives in a studio apartment as the caretaker of an Irish-German American woman who is also on SSI due to a history of chronic alcoholism and multiple medical impairments. Ricardo's exit from Cuba through the Mariel boatlift was opportunistic in nature. He reports that his father and paternal aunt had been living in Southern Florida for many years, and left Cuba believing that through their assistance he would be able to make a new life for himself in the United States. Upon Ricardo's arrival to Miami, however, he describes being rejected by both his father and aunt. He notes that his father is now remarried and that his new wife was unaware that he existed. Ricardo states that he has become extremely depressed as a result of his current family situation. Five years ago his sister–who exited Cuba through the visa granting lottery system–joined the patient in Miami. Although the sibling reunion was a joyful occasion for Ricardo, the sister was of minimal support to him since she too was facing the same family situation. Following the sister's arrival to Miami, Ricardo's depressive symptoms exacerbated leading to his first suicide attempt and subsequently to his first psychiatric hospitalization. Following a few weeks of inpatient treatment, Ricardo was discharged from the hospital without a solidified outpatient treatment plan. The patient reports doing a variety of odd jobs including menial labor to help support himself. Six months later a cousin–who had also entered the United States via the Mariel exodus–offered Ricardo a job in a small restaurant. At a later date, the patient discovered that the cousin had opened up this restaurant with "fast money" that he had made through various illegal drug dealings. Unbeknown to Ricardo, this cousin began to use him as a "delivery man" in his drug business. Following a drug raid, police officials closed the restaurant, leaving Ricardo without any means of supporting himself. Once again the patient became extremely depressed, leading to a second suicide attempt and psychiatric hospitalization. Ricardo was discharged from his second hospitalization with a schizoaffective diagnosis. The patient reports feeling tremendous emotional pain at being shunned and rejected by his father and paternal aunt. Ricardo's sister is the only one that is able to offer him some degree of emotional support. The patient states how sad he has felt at the demands that his father places on him to make something constructive out of his life without giving him any emotional or financial assistance. Ricardo attempts to please his father by visiting him often and doing chores for him without receiving any type of parental recognition or validation in return.

THE BALSERO REFUGEE/IMMIGRANT WAVE

As described earlier in this chapter, balseros represent the latest wave of Cuban immigrant/refugees entering the United States. This wave of Cuban émigrés began in 1994 when tight economic measures and continued political repression in Cuba forced thousands of Cuban individuals to exit their homeland in makeshift rafts (The National Association of Hispanic Journalists, 2001). Although the number of balseros entering the United States has decreased in the last few years, immigration laws have been enacted to grant political asylum only to those Cuban balseros that land in U.S territory (i.e., Miami, Florida). If balseros are intercepted at sea by the U.S. Coast Guard they are returned, however, to Cuba (Rankin et al., 1994). Similar to the experience of the Marielitos, the arrival of balseros in southern Florida has proven difficult for established Cuban Americans to accept. Making direct reference to the Cuban balseros, Navarro (1999) noted: "The people from today's Cuba are the children of a revolution that provided social guarantees but limited opportunities" (p. A25). Bevin (2001) has observed that this new group of Cuban refugees appear entitled, therefore, making it very difficult for the established Cuban exile community to assist them in the acculturation process specific to the American work ethic. Yet, despite the possibility that many balseros may "lack" the innate drive to succeed in a country immersed in capitalistic-economic principles because of the indoctrination of Castro's repressive regime, thousands of Cuban balseros have settled into productive lives in southern Florida and other states (Clary, 1995).

Case Vignette: Roberto

Roberto is a 37-year-old self-employed carpenter currently living in Miami with his wife. He came to the United States as a balsero. For many years Roberto planned his exit out of Cuba. Roberto's training as a carpenter assisted his escape. He built a 22 foot "lancha" (large wooden fishing boat) set a date, held secret meetings with his family, stole and stored food items and one evening he and twelve other family members journeyed to southern Florida. He reports being thrilled, exited and very much afraid. These emotions are often akin to refugees and immigrants who carefully plan their entrance into the United States (Gonsalves, 1992). He felt competent about his knowledge of the sea, and the travel course was guided by his knowledge of the stars given that he had been an active fisherman for many years. While out at sea, he reports that the boat's motor failed. Roberto was not successful at restarting it. The patient and his family drifted at sea for two days. After two days of being afloat, Roberto and his family were spotted by the U.S. Coast Guard and were brought to the Guantanamo Naval Base. Roberto and his family remained in Guantanamo for approximately three months. The patient describes conditions on the base as less than humane. There was much illness, chaos and human travesty. He and his family were admitted to the United States through the Catholic Charities Refugee Program. The family was resettled in Syracuse, New York where they remained for approximately seven years. Jointly the family decided to make a decision to relocate to Miami. This decision was based on the family's need to live in a more tropical environment as well as a more culturally relevant community. Roberto moved first to Miami and was instrumental in assisting his family with relocating and obtaining housing and employment. One year after settling in Miami, Roberto met his wife, was married and developed his own business in carpentry. He reports that his biggest issue is learning English as a second language. Having been poorly educated in Cuba he has had to struggle to learn English. He reports that due to his work schedule there is little time left for him to go to school. Roberto reports feeling emotionally frustrated at times and he presents with symptoms consonant with a diagnosis of dysthymia. Nevertheless, the patient is resilient and optimistic about the future.

FAMILY REUNIFICATION ISSUES

The family reunification issues of both Cuban Marielitos and balseros appear to be predicated on the themes of hope, rejection, disappointment, opportunity, freedom, shame and compassion. Cuban Marielitos, for example, were tainted by shame, rejection and abandonment based on the social undesirable attributes that characterized a percentage to this group including–but not limited to–mental illness, Afro-Cuban racial identity and history of incarceration. Because many Marielitos presented with a different political ideology (usually based on communist thinking), worldview, and value base that was opposite from the socio-cultural-political experience informing the Cuban exile community in the United States, members of this Cuban immigrant subgroup were perceived by their U.S. established family members as "immediate gratification seekers" who longed for "a piece of the American pie" without recognizing the importance of sacrifice, hard work and personal initiative (Boswell & Curtis, 1983; Navarro, 1999; Suarez, 1998). These perceptions, in turn, contributed to the genesis of familial abandonment, feelings of hostility and maladaptive adaptation/acculturation processes among a number of Marielitos. It may be hypothesized that U.S. based Cuban families who had exited Cuba a few decades earlier lacked an understanding of the probable poor coping mechanisms and compromised ego functioning–directly linked to continual exposure to Castro's repressive regime–that contributed to the poor adjustment of a number of Marielitos in this country (Rothe, Lewis & Castillo-Matos, 2002b; Williams & Westermeyer, 1986). Indeed, many Cuban Marielitos arriving in southern Florida were eventually admitted to a variety of systems of care and social control such as detention centers, criminal justice programs psychiatric hospitals, and substance and alcohol abuse programs.

Cuban balseros–although not completely exempt from some of the family reunification themes and dynamics impacting the Marielitos–have been perceived by the U.S. based Cuban community as "true freedom seekers" (Martinez, 2003; O'Grady, 2003). Mainland Cubans and other ethnic groups have felt compassion toward this specific émigré group. The reception of balseros upon arrival to southern Florida and other states appears to be based on the notion that individuals within this Cuban subgroup had longed to come to the United States. Impelled by the quest for liberty and the pursuit of happiness, and because of the reverberating effects of economic-political desperation, many balseros left Cuba on makeshift vessels that would often seal their destiny in death. A sense of passion and admiration has been given to the narratives of the Cuban balseros by authors in the field of humanities, filmmakers and journalists (Castro, 2001; Garcia & Viglucci, 2000).

The case of six-year-old Elian Gonzalez (Martinez, 2003) is illustrative of this point. Irrespective of the United States government or an individual's position on the case of Elian Gonzalez, the case underscored the magnitude of political-economic repression in Cuba. Elian's mother's willingness to risk her life on an inner tube raft for freedom symbolizes the tenacity and struggle for liberty of many, if not all, Cuban balseros. Cuban refugee, Carlos Erie (quoted in O'Grady, 2003), who is now the T. Lawrason Riggs Professor of History and Religious Studies at Yale University and recipient of the 2003 National Book Award for his book, *Waiting for Snow in Havana*, publicly commented on the Elian Gonzalez case and stated: "Elian Gonzalez had no autonomy, no say in his life and in a way he was just like Cuba and the Cuban people. That's how it's been for many years for Cuba. We've been pawns" (quoted in O'Grady, 2003, p. A11).

Predicated on the belief that Cuban balseros are "true freedom seekers," many individuals within this group fit more readily into the established norms of their U.S. Cuban families. It was understood by U.S. established Cuban families that the intention of many balseros was to buy into the American dream and work hard for financial success. Therefore, efforts were made by extended family members and community residents–particularly in southern Florida–to assist balseros in securing employment, housing and independent living. There was an explicit understanding that living with family was only temporary and that the expectation was that balsero family members would "move on" and develop their own lives. Bevin (2001), however, notes that this was not the case for every Cuban balsero entering the United States and many balseros have experienced the same family reunification dynamics that affected Cuban Marielitos: family abandonment, rejection and disengagement.

TREATMENT RECOMMENDATIONS

Gonzalez (2002) has noted that from an ecological-systems perspective, the mental health problems of Hispanic immigrant patients will be significantly reduced if they are assisted in mediating complex social systems, in obtaining community resources, in attaining vocational/job skills, and in learning English as a second language. Likewise, the family reunification issues of Cuban Marielitos and balseros must be addressed via an ecologically based family treatment approach. Therefore, ecological structural family therapy, bicultural effectiveness training and the social/environmental change agent role model are recommended as viable treatment approaches that may ameliorate the family reunification dynamics and conflicts presented by Cuban immigrant/refugee patients.

Ecological Structural Family Therapy

Research evidence (Szapocznik et al., 1978; Szapocznik et al., 1991; Szapocznik et al., 1997) appears to suggest that ecological structural family therapy is an effective treatment approach in addressing intergenerational conflict and acculturation differences in Hispanic families primarily of Cuban descent. Because the locus of the patient's dysfunction is not only internal but also external in nature, ecological structural family therapy stresses the interaction between the organism and its environment. Based on the theoretical and clinical work of Aponte (1974) and Minuchin (1974), this family treatment approach highlights the stress of acculturation and its disruptive impact within the structure of the Hispanic family. This treatment model pays careful attention to how normal family processes may interact with acculturation processes to create intergenerational differences and exacerbate intrafamilial conflict.

Altarriba and Bauer (1998) suggest that when applying ecological structural family therapy to Cuban immigrants an assessment of the interaction between the individual patient and his/her environment should be conducted early on during the initial phase of treatment. The diagnostic assessment process should include an appraisal of the boundaries between and among family members, the strength of the relationships between and among family members, an understanding of the hierarchal and authority structure of the family, and an examination of any inherent contradictions in the request for service.

Szapocznik et al. (1997) have empirically studied the value of ecological structural family therapy in assisting Hispanic Cuban families address their interactional problems from both a content and process level. At the content level, the cultural and intergenerational conflicts can be the focus of clinical attention making this model of family therapy particularly specific to the Cuban family. At the process level, this treatment model aims to modify the breakdown in communication processes resulting from intensified cultural and intergenerational conflicts. The content and process distinction is crucial in treating maladaptive family reunification issues often found in Cuban patients who have entered the United States via the Mariel or balsero migration wave.

Bicultural Effectiveness Training

Developed at the Spanish Family Guidance Center at the University of Miami by Szapocznik and colleagues (1984, 1986), bicultural effectiveness training–which is based on structural family theory–is delivered as a twelve-session psychoeducation treatment approach. Empirically tested with Cuban American families experiencing conflict with their adolescent children, bicultural effectiveness training is specifically designed to decrease acculturation related stresses by two-generation immigrant families. For Cuban balsero patients who may be integrating into U.S. based established family systems, this intervention model may be useful in treating family reunification dynamics.

Social/Environmental Change Agent Role Model

Given the fact that many Cuban Marielitos and balseros often lacked instrumental support from their U.S. based extended families, many attempted to negotiate complex environmental conditions (e.g., employment, housing, health care, learning English as a second language) with minimal appropriate guidance. Atkinson et al. (1993b) developed a dimensional intervention approach (social/environmental change agent role model) for the mental health treatment of ethnic-racial minority patients that recognizes the impact of the social environment in promoting or handicapping psychological growth and development. Within this treatment model, the mental health clinician treating Cuban patients can function as an agent for change or as a consultant or advisor to an identified individual patient acting to strengthen the patient's support systems.

Atkinson et al. (1993a) recommend that the following three factors should be diagnostically assessed when treating an ethnic minority patient: (1) the patient's level of acculturation, (2) the perceived cause and development of the presenting problem (internally caused versus externally-environmentally caused), and (3) the specific goals to be attained in the treatment process. In implementing this treatment model with Cuban patients, however, mental health care providers must be prepared to extend their professional role beyond that of psychotherapist to that of advocate, mediator, educator and broker (Gonzalez, 2002).

REFERENCES

Altarriba, J. and Bauer, L.M. (1998). Counseling Cuban Americans. In D. Atkinson et al. (Eds.), *Counseling American Minorities*. 5th Edition. New York: McGraw-Hill.

Aponte, H. (1974). Psychotherapy for the poor: An ecostructural approach to treatment. *Delaware Medical Journal*, 1-7.

Atkinson, D. et al. (1993a). *Counseling American minorities*. 4th Edition. Madison, WI: Brown and Benchmark.

Atkinson, D. et al. (1993b). A dimensional model for counseling racial/ethnic minorities. *The Counseling Psychologist*, 21, 257-277.

Bach, R. L. (1980). The new Cuban immigrants: Their background and prospects. *Monthly Labor Review*, 103(10): 39-46.

Bernal, G. (1982). Cuban families. In M. McGoldrick, J. K. Pearce, and J. Giordan (Eds.), *Ethnicity and family therapy* (pp. 187-207). New York: Guilford Press.

Bernal, G. and Gutierrez, M. (1988). Cubans. In L. Comas-Diaz and E. E. H. Griffith (Eds.), *Clinical guidelines in cross-cultural mental health*. New York: John Wiley and Sons.

Bernal, G. and Shapiro, E. (1996). Cuban families. In M. McGoldrick, J. K. Pearce, and J. Giordan (Eds.), *Ethnicity and family therapy* (pp. 155-168). 2nd Edition. New York: Guilford Press.

Bevin, T. (2001). Parenting in Cuban American families. In N. Webb Boyd (Ed.), *Culturally diverse parent-child and family relationships*. New York: Columbia University Press.

Boswell, T.D. and Curtis, J.R. (1983). *The Cuban American experience*. New Jersey: Rowman and Allanheld.

Castro, M. (2001, February 6). Saving Elian: Interview. *PBS Frontline*. www.pbs.org/wgbh/pages/frontline/shows/elian/interviews/castro.html

Clary, M. (1995, December 17). Miami Boy's slaying strikes raw nerve: Because suspect in mutilation killing is Cuban, recent immigrants fear taint to their image. *The Los Angeles Times*, p. 6.

Garcia, M. and Viglucci, A. (2000, April 3). As angry protests dwindle, strike called for Tuesday. *Miami Herald*, p. 1A.

Gonsalves, C. J. (1992). Psychological stages of the refugee process: A model for therapeutic intervention. *Professional Psychology: Research and Practice*, 23(5), 382-389.

Gonzalez, J. (2000). *A history of Latinos in America: Harvest of empire*. New York: Viking.

Gonzalez, M. J. (2002). Mental health intervention with Hispanic immigrants: Understanding the influence of the client's worldview, language, and religion. *Journal of Immigrant and Refugee Services*, 1(1), 81-92.

Martinez, M. C. (2003). Mothers mild and monstrous: Familial metaphors and the Elian Gonzalez case. *Southern Quarterly*, 42 (1), 22-38.

Minuchin, S. (1974). *Families and family therapy*. Cambridge, MA: Harvard University Press.

Navarro, M. (1999, February 11). Miami's generation of exiles: Side by side, yet worlds apart. *The New York Times*, p. A25.

O'Grady, M. A. (2003, December 23). Americas: A victim of Castro's tyranny tells his story. *Wall Street Journal*, p. A11.

Pedraza, S. (1995). Cuban refugees: Manifold migrations. *Cuba in Transition*, 5, 311-329.

Rankin, R., Nickens, T., and Alvarez, L. (1994, August 19). Rescued rafters will be sent to Guantanamo base camps. *Miami Herald*, p. A1.

Rothe, E. M., Castillo-Matos, H., and Busquets, R. (2002a). Posttraumatic stress symptoms in Cuban adolescent refugees during camp confinement. *Adolescent Psychiatry*, 26, 97-124.

Rothe, E. M., Lewis, J., and Castillo-Matos, H. (2002b). Posttraumatic stress disorder among Cuban children and adolescents after release from a refugee camp. *Psychiatric Services*, 53(8), 970-976.

Suarez, Z. E. (1998). Cuban American families. In Habenstein, R. W. et al. (Eds.), *Ethnic families in America*. New Jersey: Prentice Hall.

Szapocznik, J. et al. (1978). Theory and practice in matching treatment to the special characteristics and problems of Cuban immigrants. *Journal of Community Psychology*, 6, 112-122.

Szapocznik, J. et al. (1984). Bicultural effectiveness training (BET): A treatment intervention for enhancing intercultural adjustment. *Hispanic Journal of Behavioral Science*, 6(4), 317-344.

Szapocznik, J. et al. (1986). Bicultural effective training (BET): An intervention modality for families experiencing intergenerational/intercultural conflict. *Hispanic Journal of Behavioral Science*, 8(4), 303-330.

Szapocznik, J. et al. (1991). Assessing change in family functioning as a result of treatment: The structural family systems rating scale (SFSR). *Journal of Marital and Family Therapy*, 17(3), 295-310.

Szapocznik, J. et al. (1997). The evolution of structural ecosystemic theory for working with Latino families. In Garcia, J. and Zea, M.C. (Eds.), *Psychological interventions and research with Latino populations*. Boston: Allyn and Bacon.

The National Association of Hispanic Journalists. (2001). *Latinos in the United States*. Washington, DC: Author.

U. S. Bureau of Labor Statistics, Employment and Earnings. (2001). *Employment Statistics*. Washington, DC: U.S. Government Printing Office.

U. S. Bureau of the Census. (2000). *Current Population Survey*. Washington, DC: U. S. Government Printing Office.

Wenk, M. G. (1968). Adjustment and assimilation the Cuban refugee experience. *International Migration Review*, 31(1), 38-49.

Williams, C. L. and Westermeyer, J. (1986). (Eds.). *Refugee mental health in resettlement countries*. New York: Hemisphere Publishing.

Chapter 9

Counseling South American Immigrants

Jairo N. Fuertes
Vincent C. Alfonso
Janet T. Schultz

SUMMARY. The Hispanic population in the United States is growing exponentially. There are a total of 1,506,654 South Americans in
the United States who have come from Spanish-speaking countries.
Most immigrants, if not all, experience difficulties triggered by migration, discrimination, acculturation, and second language acquisition. In this chapter, we briefly discuss major issues associated with
migration and present literature and research on the construct of social support. We propose that integrating and utilizing social support
during treatment will facilitate the adjustment process for the individual. We present interventions that allow the therapist to provide sup-

---

Jairo N. Fuertes, PhD, Vincent C. Alfonso, PhD, and Janet T. Schultz, MSEd, are
affiliated with Fordham University, Graduate School of Education.

[Haworth co-indexing entry note]: "Counseling South American Immigrants." Fuertes, Jairo N., Vincent
C. Alfonso, and Janet T. Schultz. Co-published simultaneously in *Journal of Immigrant & Refugee Services*
(The Haworth Social Work Practice Press, an imprint of The Haworth Press, Inc.) Vol. 3, No. 1/2, 2005, pp.
155-169; and: *Mental Health Care for New Hispanic Immigrants: Innovative Approaches in Contemporary
Clinical Practice* (ed: Manny J. González, and Gladys González-Ramos) The Haworth Social Work Practice
Press, an imprint of The Haworth Press, Inc., 2005, pp. 155-169. Single or multiple copies of this article are
available for a fee from The Haworth Document Delivery Service [1-800-HAWORTH, 9:00 a.m. - 5:00 p.m.
(EST). E-mail address: docdelivery@haworthpress.com].

port while encouraging the client to seek support within him/herself and from other sources in the environment. *[Article copies available for a fee from The Haworth Document Delivery Service: 1-800-HAWORTH. E-mail address: <docdelivery@haworthpress.com> Website: <http://www.HaworthPress. com> © 2005 by The Haworth Press, Inc. All rights reserved.]*

KEYWORDS. Counseling, social support, South American immigrants, treatment

INTRODUCTION

United States (U.S.) Census Bureau statistics from the year 2000 (U.S. Census, 2000) indicate that 12% of the total population, about 34 million people, are of Hispanic origin. The U.S. is now the fifth largest Spanish-speaking country in the world. In South America, there are approximately 179 million people in 9 countries who are considered Hispanic by virtue of speaking Spanish as the primary language. The approximate populations of people in millions include Colombia (41), Argentina (37), Peru (28), Venezuela (24), Chile (16), Ecuador (14), Bolivia (9), Paraguay (6) and Uruguay (4).

There are a total of 1,506,654 South Americans in the U.S. who have come from Spanish-speaking countries. Of these, 509,872 are from Colombia, 298,626 from Ecuador, 278,186 from Peru, 125,218 from Argentina, 107,031 from Venezuela, 80,804 from Chile, 53,278 from Bolivia, and 53,639 total from Paraguay and Uruguay (U.S. Census, 2000).

The U.S. has the largest immigrant population of any country in the world, approximately 35 million immigrants across continents (Sarin, 2003). The number of Hispanic immigrants in the U.S. is growing rapidly, particularly from countries in Central and South America (Moss, Townsend, & Tobier, 1997; Therrien & Ramirez, 2001). For the purposes of this chapter we define the following terms: (a) immigrants are people born outside the U.S. who now reside in the U.S.; (b) adults refer to individuals age 18 and older; and (c) South American Hispanics are individuals who come from the nine Spanish-speaking countries in South America. Although we are not considering Brazilians because they speak Portuguese and not Spanish, we are aware that many Brazilians consider themselves Latin Americans or Latinos. This chapter pertains to South American Spanish-speaking adult immigrants, and focuses on issues of acculturation, poverty, discrimination, and language use that are prevalent with these populations (Bernal & Scharron-Del Rio, 2001). However, the content of this chapter may also be relevant to U.S. born Hispanics, particularly those who: (a) are visible ethnic group members and/or have parents who were born outside the U.S.; (b) do not speak English; and (c) are not fully acculturated to the U.S. ways of life.

In this brief chapter we review relevant literature on the process of migration. We also review literature on the construct of social support, since we believe that this is the primary need and the most important general intervention that mental health professionals can provide to help South American immigrants adjust to the US. We end the chapter by presenting ideas for intervention that focus on social support for issues associated with migration and adjustment.

THE EXPERIENCE OF MIGRATION

Migration is considered a major life transition that has positive and negative consequences. Even for the hardiest personality, migration is often a painful and challenging adjustment process that takes years to resolve and is fraught with difficulty, stress, and at times, even demoralization. Virtually all immigrants face to varying extents and at various points in their adjustment process, marginalization, minority status, physical health problems, socioeconomic disadvantage, collapse of social supports, and a unique learning process necessary to their adaptation in the host culture. Some of these common experiences are described below.

Discrimination

People all over the world tend to categorize themselves and others on the basis of common experiences and/or physical characteristics. The U.S. is no exception, and for many Hispanic immigrants, their skin color may facilitate the quality of new experiences in the host culture as well as their overall adjustment. It has been hypothesized that lighter-skinned, younger, and better educated immigrants adapt at a faster rate and are received more positively by the host country than those who are darker-skinned and uneducated (Smart & Smart, 1995). While age and education may be particularly important, very few people who have experienced migration to the U.S. or who have worked with immigrants and refugees would argue with a serious face that skin color is irrelevant to the interpersonal process of adjustment. This is an interesting point because racism and discrimination are also alive and well in Latin America, and even in South American countries the social strata and quality of life favors those who are White. Thus, race and skin color are deeply intertwined with socio-economic privilege, in the U.S. and South America, and the pattern is very similar in both neighboring continents. Therefore, it is reasonable to state that it is likely that all South American immigrants will experience discrimination at some time in their lives in the U.S. not just from White Americans but also from other minority or immigrant groups. This may occur for many reasons such as because of the way they speak English or Spanish, their accents, or they do not know the law or their rights.

Acculturation

Acculturation is a process by which an immigrant adapts to a new environment, including changes in language use, work setting and work hours, socio-economic status and purchasing power, gender roles and family obligations, social networks, or even factors such as weather and food. The phases of acculturation, as proposed by Williams and Berry (1991), include contact, conflict, crisis, and adaptation. The first phase is the contact phase in which immigrants tend to overestimate what they can accomplish, as they view the new country as providing endless opportunities. Williams and Berry note that during the second or middle phase, referred to as conflict and crisis (which usually occurs after 3 to 5 years), immigrants tend to experience the brunt of emotional difficulties associated with acculturation, which may include depression, anxiety, or psychosomatic symptoms. The last phase, adaptation, occurs when realistic expectations have been set, accepted, and pursued by the immigrant. In effect, the process of acculturation affects learning, behavior, values, and social activities that occur as a result of contact with a new culture (Gordon, 1964). According to Mirsky and Kaushinsky (1989), the acculturation process usually takes, on average, three to four years for most immigrants and represents a complex phenomenon that incorporates cognitive, behavioral, and affective modes of social-psychological functioning.

Second Language Acquisition

Perhaps the greatest challenge for the immigrant, and the best overall indicator of his/her ultimate adaptation to the U.S. is learning to speak English and his/her level of mastery in the use of this language. The process of learning English usually takes adult immigrants many years, particularly to learn how to read and write correctly. However, very young children and kids under the age of 12 can usually learn how to speak, read, and write English in less than a year. Most Hispanic immigrants continue to speak Spanish at home, as a recent survey conducted by Washington-based Pew Hispanic Center and the Henry J. Kaiser Family Foundation showed, and in effect most Hispanic families become bilingual and bicultural as they adapt and adjust to life in the U.S. (Zehr, 2003).

SOCIAL SUPPORT

Importance of Social Support

Over the past several decades social support has become a common phrase in the psychological research literature and in the 1990s more than 100 articles each year focused on this construct (Mutran, Reed, & Sudha, 2001). Hobfoll (2002) identified social support as a key resource that comes from the environment. For Hobfoll, "Resources are those entities that are either centrally valued in their own right (e.g., self-esteem, close attachments, health, and inner peace) or act as a means to obtain centrally valued ends (e.g., money, social support, and credit)" (p. 307). The interest in social support stems primarily from its importance as a mediating variable between stress and mental and physical pathology (e.g., Hobfoll, 2002). Social support also has been linked more specifically, however, with reduction of mortality, positive rehabilitation processes, compliance and management of diabetes, life satisfaction, general well being or quality of life, and ease of migration (e.g., Foroughi, Misajon, & Cummins, 2001; Kim & Nesselroade, 2003; Mutran et al., 2001).

A much-debated question in the research literature has been how social support works or functions, as a mediating variable. The two leading hypotheses are the buffering hypothesis and the main effect hypothesis. The former hypothesis states that the presence of social support "buffers" an individual from stress by preventing or reducing a stress reaction to a stressful stimulus (e.g., loss of work, death of a loved one, immigration) (Cobb, 1976; Wilcox, 1981). The latter hypothesis, called the main or "direct" effect views social support as influencing mental and physical health in a general manner by providing individuals with positive experiences and/or the avoidance of negative experiences (Cohen & Wills, 1985; Thoits, 1986). In other words, an individual is integrated in a social support system or network that provides him/her with protection from stress by instilling in the individual positive affect, sense of control, and self-worth. This system or network also may assist the individual in avoiding stressful situations so that stress is not experienced in the first place. Recent work by Kim and Nesselroade (2003) has demonstrated that neither of these explanations is completely satisfactory demonstrating that the mechanisms by which social support works are varied and complex. Although the precise ways in which social support affects people may not be well understood, it is clear that social support is an important phenomenon in people's lives and should continue to be studied (Hobfoll, 2002).

Definition of Social Support

Researchers have defined social support in myriad ways, which is not un-common when defining many psychological constructs. Initially, information was identified as an essential component to social support instead of material goods or even services (Cobb, 1976). Later definitions, however, included the importance of tangible assistance from the environment and behavioral trans-actions provided by a supportive network or system (e.g., Barrera & Ainlay, 1983; Turner, 1983). Pearlin, Menaghan, Lieberman, and Mullan (1981) ad-vanced the idea that when people feel supported there is a positive effect on their self-esteem and control of the environment. Later in 1988, Winnubst, Bunk, and Marcelissen defined social support as social integration, relation-ship quality, perceived helpfulness and supportiveness, and as the enactment of supportive behavior. Still, others such as Hobfoll and Vaux (1993) and House, Umberson, and Landis (1988) have conceptualized social support as a multidimensional or meta-construct or as one aspect of general classes of vari-ables. For example, these latter authors view social support and social net-works/social integration as separate, but related concepts. Central to any definition of social support, however, appears to be the belief by a person that he/she is cared for or loved by others who can provide emotional as well as tangible (i.e., material goods) assistance.

Types and Sources of Social Support

Although social support, as perhaps beauty, is in the eyes of the beholder, many researchers and clinicians would argue that there are several types and sources of support common to most people. Some types of support include information sharing, appraisal, intimate interaction, and feedback (Cohen, Mermelstein, Kamarck, & Hoberman, 1985). Sources of social support usu-ally include family, friends, colleagues, neighbors, and local community or-ganizations such as political or religious groups (Froland, Brodsky, Olson, & Stewart, 1979; Sarason, Levine, Basham, & Sarason, 1983). The type and source of support may depend on the nature and extent of the support re-quired by the person at that time. In other words, different types and sources of support may be required as a function of need and may change in the short or long-term.

Measurement of Social Support

There are probably as many measures of social support as there are defini-tions. Measures of social support vary with respect to their psychometric properties, item content, operational definition of the construct, and whether perceived (response to a hypothetical situation) or actual support (support received) is being measured (Lindner, Sarason, & Sarason, 1988; Sarason et al., 1983). Several popular measures include the Interpersonal Support Evaluation List (Cohen et al., 1985), the Social Support Questionnaire (Sarason et al., 1983), the Duke Social Support Index (Landerman, George, Campbell, & Blazer, 1989), and the Inventory of Socially Supportive Behavior (Barrera, Sandler, & Ramsay, 1981).

Mutran et al. (2001) note that although there are several measures of social support and that there is greater clarity of construct definition and measurement, "there is little effort exerted to make these [measures] appropriate for use with minority populations" (p. 67). Therefore, it is very important that researchers and clinicians alike choose the scale or questionnaire that answers their question(s) in the most effective ways and that is most appropriate for the group in question. For example, even though there is a Spanish version of the Inventory of Socially Supportive Behavior, limited reliability and validity data are available (Mutran et al., 2001). Close inspection of administration, scoring, and interpretation guidelines should assist individuals in choosing the best measure.

Social Support and Ethnic Minority Groups

Although it is generally recognized that social support is important to every individual and that it provides great protection against stressful daily and life experiences, few studies have investigated the social networks and support structures of ethnic minority groups or cultural influences in adaptation (Hobfoll, 2002; Kim & McKenry, 1998; Mutran et al., 2001). It is critical that we have a better understanding of the types and sources of social support that are valued by different ethnic groups so that we may be able to assist ethnic minorities with interpersonal and vocational adjustment. In addition, some authors have theorized that in elevated stress situations such as migration, social support may actually decrease especially after high levels of support were provided initially (Norris & Kaniasty, 1996) and that ethnic minorities may be more susceptible to resource (e.g., social support) deterioration.

One of the few, but largest studies devoted to comparing social networks and support among various groups was conducted by Kim and McKenry (1998). These investigators studied African Americans (N = 2,391), Asian Americans (N = 127), Hispanics (N = 1,004), and Caucasians (N = 9,403) to determine, what if any, differences exist among them with respect to social networks and support. Surveying individuals regarding their social activities and organizations was used to assess the social networks of the groups. Social support was assessed by asking the participants whom they would ask for assistance in three hypothetical stress situations. The mean age of respondents was 43 years with the average level of education less than high school and mean family annual income of $29,000 across groups.

The following summary of results may aid in our understanding of the differences and commonalities across ethnic minority groups and may have implications for assisting South American immigrants. A variety of statistical tests revealed the following results pertaining to social networks: (a) African American individuals had a greater tendency to attend social activities involving church compared to the other three groups; (b) Caucasians and African Americans had a greater tendency to frequent a bar or tavern than Hispanics or Asian Americans; (c) Asian Americans and Caucasians indicated more involvement in recreation activities compared to African Americans and Hispanics; (d) Asian Americans were more likely to participate in occupation-related organizations and Hispanics were the least likely to do so; (e) participation in sports groups was highest among Asian American and Caucasian respondents and participation in hobby groups was highest among Asian Americans; and (f) Asian Americans participated more often in nationality groups than African Americans and Hispanics.

A variety of statistical tests revealed the following results pertaining to social support: (a) the three ethnic minority groups had significantly greater odds of calling children if they had an emergency in the middle of the night than the Caucasian group and lower odds of calling siblings or other relatives; (b) in the case of needing to borrow $200 for an emergency all three ethnic groups had higher odds of asking children or parents for money and lower odds of asking friends, neighbors, etc., than the Caucasian group; and (c) when asked who they would ask for advice or help when feeling depressed or confused, all ethnic minority groups had significantly higher odds of asking children.

It is necessary to understand that these results pertain to and reflect group data and that individual differences are probably present within groups. In addition, these data represent patterns of behavior within a group and only significant results are presented. For example, although African Americans as a group are more likely to attend a church social it does not mean that Hispanics never attend this type of social gathering or do not find it helpful. The authors of this study conclude by stating that ethnic minority families clearly differ from Caucasian families regarding the social systems used and that the support systems that Caucasians find most useful are not necessarily the same for ethnic minorities.

IMPLICATIONS AND RELATED IDEAS
FOR COUNSELING SOUTH AMERICAN IMMIGRANTS

Before discussing possible ways and areas of intervention we would like to highlight some basic assumptions and notes regarding counseling in general and about counseling South American immigrants. The outcome literature in counseling and psychotherapy shows that when Hispanics seek mental health services they benefit as well from it as other racial and cultural groups (Sue, Zane, & Young, 1994). We also believe that immigrants can be helped psychologically and therapeutically from a variety of theoretical and technical perspectives, and that in essence there is no singular "right" approach to intervention. As the overall outcome literature shows (Wampold, 2000), all psychological perspectives to intervention work fairly well and consistently, and this is likely to be the case with South American immigrants, provided that they understand the help (i.e., in terms of language) and find it personally and culturally meaningful. We remind the reader of the importance of focusing on the individual, and not necessarily his/her ethnic group. Since no two people have the same set of experiences and circumstances, it is important not to stereotype the client or forget his/her individuality.

With respect to social support, a few assumptions are worth noting. First, we believe that humans are deeply social beings and that without human relationships and social support people cease to develop or function effectively. Certainly, the social support research reviewed above amply justifies this assumption. Secondly, we believe that for South American immigrants, just like any other immigrant group, factors such as sense of community, social support, and group belongingness become particular sources of concern as they are uprooted from their native countries and begin to adapt to a new life in the U.S. There is research that shows that social support helps people cope with an array of difficulties, and some research suggests it helps people with major life transitions and migrations. Lastly, our discussion of intervention strategies is designed to help immigrants cope primarily with "normal" problems in adaptation and adjustment, and is not presented as model of intervention for serious psychopathology or for long-standing maladaptive problems in behavior.

Intervention Strategies

Assessment. Assessment includes data gathering and allows the mental health professional to understand the etiology of the immigrant's problems and the summative effect that psychological, transitional, and/or adjustment issues have on the person's well-being. It may include assessment of the immigrants' acculturation process, experiences with discrimination, and difficulties or relevance of second-language acquisition. The process may also include formal test batteries and clinical interview questions to assess types and sources of support, coping styles and dispositions, which may help with case conceptualization and treatment planning.

The therapy relationship. A good clinician will use the information obtained from the assessment phase to help the client establish goals for treatment. However, the primary objective at the beginning of counseling should be to establish rapport with the client, to help him/her understand how counseling works, and to accept the parameters of the therapy relationship. For many clients the relationship with their counselors will be extremely important, perhaps the only source of support for them as they try to cope with or manage their problems. Many clients will want quick solutions and tangible results, and it will be up to the counselor to communicate to the client that he/she will do all that is possible to help, but the reality is often one where results are obtained with patience and perseverance. The goals for counseling can revolve around finding support, developing appropriate coping strategies, and establishing or finding appropriate work.

Understanding and appreciating social support. It is imperative to help the person understand his/her need for support, identify potential sources of support, and come to appreciate the role of social support from others in his/her life. For South American immigrants, the family, extended family, and close friends will be especially important sources of support. If family and friends are located in the country of origin, the counselor and client can work together to help the client create support in the new country, maintain effective long-distance contact with loved ones, and plan to re-unite, even if temporarily, with their family and friends. The crux of the therapeutic work at this point is to help the client set goals for making more and better use of support in the context of their circumstances. It will be important to examine whether external locus of control dispositions or indirect coping strategies being used by the person are effective. Some clients will have to learn to appreciate the importance of direct coping and the value and appropriate use of more internal locus of control strategies in managing problems where little or no support is available. In cases where there are problems with family members, it will be important to help the client review all the events, assess personal responsibility and control, and review all options available to him/her, including family counseling or any other culturally relevant outside intervention to help diffuse the conflict.

Support from the counselor may be manifested via listening, patience, and understanding. However, with South American immigrants it may behoove the counselor to become more active, even gently directive, by providing the client with appropriate "consejos" or advice. This may prove to be a tangible source of help for the client, especially if he/she sees the counselor as an expert with practical solutions. As a clinical example, the first author recently treated a 42-year-old Colombian woman, U.S. citizen, married for 9 years, who presented as very concerned about not being able to conceive a child. It became quickly apparent to the counselor that this client was taking all the responsibility (and guilt) for the difficulties in conception. A directive approach to helping her included educating her about her need for more support from her husband, the need for medical examinations for him to establish his ability to conceive, and the suggestion that they time off together to focus on one another and enhance the quality of their relationship. The client evaluated the counselor's suggestions, weighed them in her mind and planned a course of action that would be appropriate for her and her husband, and implemented a plan. While the treatment ended fairly quickly as they client felt more in control, she updated the counselor by phone that while she and her husband were still unable to conceive, their communication and relationship improved dramatically, and that they had begun to think jointly about possibly adopting a Colombian baby.

Immigrants who are going through a difficult time adjusting to the U.S. will be helped by knowing that they are going through a process which while difficult, is normal, and that in due time, the stress, longing, and loss which they feel will subside. The client will also likely need encouragement to become active in building a sense of community for him/herself, through social groups, community associations, church or religious activities, volunteering activities, participating in school activities or PTA meetings, sports, etc. Most immigrants have the option of permanently returning to their countries, and we have found it helpful to ask clients to tell us why they *should* return to their countries of origin. Clients sometimes respond to this question by talking about the reasons why they left their country, and develop a better appreciation of their freedom to stay in or leave the United States. However, the majority of South American immigrants tend to stay in the United States, often because of commitments made to their families in the U.S., because of work/job opportunities, or because in the final analysis the standard of living would be less in their country of origin.

Vocational adjustment. Another great challenge for the immigrant lies in the area of work and possibly education. Most South American immigrants come to the U.S. with dreams and ideas for better work and a higher standard of living. The reality is that many are under-employed, and if they are undocumented by virtue of not having the proper visa or work permits, they are outright exploited. Most new immigrants have tremendous difficulty finding work, and others do not know of options for studying in college or advancing in their professional development. An appropriate area for intervention lies with helping immigrants set goals for their professional development. For many, a key goal and task will be to learn to speak, read, and write English. No singular skill is more important to a new immigrant than knowing English; it is a source of information and power, and the quicker he/she learns the language the quicker he/she will realize his/her dreams in the host country. For others, the goal may be to obtain their GED, or learn a trade in night school, or to attend college. We strongly advocate helping immigrants use their full potential, and in the U.S. virtually every community has resources for helping immigrants learn, train, and develop professional skills. Counselors who plan to work with South American immigrants should have a good knowledge of low cost or free community sources, including legal advice, housing, education, and healthcare. This includes knowing how to advocate for illegal immigrants who are being exploited or need medical or legal help, or knowing the procedures available to some to receive the proper work permits or visas to be legal residents in the U.S.

Flexibility in gender and parental roles. Many immigrants also will also have to contend with flexible gender roles in the U.S. For many immigrants, their countries of origin will prescribe more traditional roles for the genders with regard to a host of behaviors including education, work, family responsibilities, and dating. This is often a challenge for couples and for parents of children who quickly learn new norms of behavior from other family members, peers, and various media. It is important for counselors to help individuals and families cope with these issues. Many immigrant women will benefit from gender-aware therapy, but it will important to temper this kind of support with serious consideration of the expectations and traditions of her family, religion, and culture. Since children acculturate much more quickly and fully to the U.S., conflicts with parents can arise, with respect to autonomy and independence from parents, marriage and dating practices, and vocational and professional aspirations. As noted in the review of the social support literature, ethnic groups tend to expect and seek support from children in the household, particularly grown children. A significant challenge for both parents and children is to balance conflicting expectations and find compromise or solutions to dilemmas to which simple solutions do not apply.

CONCLUSION

This brief chapter has reviewed literature on the process of migration for immigrants. We reviewed the extant literature on social support, and presented areas for intervention. We would like to point out that there is a need for trained counselors who can work with the growing number of South American immigrants to the U.S., and that ethical and professional standards, for example from the American Psychological Association (1993) require that formal training and supervision be in place before individuals are sent to work with culturally and linguistically diverse populations

REFERENCES

APA Office of Ethnic Minority Affairs (1993). Guidelines for providers of psychological services to ethnic, linguistic, and culturally diverse populations. *American Psychologist, 48*, 45-48.

Barrera, M. Jr., & Ainlay, S. L. (1983). The structure of social support: A conceptual and empirical analysis. *Journal of Community Psychology, 11*, 133-143.

Barrera, M. Jr., Sandler, I. N., & Ramsay, T. B. (1981). Preliminary development of a scale of social support: Studies on college students. *American Journal of Community Psychology, 9*, 435-447.

Bernal, G., & Scharron-Del-Rio, M. R. (2001). Are empirically supported treatments valid for ethnic minorities? Toward an alternative approach for treatment research. *Cultural Diversity and Ethnic Minority Psychology, 7*, 328-342.

Cobb, S. (1976). Social support as a moderator of life stress. *Psychosomatic Medicine, 38*, 300-314.

Cohen, S., Mermelstein, R., Kamarck, T., & Hoberman, H. M. (1985). Measuring the functional components of social support. In I. G. Sarason & B. R. Sarason (Eds.), *Social support: Theory, research, and applications* (pp. 73-94). Dordrecht, The Netherlands: Martinus Nijhoff.

Cohen, S., & Wills, T. A. (1985). Stress, social support, and the buffering hypothesis. *Psychological Bulletin, 98*, 310-357.

Foroughi, E., Misajon, R., & Cummins, R. A. (2001). The relationships between migration, social support, and social integration on quality of life. *Behaviour Change, 18*, 156-167.

Froland, C., Brodsky, G., Olson, M., & Stewart, L. (1979). Social support and social adjustment: Implications for mental health professionals. *Community Mental Health Journal, 15*, 82-93.

Gordon, M. M. (1964). *Assimilation in American life.* New York: Oxford University Press.

Hobfoll, S. E. (2002). Social and psychological resources and adaptation. *Review of General Psychology, 6*, 307-324.

Hobfoll, S. E., & Vaux, A. (1993). Social support: Social resources and social context. In L. Goldberger & S. Breznitz (Eds.), *Handbook of stress: Theoretical and clinical aspects* (pp. 685-705). New York: The Free Press.

House, J., Umberson, D., & Landis, K. R. (1988). Structures and processes of social support. *Annual Review of Sociology, 14*, 293-318.

Kim, J. E., & Nesselroade, J. R. (2003). Relationships among social support, self-concept, and well being of older adults: A study of process using dynamic factor models. *International Journal of Behavioral Development, 27*, 49-65.

Kim, H. K., & McKenry, P. C. (1998). Social networks and support: A comparison of African Americans, Asian Americans, Caucasians, and Hispanics. *Journal of Comparative Family Studies, 29*, 313-334.

Landerman, R., George, L. K., Campbell, R. T., & Blazer, D. G. (1989). Alternative models of the stress-buffering hypothesis. *American Journal of Community Psychology, 17*, 625-642.

Lindner, K. C., Sarason, I. G., & Sarason, B. R. (1988). Assessed life stress and experimentally provided social support. In C. D. Spielberger, I. G. Sarason, & P. B. Defares (Eds.), *Stress and anxiety* (Vol. 11) (pp. 231-240). Washington: Hemisphere.

Mirsky, J., & Kaushinsky, F. (1989). Migration and growth: Separation-individuation processes in immigrant students in Israel. *Adolescence, 24*, 225-240.

Moss, M. L., Townsend, A., & Tobier, E. (1997, December). Immigration is transforming New York City. New York: Taub Urban Research Center, Robert F. Wagner School of Public Service, New York University. Retrieved from: http://www.urban.nyu.edu/research/immigrants/immigrants.html.

Mutran, E. J., Reed, P. S., & Sudha, S. (2001). Social support: Clarifying the construct with applications for minority populations. *Journal of Mental Health and Aging, 7*, 67-78.

Norris, F. H., & Kaniasty, K. (1996). Received and perceived social support in times of stress: A test of the social support deterioration deterrence model. *Journal of Personality and Social Psychology, 71*, 498-511.

Pearlin, L. I., Menaghan, E. G., Lieberman, M. A., & Mullan, J. T. (1981). The stress process. In H. B. Kaplan (Ed.), *Psychosocial stress: Trends in theory and research* (pp. 3-32). New York: Academic.

Sarason, I. G., Levine, H. M., Basham, R. B., & Sarason, B. R. (1983). Assessing social support: The social support questionnaire. *Journal of Personality and Social Psychology, 44*, 127-139.

Sarin, R. (2003). As migration grows, immigrants face greater barriers. *Environmental Science, 16*, 8.

Smart, J. F., & Smart, D. W. (1995). Acculturative stress of Hispanics: Loss and challenge. *Journal of Counseling & Development, 73*, 390-396.

Sue, S., Zane, N., & Young, K. (1994). Research on psychotherapy with culturally diverse populations. In A. E. Bergin & S. L. Garfield (Eds.), *Handbook of psychotherapy and behavior change* (4th ed., pp. 783-817). New York: Wiley.

Therrien, M., & Ramirez, R. (2001). Diversity of the country's Hispanics highlighted in US Census Bureau Report, Washington, DC. Retrieved from: http://www.cenus.gov/Press-Release/www/2001/cb01-41.html

Thoits, P. A., (1986). Social support as coping assistance. *Journal of Consulting and Clinical Psychology, 54*, 416-423.

Turner, R. J. (1983). Direct, indirect, and moderating effects of social support on psychological distress and associated conditions. In H. B. Kaplan (Ed.), *Psychosocial stress: Trends in theory and research* (pp. 105-155). New York: Academic.

U.S. Census Bureau (2000). Census 2000 Summary File 3 (SF 3). *Place of birth for the foreign-born population*. Retrieved from: http://www.factfinder.census.gov/servlet/DTTable?_ts=70897381609

Wampold, B. E. (2000). Outcomes of individual counseling and psychotherapy: Empirical evidence addressing two fundamental questions. In S. D. Brown, & R. W. Lent (Eds.), *Handbook of counseling psychology* (3rd ed., pp. 711-739). New York: Wiley.

Wilcox, B. L. (1981). Social support, life stress, and psychological adjustment. A test of the buffering hypothesis. *American Journal of Community Psychology, 9*, 371-386.

Williams, C. L., & Berry, J. W. (1991). Primary prevention of acculturative stress among refugees–Application of psychological theory and practice. *American Psychologist, 46*, 632-641.

Winnubst, J. M. A., Buunk, B. P., & Marcelissen, F. H. G. (1988). Social support and stress: Perspectives and processes. In S. Fisher & J. Reason (Eds.), *Handbook of life stress, cognition, and health* (pp. 511-528).

Zehr, M. (2003). English-learners & immigrants. *Education Week, 22* (16), 11.

Chapter 10

Central American Survivors of Political Violence: An Examination of Contextual Factors and Practice Issues

David W. Engstrom
Lissette M. Piedra

SUMMARY. Despite compelling, well-documented findings on the levels of stress and trauma among Central American refugees, this group continues to be underserved. A host of issues contributes to this underservice, ranging from macro-level imposed obstacles, such as citizenship and health insurance as determining factors for accessing social and health services, to institutional factors that impede service utilization, such as an insufficient number of translators or a cumbersome and confusing bureaucracy. This chapter adopts a human rights framework as a strategy for working with groups of Central Americans who have experienced political violence. The ongoing effects of political violence on Central Americans, as they relate to mental and physical health prob-

David W. Engstrom, PhD, is Associate Professor, San Diego State University.
Lissette M. Piedra, PhD, MSW, is Part-Time Lecturer, University of Chicago.

[Haworth co-indexing entry note]: "Central American Survivors of Political Violence: An Examination of Contextual Factors and Practice Issues." Engstrom, David W., and Lissette M. Piedra. Co-published simultaneously in *Journal of Immigrant & Refugee Services* (The Haworth Social Work Practice Press, an imprint of The Haworth Press, Inc.) Vol. 3, No. 1/2, 2005, pp. 171-190; and: *Mental Health Care for New Hispanic Immigrants: Innovative Approaches in Contemporary Clinical Practice* (ed: Manny J. González, and Gladys González-Ramos) The Haworth Social Work Practice Press, an imprint of The Haworth Press, Inc., 2005, pp. 171-190. Single or multiple copies of this article are available for a fee from The Haworth Document Delivery Service [1-800-HAWORTH, 9:00 a.m. - 5:00 p.m. (EST). E-mail address: docdelivery@haworthpress.com].

lems, are reviewed and a case vignette is used to illustrate how political violence affects individuals and how macro-level forces and institutions create barriers to access and use of health care and social services. Treatment approaches for helping survivors of political violence in the context of a human rights framework are suggested. *[Article copies available for a fee from The Haworth Document Delivery Service: 1-800-HAWORTH. E-mail address: <docdelivery@haworthpress.com> Website: <http://www.HaworthPress.com> © 2005 by The Haworth Press, Inc. All rights reserved.]*

KEYWORDS. Central American refugees, political violence, stress, trauma

INTRODUCTION

The story of Central American refugees in the last 30 years is a sharp departure from what is typically known as the "immigrant story." Unlike many immigrants who have made the United States their home, Central American refugees' adaptation to this society is affected by their exposure to high levels of political violence in their countries of origin; also, traumatic experiences are all too common during the emigration exodus itself. Many Central American refugees left behind lives strongly embedded in traditional rural values and lifestyles, ending up with a radically different urban existence in a foreign and often hostile environment. These experiences, along with all the socioeconomic problems and hardships that follow from undocumented immigration status in the United States, influence the immigrants' well-being and shape their adaptation to this country. Many have lived in constant dread of being deported, because they equate repatriation with certain bodily harm or death.

This chapter adopts a human rights framework as an important strategy for understanding and working with Central American groups. The experiences of Central American refugees and the circumstances surrounding their immigration to the United States are particularly relevant for mental health and other social service professionals. It is important for mental health professions to have at least a basic knowledge of the social and political context of the Central American exodus, and the ongoing social and political obstacles that interfere with these immigrants' well-being and their access to services.

We begin our discussion by providing a demographic overview of Central Americans in the United States, before addressing political violence. We pay particular attention to Salvadorans, Guatemalans, and Nicaraguans as Central

Americans whose migration has been forced, in many cases, by the brutalities of civil war, political violence, egregious human rights abuses, oppression, and poverty. Finally, the continuing effects of political violence on Central Americans are reviewed as they relate to mental and physical health problems.

We define *political violence* as any direct or indirect state-sponsored violence that includes but is not limited to torture, disappearances of family and friends, pervasive fear of government and/or guerilla reprisals, and witness of massacres, executions, and armed conflict. Throughout our discussion, we use the case of Ernesto, a Guatemalan refugee, to illustrate how political violence affects individuals and creates access barriers to health care and social services. We conclude by suggesting treatment approaches to helping survivors of political violence, in the context of an overarching human rights framework.

DEMOGRAPHIC PROFILE

Central Americans are the third largest Hispanic group in the United States. The 2000 Census counted nearly 1.7 million Central Americans in the United States, a 37% increase from 1990 (United States Census Bureau, 2001a). *Central American* is used to delineate those who trace their recent or distant origins to the countries that bridge North and South America. Like *Hispanic* or *Latino*, the term *Central American* provides a convenient way to categorize people, but it masks the sociodemographic heterogeneity within and divergent immigration history of this population (Cafferty and Engstrom, 2001). Of persons identified in 2000 as Central American, 39% were Salvadoran, 22% Guatemalan, 13% Honduran, 11% Nicaraguan, 5% Panamanian, and 4% Costa Rican.

The majority of Central Americans are recent immigrants to the United States. According to the 2000 Census, 76% of Central American residents are foreign-born, almost seven times the national average. The difference is even more pronounced among adult Central American residents: more than 90% of them are foreign-born. Approximately 45% of foreign-born Central Americans currently living here entered the United States during the 1990s, and another 37% during the 1980s. With the exception of foreign-born Costa Ricans (24%), less than 10% of all other groups entered the United States before 1975 (United States Census Bureau, 2003).

Central Americans are concentrated in a handful of states and urban areas. Five states account for 71% of the Central American population: California (34%), Florida (12%), New York (11%), Texas (9%), and New Jersey (5%). Nearly two-thirds of Central Americans reside in five metropolitan areas: Los

Angeles, New York, Miami, Washington, D.C., and Houston. Los Angeles alone is home to more than one-quarter of all the Central Americans in the United States (United States Census Bureau, 2003).

As would be expected of an immigrant population, Central Americans are considerably younger in median age than the general population of the United States (29 versus 35.4 years). Guatemalans are the youngest, with a median age of 27.8 years, and Panamanians the oldest, at 32.6 years. Compared to the general population, Central Americans also have larger-than-average household and family sizes and a greater percentage of households headed by single males or single females (United States Census Bureau, 2003).

Many Central Americans have low levels of education, though this varies by country of origin. According to the 2000 Census, more than one-half of adult Central Americans never graduated from high school, and 8% have received no formal schooling at all. Looking at specific Central American groups, more than half of Salvadorans, Hondurans, and Guatemalans never graduated from high school, compared with 15% of Panamanians and 27% of Costa Ricans (United States Census Bureau, 2003). Low levels of educational attainment correspond with reduced occupational opportunity, so Central Americans are predictably concentrated in low-wage service and blue-collar occupations; only 7% work as managers and professionals. Central American males have slightly higher labor force participation than the general population (94.5%), whereas Central American females have a considerably lower participation rate (58.1%) (United States Census Bureau, 2001b).[1]

Not surprisingly, given their recency of migration, generally low educational attainment, and high concentration in low-wage occupations, all Central American groups have below-average income and higher rates of poverty. The median family income of Central Americans is $34,150, or about $16,000 less than the national average. Twenty percent of Central Americans find themselves below the poverty line, compared with a national poverty rate of 14%. Extending the poverty threshold to 200% of poverty captures one-half of all Central Americans, compared with 30% of the general population. Among Central Americans, Panamanians (13%) and Costa Ricans (16%) have the lowest rates of poverty and Hondurans (24%) and Guatemalans (22%) the highest (United States Census Bureau, 2003).

POLITICAL VIOLENCE IN CENTRAL AMERICA

Although the demographic profile of Central Americans suggests a worrisome socioeconomic status in this country, these numbers pale in comparison to the political and economic contexts from which many fled. The scale and scope of political violence in Central America, and the terror the violence inspired, are difficult to fully imagine. Metaphors, perhaps more than cold statistics, capture the human cost of the region's civil wars during the 1970s to 1990s. To describe how endemic violence shaped El Salvador, Guatemala, and Nicaragua, anthropologists have used phrases such as "the culture of fear" (Green, 1994), "a painful purgatory" (Tully, 1995), and "a landscape of violence" (Jenkins, 1991); other experts have used words such as "culture of terror" (Hovey, 2000b), "escape from terror" (Morrison and May, 2001), "traumatized societies" (Summerfield, 1991), and "the collective nightmare" (Aron, 1996). Most of the victims of this violence were civilians and most of them were killed "in circumstances of great cruelty" (Pearce, 1998: 591). The terms *massacre, death squads, torture,* and *disappearance* are commonly associated with political violence in Central America.

The statistics that quantify this violence are staggering in their own right. During the last three decades of the century, an estimated 300,000 persons were killed in Central American conflicts, and many more injured and traumatized (Pearce, 1998). In Guatemala, an estimated 42,000 people "disappeared" (Green, 1994), among them 6,159 children (Amnesty International, 2000), leaving their families devastated. According to Summerfield (1991: 1028), "state-sponsored violence [in Guatemala] . . . produced 150,000 orphans in the 1980s, and this in a nation of 8 million." In Nicaragua, conflict between government forces and the Contras produced 60,000 casualties (Summerfield and Toser, 1990) and destroyed the educational, health, and social service infrastructure of significant parts of the country (Tully, 1995). In El Salvador, political violence killed an estimated 75,000 in the 1980s; also, 6,000 people "disappeared," in addition to "countless rapes, tortures, and other abuses of human rights" (Bowen, Carscadden, Beighle, and Fleming, 1992: 269). Death squads in El Salvador terrorized entire communities (Oakes and Lucas, 2001).

EXILE AND ITS CONSEQUENCES

The devastating consequences of political violence in these Central American countries can best be understood by examining macro forces as they impinge on individual persons and shape the range of their life choices. To this end, we present the story of Ernesto,[2] a young Mayan man, who fled the political violence in Guatemala during the early 1970s. The Guatemalan highlands or *altiplano,* where many Mayans live, was the locus of almost genocidal violence in the 1980s. Although this is the case study of one individual, it is a life story that reflects the magnitude of loss visited upon many Central American refugees and the challenges they face in adapting to a new society. The story also highlights the alignment of societal forces and institutions against some of society's most vulnerable members.

Ernesto had been living illegally in the United States for several years, working as a day laborer and supplementing his income with occasional landscaping work. He initially slept on the street, but met up with other Guatemalans who invited him to live in their already cramped house. Initially wary and secretive, over time he became friendly with several coworkers and housemates, with whom he shared snippets of his life in Guatemala–including the fact that he had witnessed many "bad things." Mostly he confided his deep fear that the Immigration and Naturalization Service (INS) would catch him and send him back. This very reasonable fear was in fact realized one day. When traveling by car to a job with other Central Americans, the Border Patrol pulled them over, asked for papers, and detained all the passengers.

Fear of removal is not unusual among undocumented immigrants. Undocumented Central American immigrants lived with the constant fear of being detected, deported, and sent back into harm's way. This terror is particularly acute among those who have already been traumatized by political violence (Leslie, 1993).

In addition, the lack of legal immigration status for most Central Americans made their lives in the United States immensely more stressful and dangerous. Like other refugee groups that fled persecution, Central Americans often entered the United States with few tangible resources to remake their lives. Unlike for other refugee groups, the U.S. government's long-standing policy was to classify them as "illegal immigrants." This status meant that they were ineligible for all but a handful of publicly funded social service, health care, and income maintenance programs (Chavez, Flores, and Lopez-Garza, 1992). Moreover, the lack of "papers" meant that employment opportunities were few and the possibility of exploitation great (Hall, 1998). Nevertheless, Central Americans managed to create enclaves and networks that provided support and access to information and other forms of human capital (Jacob, 1994; Coutin, 1998).

The historic backdrop of Ernesto's life is worthy of examination because it represents the difficult position in which many Central Americans found themselves. On a societal level, one primary and immediate effect of the political violence Ernesto and many others encountered was that they had to search for safety. Millions of Central Americans fled the villages and towns of their birth. Some moved to less violent places within the country of origin (Morrison and May, 2001); some crossed into Mexico to seek refuge; many journeyed north to the United States. This is not to say that other factors did not enter into the decision to migrate. The Central American exodus and mass displacement were additionally fueled by extreme income and resource inequity, sluggish economic conditions, increasing globalization, and a lack of opportunity (Hamilton and Chinchilla, 1996). Nevertheless, much of the political violence in the region was rooted in racial and ethnic conflicts between the ruling elite and indigenous populations, in the economics of modernization (particularly its effects on land distribution and agricultural labor), and in subsequent land disputes (Miller, 1996; Morrison and May, 2001). It is difficult and probably inaccurate to point to any one cause as primary.

When he finally fled his war-torn country, Ernesto, like hundreds of thousands of other Central Americans who have sought sanctuary and opportunity in the United States, migrated to California. Like most others, he first had to cross the length of Mexico. Other than frequently being hungry, his journey through Mexico was uneventful. The stories of other Central Americans were not so benign. Though little empirical evidence is available about the transit experience through Mexico, anecdotal information suggests that Central America refugees were often subjected to additional traumatic experiences, including robbery, assault, rape, murder, separation from loved ones, detention, and forced repatriation (Menjivar, 1994; Jenkins, 1991; Malakoff, 1994). To circumvent ever-increasing U.S. border enforcement, many had to rely on coyotes (paid guides and people smugglers) who also were often violent and exploitative (Postero, 1992).

Once in the United States, many refugees found that the political climate created unforeseen obstacles. In the 1980s and 1990s, the U.S. government was hostile to the presence of Central Americans, and consistently characterized them as illegal immigrants rather than refugees. The INS attempted to stop Central Americans from entering at the border and tried to apprehend them once they had made it to the interior of the country. Still viewing Central America through a Cold War prism, and politically supporting military dictatorships there, the U.S. government found it politically untenable to acknowledge that the Salvadorans and Guatemalans who were crossing the borders into Mexico and the United States were actually fleeing political persecution. The U.S. government's treatment of Nicaraguan refugees stood in sharp contrast. It was more willing to recognize the legitimacy of Nicaraguan persecution at the hands of the communist Sandinistas.

The illegal status of the Central American refugees was challenged on many fronts. Human rights groups formed the "sanctuary movement" to contest U.S. policy and to assist Central American refugees by hiding them and providing services for them (Tomsho, 1987). Even more compelling was the effort mounted by Central Americans themselves, as they filed hundreds of thousands of asylum requests that effectively clogged the INS asylum bureaucracy even while they gave the applicants a temporary right to be in the United States. Because of class-action court challenges and strenuous advocacy by immigrant-rights groups, the U.S. government finally began to change some of its policies regarding the legal immigration status of Central American immigrants. For example, in 1990 the Justice Department granted "Temporary Protected Status" to Salvadorans who had entered the country prior to September 1990. To deal with continuing legal and asylum issues, Congress passed the Nicaraguan Adjustment and Central America Relief Act of 1997. Even so, these policy actions benefited only some Central Americans, and for those who did benefit, the results were often less than full legal immigration status.

FILING FOR ASYLUM

Even before being apprehended by the INS, Ernesto had heard about asylum through his Guatemalan network. During his initial INS processing, Ernesto stated that he wanted to apply for political asylum, to avoid immediate deportation. Like many other Central Americans, other than stopping the deportation process, Ernesto had little idea of what was involved in requesting asylum; in fact, this strategy had great psychological costs for many who used it. Asylum was then and still is an adversarial process in which applicants must prove the validity of their fear of persecution. It places a premium on documentation and a rational and coherent narrative. In the absence of physical evidence, the narrative of persecution had to provide the circumstantial evidence necessary to validate a claim for amnesty. To proceed with asylum claims, many Central Americans had to revisit traumatic events, often with little or no psychological support from either lawyers or mental health counselors (Postero, 1992). Even in cases where there is support, the asylum process can be traumatic, because the clients may not be prepared to revisit painful memories; the ordeal may result in their experiencing increased psychological and physiological symptoms. "The process of achieving refugee status in what is called the pre-asylum period is a tortuous process in itself," writes Baker (1992: 93).

Ironically, the initial traumas often produce fragmentary and disjointed stories, rather than the straightforward, chronologically precise ones required for asylum hearings (Kinzie and Jaranson, 2001). Even when the stories made sense, often it did not matter. Asylum decisions seldom favored Central Americans. For example, only 4% of Salvadoran and 5% of Guatemalan cases decided in 1987 ended with a grant of asylum (Engstrom, 2001).

Ernesto was fortunate. He was granted asylum. Nevertheless, the complexities inherent in filing for asylum, encountered by thousands of Central Americans, are reflected in Ernesto's case. Upon learning that Ernesto had applied for asylum, one of his landscaping clients put him in contact with an immigration attorney. Having worked extensively with Central American asylum seekers, this attorney knew that a psychological affidavit documenting the effects of violence and persecution on Ernesto was necessary. The attorney referred Ernesto to a social worker skilled in working with survivors of torture and other forms of political violence.

Despite the clinician's best efforts, recounting his horrific experiences in Guatemala was stressful for Ernesto and left him with severe headaches for several days after the first session. He was reluctant to return and did so only because of the urging of the attorney and his underlying hope of receiving asylum. After several sessions, his initially jumbled and disjointed story of violence and flight eventually took the form of a coherent narrative; the psychological evaluation documented his symptoms as consistent for someone who had experienced out-of-the-ordinary life-threatening events. This provided additional evidence to support his asylum claim. Although Ernesto knew that the purpose of the evaluation was to gain documentation for his case, he nevertheless became severely depressed after the information was extracted, and had to be placed on antidepressants. He never followed through with a referral for therapy, because his experiences during the initial evaluation and revisiting of past trauma had been too painful.

PERSONAL LOSSES AND THE CONSEQUENCES THEREOF

The distorting effects of violence and profound loss are revealed in Ernesto's life story. At the age of 10, he witnessed the death of his mother at the hands of Guatemalan security forces. This grave loss was exacerbated when his father quickly remarried and established a family situation so abusive that Ernesto ran away. He worked irregular odd jobs in a nearby village and lived with his uncle and cousins. Although he was required to work for his keep, this new family provided him with care and shelter. He eventually married a young woman from a neighboring village and had two sons with her, though he lived with her only for short periods. When his extended family was victimized by the local militia and his own life was threatened, Ernesto fled to California, resulting in a prolonged absence and estrangement from his wife and sons.

Falicov (2002) describes the concept of "ambivalent losses" in association with the migration process, in which the gains of migrating are entangled with the losses that such a choice entails. However, the concept of ambivalent losses is difficult to apply to refugees whose migration was forced: their history of losses goes well beyond what is commonly encountered by immigrants. A more useful heuristic is to distinguish existential losses from nonexistential losses. *Existential losses* involve a fundamental change in how the person views himself or herself and how that person lives out his or her life. For example, Ernesto's life was punctuated with episodes of violence, but that violence had different meanings of loss for him at different points in time. During his years of living in the village, Ernesto repeatedly came across dead, mutilated bodies left in the streets as a warning to villagers of the consequences of supporting insurgents. The power and meaning of such a message can be understood in terms of the loss that death brings to the survivor–the loss of a spouse, a mother, a sibling, a friend, a neighbor. In a society regulated by a reign of terror, the losses most deeply felt and that cause the most injury are those that encroach on a person's relationship network:

> Traumatic events call into question basic human relationships. They breach the attachments of family, friendship, love and community. They shatter the construction of the self that is formed and sustained in relations to others. They undermine the belief systems that give meaning to human experience. They violate the victim's faith in the natural or divine order and cast the victim into a state of existential crisis. (Herman, 1992: 51)

Compare, for example, the impact that two different events had on Ernesto and their consequences for his life. Ernesto once witnessed the terror of villagers who were rounded up and forced into a church, whereupon security forces selectively pulled a couple of villagers from the crowd and publicly tortured and executed them. In time, Ernesto learned that whenever rebel guerillas attacked the army, it was safer to escape to the mountains and hide. Later, while working with his uncle and cousins on their small plot of farmland, local government security forces descended on them and accused his uncle of helping the guerillas. The soldiers severely tortured his uncle, raped his cousin, and beat Ernesto, threatening to return for him the next day. Frightened for his life, Ernesto fled to a nearby village and later migrated to the United States.

Although both occurrences are marked by unspeakable loss, the second event was far more immediate and personal (injury to loved ones, bodily harm to himself) and engendered a flight response of complete disconnection, similar to the way Ernesto had reacted when faced with the loss of his mother (through death) and the loss of his father (through abuse). In the landscape of losses, personal and immediate losses have the greatest impact on a person; social services can play an important role in the healing process by helping the client mourn those losses.

The issue for Central American refugees has less to do with ambivalent losses and more to do with unrecognized and unmourned losses. Such losses have ongoing consequences for individuals and their ability to sustain relationships. Ernesto's traumatic early childhood experiences (the loss of primary caregivers), compounded by the social stressors imposed by a violent society (civil war, torture, and extreme poverty) had a corrosive effect on his ability to participate in and enjoy the deeply pleasurable relationships that a family can provide. Early experiences with caregivers profoundly inform the way we relate to others. Bereft of the love, support, and protection of his parents at an early age, Ernesto grew to depend solely on himself. Even his arrangement with his uncle and cousins required a degree of premature self-sufficiency, inappropriate in a child so young. Though adaptive at the time, austere self-reliance ultimately came at great cost to Ernesto. These early traumatic experiences later caused serious problems in his relationship with his wife and children.

MENTAL AND PHYSICAL HEALTH CONSEQUENCES OF POLITICAL VIOLENCE

In matters of public health, the individual is never the sole unit of analysis (Levins and Lewontin, 1985). Because most human beings live their lives in connection with families and groups, the harm created by political violence radiates from individuals to their family members. For some, grief over the loss of family members (who may have been killed or simply disappeared) becomes a primary factor in their lives. For example, research has documented that the spouses of torture survivors often suffer from post-traumatic stress disorder (PTSD), depression, and physical disorders (Allden, 1998). Parents whose children were exposed to violence must also deal with guilt stemming from their inability to protect their children. Moreover, "the family may have shared the extremely stressful experience of flight into exile" (Bojholm and Vesti, 1992: 301-2). Therefore, the physical and mental health issues of one individual also affect the social systems in which that person is embedded.

Several studies specifically document the pervasiveness of the political violence experienced by Central Americans and the mental and physical health consequences of that violence. In a sample of 31 Salvadoran women living in Salvador, Bowen and colleagues found high frequencies of trauma experiences and correspondingly high rates of PTSD symptoms. More than half of these women had personally experienced physical assault, 32% had been raped, and 19% had been tortured; 61% had witnessed an assault on one or more family members, and 42% had witnessed the death of family members (Bowen et al., 1992). Locke and colleagues (1996) found, in a U.S. sample of mothers and children from El Salvador, Guatemala, and Nicaragua, that virtually all of the women had been exposed to at least three types of traumatic events, which included witnessing the detention and/or murder of others, being subjected to or witnessing bombing or artillery fire, seeing corpses on the streets, and undergoing beatings and/or rape. Among the children in the study, more than two thirds (68%) had "direct[ly] observ[ed] events that would be considered traumatic according to the definition set out in the DSM-III-R" (Locke et al., 1996: 824). Forty-five percent of these children could be considered "possibly depressed," and nearly all the children reported at least one somatic complaint. Another striking aspect of this study is that many of the mothers interviewed were reluctant to seek medical care, because of fear of detection and/or uncertainty about access to the health care system.

Even for those who do seek medical attention, the relationship of political violence to current mental/physical health issues goes largely unexplored. In perhaps one of the largest studies to date, Eisenman and colleagues found that, of Central American adult primary-care patients in Los Angles, 83% of Salvadorans and 67% of Guatemalans reported exposure to political violence. Indeed, 12% of Salvadorans and 7% of Guatemalans reported having been physically tortured. Eisenman's study concluded that Central Americans (and other Hispanic immigrants) who had been exposed to political violence were more likely than those not exposed to meet "symptom criteria for PTSD, depression, and any other mental health disorder" (Eisenman et al., 2003: 631). Even so, only 3% of 267 patients had ever told a clinician about their histories, and none had ever been asked by their current physicians about exposure to political violence—a troubling finding for a group whose main access to the health care system is through primary health care facilities.

Even in the absence of specified political violence, the rates of PTSD, depression, generalized stress, and suicidal ideation among Central Americans are striking. One California study found that Central Americans reported more PTSD symptoms than Mexican immigrants. Fifty-two percent of Central Americans who had fled political violence had PTSD symptoms, the highest rate of any subgroup (Cervantes et al., 1989). Plante and colleagues studied 54 Salvadoran immigrants, the majority of whom had fled from the civil war, and found that "these immigrants . . . experience significant degrees of general stress" (Plante et al., 1995: 476). In a study of Latino mothers' use of emergency pediatric services, Zambrana and Ell found high levels of mental distress, specifically nervousness and depression, with Central Americans reporting more mental distress than Mexicans (Zambrana and Ell, 1994).

Acculturative stressors also raise mental health issues among Central Americans. Leslie and Leitch (1989) found high levels of stressful life events in a sample of 91 Central Americans living in Washington, DC. In a study of 78 Central Americans in Los Angeles, Hovey reported that those with high levels of acculturative stress also scored high on a depression scale (Hovey, 2000b). A subsequent study by Hovey found that high acculturative stress was associated with "heightened levels of depression and suicidal ideation" (Hovey, 2000a: 125).

Other researchers have identified other symptoms with political violence. In a sample of 71 adult Central Americans who were exposed to political violence, Farias (1991) found that males and females presented different symptoms. For example, males were more likely to suffer from nightmares, fear of falling, and fear of losing control, whereas females reported higher levels of "intranquility," headaches, and other somatic pain. Though it did not control for political violence, a study by Murguía and colleagues (2003) found that, in a sample of 76 Central American adults, 84% of respondents suffered from migraines and 40% had experienced *ataques de nervios* (attacks of the nerves).

Ernesto's case highlights the far-reaching mental and physical health consequences of political violence on the individual and on families. Since arriving in the United States, Ernesto suffered from migraines and often had graphic nightmares. Sometimes he had difficulty concentrating, and at other times he was confused and anxious. Certain odors and sounds triggered violent flashbacks.

After receiving asylum, Ernesto filed paperwork to bring his family to the United States. Shortly after being reunited with his family, though, Ernesto grew dismissive of his wife and began to avoid spending time with his two children. Instead, Ernesto occupied all his time with work, an important source of self-esteem for him. Indeed, the primary satisfaction Ernesto derived from life was being viewed as a hard and honest worker, an outlook inherited from his early childhood. Although he was unable to connect emotionally with his two young sons, he took pride in providing for their material needs. His wife and children, however, found relating to Ernesto difficult and at times unbearable.

Ernesto's responses to traumatic experiences contributed to his decreased capacity to provide the type of emotional nurturance commonly expected from a husband and a father. Ernesto's experience upon reunification with his family underscores the need for continuing psychosocial supports for all family members impacted by political violence. Although Ernesto may have ongoing difficulties in attending to his children's emotional needs, the effects may be mitigated by continuing social supports for his children and wife through local, community- and school-based services. It is important for a family like this to have available not only helping professionals, but also ones with whom they can collaborate in navigating various systems to meet their physical health, mental health, and educational needs. Such helpers may include mental health practitioners, social service caseworkers, a family physician, schoolteachers and school nurses, and spiritual leaders. Each professional who comes into contact with such a family is in the critical position of not only providing needed services, but also orienting them and providing information that will facilitate their transition into American culture. This level of help requires that providers know and understand the individuals and families they work with, that they be sensitive to the issues their clients face, and that they understand that families like Ernesto's have long-term needs that warrant long-term helping commitments.

MENTAL AND PHYSICAL HEALTH INTERVENTIONS

Given the lasting social and psychological effects of political violence and the challenges of exile-related stressors, it is apparent that we need a new conceptualization of mental health services for refugees that combines clinic-based services with community-based services (Miller, 1999). This is consonant with the social-work ideal of providing services for clients in the context of their environment. Miller (1999) posits that, although recovery from trauma induced by political violence is an important feature of any social service program for refugees, assistance with exile-related stressors is also essential. Exile-related stressors concern the many losses that accompany relocation: the loss of community and social networks; the loss of meaningful life projects, daily activities, and social roles; and the losses and continuing stressors related to changes in economic status and economic survival (Miller, 1999). Coping with losses and creating new relationships, social structures, and social roles are important tasks in adapting to a new environment and ultimately affect the quality of one's daily life. To address the question of how to reach the largest number of people with the existing and available mental health services, Miller employs an ecological model. This model emphasizes the relationships between people and the settings they live in; the identification of naturally occurring resources within communities that can promote healing and healthy adaptations; the enhancement of coping and adaptational strategies that enable individuals and communities to respond effectively to stressful events and circumstances; and the development of culturally grounded community interventions that actively involve community members in the process of solving their own problems (Miller, 1999: 288).

An ecological approach would enlist the help of non-mental health experts to improve refugees' access to services and supports that will enhance their quality of life. For example, though it is unlikely that refugees will seek out mental health services at a clinic, they *are* likely to attend classes to learn English. ESL (English as a second language) teachers could be trained to identify signs of mental distress and to refer students who seem to need professional help. Another important avenue of intervention, which is often overlooked, is the use of ethnomedical approaches by Central Americans to address physical and mental health issues (Murguía et al., 2003). Murguía and his colleagues suggest that ethnomedical approaches could be used in conjunction with standard U.S. medical practice to increase compliance with a treatment plan and to foster relationships with clients.

All these approaches require a minimal level of linguistic accessibility and a flexible institutional structure that allows the use of nontraditional methods and practices. However, the linguistic barriers and cumbersome bureaucracies that are the norm today continue to be serious obstacles for refugees (Hall, 1988; Leslie, 1993; Palinkas, 1995; Zambrana and Ell, 1994). Central Americans have the highest level of linguistic isolation of any Hispanic group. Thirty-five percent of Central Americans aged five or older live in households that can be classified as *linguistically isolated*; that is, households in which English is spoken "less than very well" (United States Census Bureau, 2003). The use of translators becomes crucial in this scenario, but often there is only a limited number of translators on hand, compounding the problems of access to an already difficult and cumbersome health care bureaucracy.

Most problematic is a health care system that requires a person to have health insurance before he or she can access basic primary health care (Chavez, Flores, and Lopez-Garza, 1992). The majority of foreign-born Central Americans (52.4%) have no health insurance, compared to the 13.5% of the total U.S. population that the 2000 Census identified as uninsured. Only 30.9% of Central Americans have employment-based health insurance–the lowest of all foreign-born groups, including Mexicans, that have that type of insurance (United States Census Bureau, 2001b).

When and if immigrants do enter the social service system, social workers can play an important role in helping survivors of political violence rebuild their lives, simply by recognizing the political context of their clients' trauma. Political violence is different from other human-induced traumas (such as domestic violence and sexual assault) in that it is created through and committed by socially sanctioned institutions and actors, usually backed by powerful governmental resources. Although most clinicians who work with trauma survivors pay particular attention to issues such as safety and trust, these issues have different meanings for survivors of political violence. It is here that we can use knowledge gained from treating survivors of torture (an extreme form of political violence) to inform practice for helping people affected by political violence. Lira emphasized the "importance of incorporating political and cultural meaning into the therapeutic process. Put simply, a torture survivor is not simply another instance of posttraumatic stress disorder" (1998: 54). As part of treatment, social workers are in a powerful position to help their clients by emphasizing that the violence experienced by survivors falls well outside the norms of acceptable behavior.

It is important for clinicians to recognize that it is counterproductive and harmful to explore the trauma directly if clients are not ready or willing to do so. One of the most helpful approaches clinicians can take with trauma survivors is to allow them the right to decide if and when to discuss traumatic events. In many cases, clients will present with psychosomatic symptoms; addressing these symptoms may be the most appropriate way to assist them. It may open the door for addressing other problems. If Central Americans clients do disclose traumatic life events, it is important for clinicians to believe what they say, even though the content of such stories may seem too fantastic or too jumbled to be true. To do otherwise only validates their political persecution and aligns clinicians as (institutional) agents who condone abusive institutional structures and actions. Survivors of political violence often suffer from survivor's guilt, and sometimes an underlying fear that they may somehow have been responsible for the horrendous acts inflicted upon them. Regardless of how the guilt is manifested, survivors need a clear message that *they are not responsible* for the trauma and harm of political violence. Clinicians can, however, encourage and support such clients to take care of themselves in the face of trauma and loss. In this way, clinicians can avoid pathologizing survivors of political violence, by reframing psychological problems such as PTSD, depression, and anxiety as normal responses to abnormal circumstances and emphasizing that help is available.

One of the most compelling issues for clinicians who work with Central American refugees is recognition of those who have survived political violence. As noted previously, the literature suggests that few social service and health care professionals are aware of the many and varied forms of political violence, and fewer still recognize its symptoms (Iacopino, 1998: 46). Because survivors seldom self-disclose, social workers must take greater care in assessing the likelihood that a person has been subjected to political violence, in order to create a space for discussion of such painful issues if the client chooses to do so. This requires that clinicians working with Central Americans have some knowledge of the political and human rights conditions of the countries from which their clients originated. Reports from Amnesty International, Human Rights Watch, and the U.S. State Department on human rights abuses can alert social workers to those Central Americans most likely to have been persecuted and to the types of political violence to which they might have been exposed. Other risk factors associated with exposure to political violence include political and antigovernment activity in the country of origin, a history of arrest and detention, family members missing or killed, and/or membership in a minority group. Being aware of the political and human rights conditions of their clients' countries of origin can help social workers be better prepared to listen for signs that a client may want to broach the subject of political violence and trauma.

Human rights abuses are not just a matter of the past. Although in many ways the current human rights picture in Central America has improved, there remain too many human rights violations. People still disappear and torture is still used. Many Central American immigrants to the United States still have family members living in the country of origin and have reason to fear for the safety of those loved ones. Moreover, many of the leaders who orchestrated the reigns of terror have not been brought to justice or held accountable for their actions, making closure difficult for some Central American refugees.

CONCLUSION

Despite compelling, well-documented findings on the levels of stress and trauma among Central American refugees, this group continues to be underserved. Their access to service involves a host of issues ranging from macro-level imposed obstacles (such as the role of citizenship and health insurance as determining factors for accessing social and health services) to institutional factors that impede service utilization (such as insufficient numbers of translators and a cumbersome and confusing bureaucracy). On the individual level, the range and scope of losses a person has experienced from political violence directly impacts his or her well-being and the well-being of those closest to that person. Although many refugees demonstrate incredible resilience and courage in the face of horrendous circumstances, some also find it very difficult to form and participate in relationships with others who could serve as a source of comfort and enrichment–family and treatment providers. Understanding Central Americans from a human rights perspective is the first step in developing a comprehensive social and health service system that is well-suited to address the issues this population faces.

NOTES

1. Because 90% of the Central American adults residing in the United States are in fact foreign-born, the data in this report can accurately be extrapolated to apply to this population.

2. All identifying information has been changed so that the information provided would be unrecognizable even to the person on whom this vignette is based.

REFERENCES

Allden, K. (1998). The Indochinese psychiatric clinic: Trauma and refugee mental health. *Journal of Ambulatory Care Management* 21(2): 20-29.

Amnesty International. (2000). *Guatemala: "Disappearances" Briefing to the UN Committee against Torture.* London: Amnesty International.

Aron, A. (1996). The collective nightmare of Central American refugees. In D. Barrett (ed.), *Trauma and Dreams* 140-7. Cambridge, MA: Harvard University Press.

Baker, R. (1992). Psychological consequences of torture refugees seeking asylum and refugee status in Europe. In M. Basoglu (ed.), *Torture and Its Consequences* 82-105. New York: Cambridge Press.

Bojholm, S., and Vesti, P. (1992). Multidisciplinary approach in the treatment of torture survivors. In M. Basoglu (ed.), *Torture and Its Consequences* 143-63. New York: Cambridge Press.

Bowen, D. J., Carscadden, L., Beighle, K., and Fleming, I. (1992). Post-traumatic stress disorder among Salvadoran women: Empirical evidence and description of treatment. *Women and Therapy* 13: 267-80.

Cafferty, P. S. J., and Engstrom, D. W. (eds.). (2001). *Hispanics in the United States: An Agenda for the Twenty-First Century.* New Brunswick, NJ: Transaction Publishers.

Cervantes, R. C., Salgado de Snyder, V. N., and Padilla, A. M. (1989). Posttraumatic stress in immigrants from Central America and Mexico. *Hospital & Community Psychiatry* 40(6): 615-19.

Chavez, L. R., Flores, E. T., and Lopez-Garza, M. (1992). Undocumented Latin American immigrants and U.S. health services: An approach to a political economy of utilization. *Medical Anthropology Quarterly* 6(1): 6-26.

Coutin, S. B. (1998). From refugees to immigrants: The legalization strategies of Salvadoran immigrants and activities. *International Migration Review* 32(4): 901-25.

Eisenman, D. P., Gelberg, L., Liu, H., and Shapiro, M. F. (2003). Mental health and health-related quality of life among adult Latino primary care patients living in the United States with previous exposure to political violence. *JAMA: The Journal of the American Medical Association* 290(5): 627-34.

Engstrom, D. W. (2001). Hispanic immigration in the new millennium. In P. S. J. Cafferty and D. W. Engstrom (eds.), *Hispanics in the United States: An Agenda for the Twenty-First Century* 31-68. New Brunswick, NJ: Transaction Publishers.

Falicov, C. J. (2002). Ambiguous loss: Risk and resilience in Latino immigrant families. In M. M. Suarez-Orozco and M. Paez (eds.), *Latinos: Remaking America* 274-88. Berkeley: University of California Press.

Farias, P. (1991). Emotional distress and its socio-political consequences. *Culture, Medicine, and Psychiatry* 15: 167-92.

Green, L. (1994). Fear as a way of life. *Cultural Anthropology* 9(2): 227-56.

Hall, L. K. (1988). Providing culturally relevant mental health services for Central American refugees. *Hospital & Community Psychiatry* 39(11): 1139-44.

Hamilton, N., and Chinchilla, N. S. (1996). Global economic restructuring and international migration: Some observations based on the Mexican and Central American experience. *International Migration* 34(2): 194-231.

Herman, J. (1992). *Trauma and recovery: The aftermath of violence–From domestic abuse to political terror.* New York: Basic Books.

Hovey, J. D. (2000a). Acculturative stress, depression, and suicidal ideation in Mexican immigrants. *Cultural Diversity & Ethnic Minority Psychology* 6(2): 134-51.

Hovey, J. D. (2000b). Psychosocial predictors of depression among Central American immigrants. *Psychological Reports* 86(3, pt. 2): 1237-40.

Iacopino, V. (1998). Commentary. *Journal of Ambulatory Care Management* 21(2): 43-51.

Jacob, A. G. (1994). Social integration of Salvadoran refugees. *Social Work* 39(3): 307.

Jenkins, J. H. (1991). The state construction of affect: Political ethos and mental health among Salvadoran refugees. *Culture, Medicine and Psychiatry* 15(2): 139-65.

Kinzie, J. D., and Jaranson, J. M. (2001). Refugees and asylum-seekers. In Ellen Gerrity, Terence M. Keane, and Farris Tuma (eds.), *The Mental Health Consequences of Torture* 111-20. New York: Kluwer Academic/Plenum Publishers.

Leslie, L. A. (1993). Families fleeing war: The case of Central Americans. *Marriage and Family Review* 19(1/2): 193-205.

Leslie, L. A., and Leitch, M. L. (1989). A demographic profile of recent Central American immigrants: Clinical and service implications. *Hispanic Journal of Behavioral Sciences* 11(4): 315-29.

Levins, R., and Lewontin, R. C. (1985). *The dialectical biologist.* Cambridge, MA: Harvard University Press.

Lira, E. (1998). Commentary. *Journal of Ambulatory Care Management* 21(2): 51-55.

Locke, C. J., Southwick, K., McCloskey, L. A., and Fernández-Esquer, M. E. (1996). The psychological and medical sequelae of war in Central American refugee mothers and children. *Archives of Pediatrics & Adolescent Medicine* 150(8): 822-8.

Malakoff, M.E. (1994). Refugee children and violence. In C. Chiland and J.G. Young (eds.), *Children and Violence* 145-59. Northvale, NJ: Jason Aronson, Inc.

Menjivar, C. (1994). Salvadoran migration to the United States in the 1980s: What can we learn about it and from it? *International Migration* 32(2): 371-401.

Miller, K. E. (1996). The effects of state terrorism and exile on indigenous Guatemalan refugee children: A mental health assessment and an analysis of children's narratives. *Child Development* 67(1): 89-106.

Miller, K. E. (1999). Rethinking a familiar model: Psychotherapy and the mental health of refugees. *Journal of Contemporary Psychotherapy* 29(4): 283-306.

Morrison, A. R., and May, R. A. (2001). Escape from terror: Violence and migration in post-revolutionary Guatemala. *Latin American Research Review* 29(2): 111.

Murguía, A., Peterson, R. A., and Zea, M. C. (2003). Use and implications of ethnomedical health care approaches among Central American immigrants. *Health & Social Work* 28(1): 43-51.

Oakes, M. G., and Lucas, F. (2001). How war affects daily life: Adjustments in Salvadoran social networks. *Journal of Social Work Research* 2(2): 143-55.

Palinkas, L. A. (1995). Health under stress: Asian and Central American refugees and those left behind. *Social Science & Medicine* 40(12): 1591-96.

Pearce, J. (1998). From civil war to "civil society": Has the end of the Cold War brought peace to Central America? *International Affairs* 74(3): 587-615.

Plante, T. G., Manuel, G. M., Menendez, A. V., and Marcotte, D. (1995). Coping with stress among Salvadoran immigrants. *Hispanic Journal of Behavioral Sciences* 17(4): 471-9.

Postero, N. G. (1992). On trail in the promised land: Seeking asylum. In E. Cole, O. M. Espin, and E. D. Rothblum (eds.), *Refugee Women and Their Mental Health: Shattered Societies, Shattered Lives*. New York: The Haworth Press, Inc.

Summerfield, D. (1991). Guatemala: Health, human rights, and landlessness. *The Lancet* 337: 1028-9.

Summerfield, D., and Toser, L. (1990). Nicaragua: The psychological impact of "low-intensity" warfare. *The Lancet* 336: 678-9.

Tomsho, R. (1987). *The American sanctuary movement*. Austin, TX: Texas Monthly Press.

Tully, S. R. (1995). A painful purgatory: Grief and the Nicaraguan mothers of the disappeared. *Social Science & Medicine* 40(12): 1597-1610.

United States Census Bureau. (2001a). *The Hispanic population: Census brief 2000*. Washington, DC: U.S. Census Bureau.

United States Census Bureau. (2001b). *Profile of the foreign-born population in the United States: 2000*. Washington, DC: U.S. Census Bureau.

United States Census Bureau. (2003). GCT-T1. Population estimates. 2002 *Population estimates*. Retrieved September 14, 2003 from http://factfind.gov/servletBasicFactsServlet

Zambrana, R. E., and Ell, K. (1994). The relationship between psychosocial status of immigrant Latino mothers and use of emergency pediatric services. *Health & Social Work* 19(2): 93-105.

Chapter 11

The Future of Culturally Competent Mental Health Care for Latino Immigrants

William A. Vega

SUMMARY. This chapter underscores the importance of cultural competence in the provision of effective mental health services to Latino immigrants. Culturally competent mental health care must be understood within the context of a social-political-economic framework that is changing on a continual basis. Health and mental health care reform for Latino immigrants must be linked to both practice-based research efforts and timely diffusion of best practice innovations. Cultural competence must be integrated as a valued component of the organizational structure of mental health systems of care. *[Article copies available for a fee from The Haworth Document Delivery Service: 1-800-HAWORTH. E-mail address: <docdelivery@haworthpress.com> Website: <http://www.HaworthPress.com> © 2005 by The Haworth Press, Inc. All rights reserved.]*

KEYWORDS. Cultural competence, mental health, Latino immigrants

William A. Vega, PhD, is Professor of Psychiatry, Robert Wood Johnson Medical School.

[Haworth co-indexing entry note]: "The Future of Culturally Competent Mental Health Care for Latino Immigrants." Vega, William A. Co-published simultaneously in *Journal of Immigrant & Refugee Services* (The Haworth Social Work Practice Press, an imprint of The Haworth Press, Inc.) Vol. 3, No. 1/2, 2005, pp. 191-198; and: *Mental Health Care for New Hispanic Immigrants: Innovative Approaches in Contemporary Clinical Practice* (ed: Manny J. González and Gladys González-Ramos) The Haworth Social Work Practice Press, an imprint of The Haworth Press, Inc., 2005, pp. 191-198. Single or multiple copies of this article are available for a fee from The Haworth Document Delivery Service [1-800-HAWORTH, 9:00 a.m. - 5:00 p.m. (EST). E-mail address: docdelivery@haworthpress.com].

Available online at http://www.haworthpress.com/web/JIRS
© 2005 by The Haworth Press, Inc. All rights reserved.
Digital Object Identifier: 10.1300/J191v3n01_11

No health care professional or health care researcher could fail to notice the U.S. health care system's prime contradiction, very high cost and serious gaps in quality of care (Institute of Medicine, 2001). This contradiction is exemplified by disparities in care to minorities and a poor showing on traditional morbidity and mortality indicators when contrasted with other developed nations in Europe and Asia. A central issue in improving quality of care for Latino immigrants and addressing mental health care disparities affecting all Latinos is whether the impediments to change are sufficiently modifiable. In short, can the least socially powerful sectors of American society that suffer the greatest deficits in access and quality of care be adequately served by their health care system? The obstacles are daunting. Efforts during the past decade to organize health care around market principles and to offer medical care services at decreased cost are crumbling in the face of consumer demands for higher quality and coordination of care, punctuated by litigation and advocacy. Simultaneously, the expanding number of uninsured in the U.S. continues to grow due to chronic poverty and job loss, restrictions in benefit coverage is increasing among the employed, continuing immigration is increasing ethnic diversity, and general economic weakness is producing chronic budget shortfalls at the federal and state levels thus forcing reductions in basic health care services.

In the face of this turmoil, or perhaps because of it, unprecedented attention and support for culturally competent health care is now evident. This is a surprising turn of events given the recent historical context that has provided a foundation for minority health care. It is even more impressive that some professional organizations are embracing cultural competence as one strategy for improving access and quality of care problems despite the open-ended implications and the dearth of empirically generated information about best practices for patients from minority ethnic groups. Specific to mental health, several recent reports published by the U.S. Surgeon's Office, the National Institutes of Health, the President's New Freedom Report on Mental Health, and the Institute of Medicine send a clear message: persuasive evidence of disparities in health and quality of care must be addressed by a rapid development of new knowledge and implementation of culturally competent care (Institute of Medicine, 2002; DHHS, 2001; DHHS, 1998; NIMH, 2001; DHHS, 2003). This effort must be matched by a strong effort to increase the labor supply of mental health professionals from affected minority groups. While these reports for the most part did not provide new directions regarding the science and practice of cultural competence, they provided remarkable visibility to new audiences. They also highlighted the challenge of filling knowledge gaps, addressing educational deficits, meeting professional training requirements, and developing, implementing, and evaluating operational models of cultural competence in health care settings. Therefore, as professional resistance transitions toward wider acceptance of cultural competence in health care, the challenge of defining and organizing the field becomes the first order of business.

Perhaps timing is the truly compelling factor. The universally acknowledged shift in demographics of minorities in the U.S. is occurring during a period of rapid reorganization of treatment programs and clinical intervention techniques. Merging an awareness of changing patient characteristics and organizational self-study is likely to benefit all consumers of health services by forcing a thoroughgoing review of quality of care and patient care accountability practices. It is extraordinary that the current broad based movement in improve mental health care could emerge from somewhat isolated but long-standing efforts of a relatively small group of advocates–what Rodgers called "innovators"–who, at least in theory, would represent only about 2.5% of practitioners (Rodgers, 2003). Currently, we appear to be in the middle phase of "early adopters" who are presumably better rooted in local practice networks (compared to innovators) and are opinion leaders. If this is true, culturally competent mental heath care is at a much stronger point today than even five years ago, and has gained acceptance by perhaps 10% to 15% of practitioners–yet remaining short of the hypothetical "tipping point." As exemplified by this volume, the rate of dissemination of new information to improve culturally competent care is now accelerating rapidly. Nonetheless, it has not attained the status of a consensus clinical formulation or guidelines which would signal acceptance by the "early majority," and is possibly a decade or more short of becoming a "standard of practice" which exemplifies acceptance by the "late majority" in diffusion theory. The continued diffusion will in part depend on the ability to define sub-specializations including theory and methodology, conduct research to provide concrete information for diffusion, and evaluate outcomes in order to provide "evidence based" practices to health care providers. This volume represents an important part of this diffusion effort.

CULTURAL COMPETENCE: THE STATE OF THE ART

As perhaps one of the most complex words in the English language, the meaning of culture is not easily captured in 20 word definitions, especially as applied to treatment and health services research. The definition of cultural competence is no less challenging precisely because the range of activities and situations implicated is so profound and varied. As Bentancourt, Green, and Carrillo (2003) pointed out, there are really three domains that emerge in the literature: processes of care, clinical knowledge, and organizational impediments and strategies. These are conceptual domains not components of a delivery system, therefore, they must be operationalized. The three domains are complex, overlapping and inseparable in practice, especially in large-scale health care delivery systems. Insightful research is needed to evaluate administrative and treatment practices in diverse organizational settings using criteria sensitive to access to care, equity of treatment coverage, and quality of patient care. Just as critical is formulating and disseminating information that is useful and understandable, and advocating changes that are feasible.

The lessons from other areas of health care reform vividly highlight that innovative evidence based practices with powerful outcomes are often dropped or slow to be disseminated, accepted, and to attain significant penetration into the health care system. To hasten the pace it is critically important to create strong ties between the production of new knowledge and practice. Health care organizations and mental health practitioners who work for them, especially those outside academic medical centers, require convincing that culture competence is consistent with their reward structure and ethical framework, including satisfying reaccrediting and licensure standards, professional education requirements, cost effectiveness expectations, improved patient care and management.

Berwick (2003) identifies five indicators of the facility for an innovation to be accepted: (1) the perceived benefit of the change, (2) the compatibility with values, beliefs, past history, and current needs of individuals affected, (3) the complexity of the innovation with simple innovations moving faster because inevitably innovations are mutated as they are implemented in specific contexts, (4) the feasibility of implementing the innovation linked to scale of change required, and (5) the ease with which the innovation can be modeled by others and easily observed and replicated. Cultural compatibility is not likely to "spread" uniformly, and history has already demonstrated that the early stages of diffusion have proceeded slowly, spearheaded in health care organizations and government agencies primarily in "early adopter" states like California, where Kaiser Permanente took the lead, and within foundations and federal agencies such as the Substance Abuse and Mental Health Service Administration. Introducing cultural competent mental health practices differs from introducing singular technological inventions such as a new medical procedure or medications that are easily grasped and linked to specific outcomes. There is a much larger task of conducting important preparatory work that must continue apace of implementation for adoption to progress effectively. Foremost among these challenges is making the case for "benefit" especially in the current market driven clinical environment. The complexity of cultural competence as a field, which this volume illustrates, is only now being appreciated. It poses both an economic burden on health care systems because it costs money to train professional personnel and to sustain lost revenue from patients not serviced, and a personal burden on clinical staff and others who must learn a new body of information and take the time and energy to apply it.

We know very little about what mental health administrators and clinicians think about cultural competence or its value and priority in professional education and clinical care in the United States. The same could be said about federal research agencies such as the NIH, who thus far have not linked cultural competence to research in any tangible way. Thus, little is known about how cultural competence could be or is actually being perceived-as an unavoidable nuisance or a gateway to improving quality of care. It is evident that fledgling efforts to link cultural competence to evidence based practices have not advanced sufficiently for three reasons: the absence of tangible research evidence that cultural competence knowledge, skills, and practices can change aspects of clinical care that are highly valued such as outcomes, that organizational effectiveness will be improved with better compliance, and a lack of solid research articles linking culturally competent practices to generally higher quality of care including improved access and continuity of care. This is not meant to imply that these obstacles will not be reversed at some future time, rather the point is to show that there must be progress on these three fronts to advance the diffusion of cultural competent information and skills as discussed in this volume.

Effective communication is the central feature of any strategy for diffusion of innovations in health care organizations. It is a two-part strategy that requires significant front-end investment in research, and influencing executive administrator and practitioner opinion leaders to support a long-range commitment toward comprehensive change, appropriate information systems, feedback, and maintaining momentum for change supported by incentives and accountability mechanisms to track progress.

SCOPE OF THE EFFORT IN MENTAL HEALTH SERVICES

There are many aspects of cultural competence in mental health care akin to general health care. The most obvious is language comprehension and personal representations of illness. However, these examples have different manifestations in mental health care because both are fully dependent on verbal and non-verbal communication by a patient and an accurate interpretation by a therapist without reliance on biological tests. Most Latino mental health research to date has focused on the very significant problem of developing a body of knowledge around these clinical issues and imparting that knowledge to health care professionals, as reflected in this volume. This task has been widely based and has generated many important and high quality publications and reports. Many more are needed especially focused on overcoming disparities and improving outcomes.

The second part of this process, changing organizational culture and motivating individual clinicians to accept and implement new practices as part of their essential mission is equally important. The organizational linkage, articulation, and implementation of these two processes presents a dilemma for advocates who want to move culture into formal systems of medical care. What is the best game plan? Each situation is in some sense a case study yet there are also common issues and experiences that should enter the professional literature for wider dissemination.

The importance of learning new culturally competent skills and developing a supporting knowledge base is gaining wider acceptance in somatic medicine and mental health. There remains skepticism about the ultimate value of culturally competent practices. This latent resistance places an enormous burden on researchers to use the extant knowledge base to provide a first generation logic structure (e.g., criteria for inclusion and classification of information) and for building a respected and versatile foundation of information. The very act of culling and ordering the quickly amassing information will lead to identifying additional gaps in knowledge and new, better focused research. This infers that cultural competence is a dynamic field that will require an agenda for research, financial support, and rapid transfer of that research to practice. How much and what type of information is most needed for improving health care? It is a sobering reality that major constraints exist to the amount of information that can be imparted to health care professionals, therefore, we must ascertain *empirically* what information is the most useful for a specific purpose and audience.

The soft underbelly of the cultural competence movement has been and continues to be the lack of information regarding about how care improves for Latinos by receiving and using new information. Cultural competence has been long on face validity but a continuing absence of evaluation research will undermine the credibility of the field. As many researchers have noted, its not enough to demonstrate that health care practitioners learn the information, feel more efficacious about doing their job, or are more satisfied. This is a necessary intermediate goal to gain and sustain support. Ultimately, it must be demonstrated that learning new information will actually change patient care in clear cut ways such as improving, (1) access to care, (2) diagnostic assessment, (3) medication (dosing, monitoring, compliance), (4) non-medicinal intervention effectiveness, (5) follow-up, (6) prevention services, and (7) treatment outcome. This is a formidable list and some division of labor is required at both the knowledge production side and the health practitioner side.

The key point is that the moment of truth has arrived, and we must decide on some rational basis about which information works for whom, develop methods to successfully impart that information, and then assess whether it makes any difference for both practitioners and patients. Doubtless, increasing the pool of Latino health and mental health professionals will facilitate acceptance and implementation of practices that improve Latino patient care, and they are needed for the long process of research, evaluation, and refinement of knowledge, methods, and technologies that will follow in the years ahead. For the next few decades at least one thing is certain, most Latinos will receive mental health care from non-Latinos so these professionals need the best preparation possible for their mission.

CONCLUSION

Demonstrating that cultural information infused into mental health practice is beneficial is very important. However, it will not guarantee organizational or personal readiness to offer improved care beyond symbolic acceptance. Cultural competence must be integrated as a valued component of organizational culture to assure implementation and survival. I summarize by accentuating the interdependency between new knowledge development, professional acceptance, effective implementation of information/technology transfer, and mental health and medical care organizational change as essential for transforming culturally informed practices into accepted standards of care. With great enthusiasm and an optimistic view to the future, I can report that all of these activities are taking place in one form or another across the nation at this time. We have reached a point where developing culturally competent practices should be considered a specialized interdisciplinary concentration reflecting its unique characteristics, professional functions, and intellectual requirements.

REFERENCES

Berwick, D.M. (2003). Disseminating innovations in health care. *JAMA*, 289(15), 1969-1975.

Betancourt, J.R., Green, A.R., Carrillo, J.E. & Ananeh-Firempong, O. (2003). Defining cultural competence: A practical framework for addressing racial/ethnic disparities in health and health care. *Public Health Reports*, 118(4), 293-302.

Institute of Medicine. (2001). *Crossing the quality chasm: A health system for the 21st Century.* Washington, DC, National Academies Press.

Institute of Medicine. (2002). *Unequal treatment: Confronting racial and ethnic disparities in health care.* Washington, DC, National Academies Press.

National Institute of Mental Health. (2001). *An investment in America's future: Racial/ethnic diversity in mental health research careers.* Report by the National Advisory Council Workgroup on Racial/Ethnic Disparities Research. Rockville, MD, NIMH.

New Freedom Commission on Mental Health. (2003). *Achieving the promise: Transforming mental health care in America.* Final Report. DHHS pub no SMA-02-3832. Rockville, MD, Department of Health and Human Services.

PHS. (2001). *Surgeon General's report on mental health disparities in minority populations.* Washington, DC, Public Health Service.

Rodgers, E. (2003). *Diffusion of Innovations.* Free Press: New York, NY

U.S. Department of Health and Human Services. (1998). *Racial and ethnic disparities in health: Response to the President's initiative on race.* Washington, DC, DHHS.

Appendix

RESOURCE LIST OF SELECTED
NATIONAL HISPANIC ORGANIZATIONS

ASPIRA Association, Inc.

A nonprofit organization devoted to the education and leadership development of Puerto Rican and other Latino youth.

Contact: National Office
1444 Eye Street, N.W., Suite 800, Washington DC 20005
Telephone: (202) 835-3600, Fax: (202) 835-3613
http://www.aspira.org

CENTRO: Puerto Rican Studies at CUNY

CENTRO is a university-based research institute dedicated to the study and interpretation of the Puerto Rican experience in the United States. It is also the world's only repository of archival and library materials dedicated exclusively to the Puerto Rican diaspora.

Contact: Center for Puerto Rican Studies
Hunter College, 695 Park Avenue, Room E1429,
New York, NY 10021
Telephone: (212) 772-5688, Fax: (212) 650-3673
http://www.centropr.org

[Haworth co-indexing entry note]: "Appendix." Co-published simultaneously in *Journal of Immigrant & Refugee Services* (The Haworth Social Work Practice Press, an imprint of The Haworth Press, Inc.) Vol. 3, No. 1/2, 2005, pp. 199-209; and: *Mental Health Care for New Hispanic Immigrants: Innovative Approaches in Contemporary Clinical Practice* (ed: Manny J. González, and Gladys González-Ramos) The Haworth Social Work Practice Press, an imprint of The Haworth Press, Inc., 2005, pp. 199-209. Single or multiple copies of this article are available for a fee from The Haworth Document Delivery Service [1-800-HAWORTH, 9:00 a.m. - 5:00 p.m. (EST). E-mail address: docdelivery@haworthpress.com].

Available online at http://www.haworthpress.com/web/JIRS
© 2005 by The Haworth Press, Inc. All rights reserved.
Digital Object Identifier: 10.1300/J191v3n01_12

Congressional Hispanic Caucus

The El Paso Office offers assistance to constituents in dealing with federal government agencies, to organizations in seeking federal grants, to students in seeking a Congressional nomination to U.S. military academies, and also to constituents in visiting the nation's capital.

Contact: 1527 Longworth House Office Building, Washington, DC 20515
Telephone: (202) 225-4831, Fax: (202) 225-2016
http://wwwc.house.gov/reyes

Cuban American National Council, Inc.

A non-profit and tax-exempt 501 (C) (3) organization which provide education, housing and community development services to needy individuals from diverse racial and ethnic groups with a focus on Hispanics and minorities.

Contact: 1225 SW 4 Street, Miami, FL 33135
Telephone: (305) 642-3484, Fax: (305) 642-9122
http://www.cnc.org/index.html

Hispanic Advocacy and Community Empowerment Through Research (HACER)

A non-profit, community based research and advocacy organization committed in identifying research needs and delivering quality research products that strengthen the Latino community. HACER provides the Minnesota Latino community the ability to create and to control information about itself in order to affect institutional decisions and public policy.

Contact: HACER 330 HHH Center
301 19th Avenue South, Minneapolis, MN 55455
Telephone: (612) 624-3326
www.hacer-mn.org

Hispanic Association of Colleges and Universities (HACU)

HACU represents more than 350 colleges and universities committed to Hispanic higher education success in the U.S., Puerto Rico, Latin America and Spain. It is the only national educational association that represents Hispanic-Serving Institutions (HSIs). It provides faculty grants training, research programs, undergraduate and graduate research internship/fellowship programs, pre-collegiate programs, and technical assistance.

Contact: *National Headquarters*
8415 Datapoint Drive, Suite 400, San Antonio, TX 78229
Telephone: (210) 692-3805, Fax: (210) 692-0823
http://www.hacu.net

Hispanic Community Resource Helpline

A national information and referral service that provides support for Hispanics who need information about educational, health and human service providers.

Contact: *529 14th Street, N.W., Suite 740, Washington, DC 20045*
Telephone: (202) 661-8016, 1-800-473-3003, Fax: (202) 637-8801
http://www.selfreliancefoundation.org/hotline.htm

Hispanic Education Foundation

A national organization that promotes educational opportunities for Hispanics by providing scholarships, training and additional education.

Contact: *P.O. Box 2102, Longmont, CO 80502*
Telephone: 1-800-892-5558 ext. 88084
http://bcn.boulder.co.us/univ_school/hef/

Hispanic Federation

A membership organization of 76 Latino health and human services agencies that provides immigration services, health care, economic development, job training, AIDS prevention, youth services, leadership development, and housing to all Latinos who live in New York, New Jersey and Connecticut.

Contact: *130 William Street, 9th floor, New York, NY 10038*
Telephone: (212) 233-8955, Fax: (212) 233-8996
HF Hotline: (212) 732-HELP (4357)
http://www.hispanicfederation.org

Hispanic Scholarship Fund (HSF)

A national leading organization supporting Hispanic higher education by providing the Latino community with college scholarships and educational outreach support.

Contact: 55 Second Street, Suite 1500, San Francisco, CA 94105
      Telephone: 1-877-HSF-INFO (1-877-473-4636), Fax: 415-808-2302
      http://www.hsf.net

Hispanic-Serving Health Professions Schools, Inc. (HSHPS)

HSHPS is a non-profit organization that represents over twenty medical schools and three schools of public health across the United States. The mission of the HSHPS is to improve the health of Hispanics through academic development, research initiatives and training.

Contact: 1411 K Street, N.W., Suite 200, Washington, DC 20005
      Telephone: (202) 783-5262, Fax: (202) 628-5898
      http://www.hshps.com

Institute for Cuban and Cuban-American Studies (ICCAS)

The Institute for Cuban and Cuban-American Studies (ICCAS) is part of the *University of Miami.* ICCAS serves as a world-class academic center for the research and study of Cuban and Cuban-American topics.

Contact: 1531 Brescia Avenue, P.O. Box 248174,
      Coral Gables, FL 33124-3010
      Telephone: (305) 284-CUBA (2822), Fax: (305) 284-4875
      http://www.miami.edu/iccas/mission.htm

Interamerican College of Physicians and Surgeons (ICPS)

The ICPS is a not-for-profit, tax-exempt, non-governmental organization. It is the largest association of Hispanic physicians in the nation. The goals of ICPS are to improve the health of the Hispanic community, to reduce the incidence of preventable diseases, to improve educational and leadership opportunities for Hispanic physicians, and to encourage Hispanic youths to pursue careers in the healthcare field.

Contact: 1616 H Street, N.W., Suite 400, Washington, DC 20006
      Telephone: (202) 467-4756, Fax: (212)467-4758
      http://www.icps.org/main.htm#

Inter-University Program for Latino Research (IUPLR)

IUPLR is the only nationwide university-based research organization, containing 18 Latino research centers. Its goals are to expand the pool of scholars and leaders, to strengthen the capacity of Latino research centers, and to facilitate the availability of policy-relevant, Latino-focused research. It offers training programs, sponsors interdisciplinary research, and creates links between scholars, policy experts, public officials, and community advocates.

Contact: IUPLR
University of Notre Dame
230 McKenna Hall, P.O. Box 764, Notre Dame, IN 46556-0764
Telephone: (574) 631-3481, Fax: (574) 631-3884
http://www.nd.edu/~iuplr/

Latin American Association

A non-profit organization that provides Latino families and individuals with basic transition services in order to facilitate integration into the mainstream community, and advocates on behalf of Latinos.

Contact: 2750 Buford Highway, Atlanta, GA 30324
Telephone: (404) 638-1800, Fax: (404) 638-1806
http://www.latinamericanassoc.org

Latin American Health Institute (LHI)

A community-based organization serves Latino families, individuals, health care providers and institutions by providing technical assistance, fiscal sponsorship, and program oversight.

Contact: 95 Berkeley Street, Boston, MA 02116
Telephone: (617) 350-6900, Fax: (617) 350-6901
http://www.lhi.org/lhi/

League of United Latin American Citizens (LULAC)

LULAC advances the economic condition, educational attainment, political influence, health and civil rights of Hispanic Americans through community-based programs operating at more than 600 LULAC councils nationwide. The organization involves and serves all Hispanic groups.

Contact: 2000 L Street, N.W., Suite 610, Washington, DC 20036
Telephone: (202) 833-6130
http://www.lulac.org

MANA, A National Latina Organization

MANA is a nonprofit, advocacy organization. Its mission is to empower Latinas through leadership development, community service, and advocacy.

Contact: 1725 K Street, N.W., Suite 501, Washington, DC 20006
        Telephone: (202) 833-0060, Fax: (202) 496-0588
        http://www.hermana.org/

Migrant Legal Action Program (MLAP)

The Migrant Legal Action Program (MLAP) provides legal representation and a national voice for migrant and seasonal farmworkers. MLAP works to enforce rights and to improve public policies affecting farmworkers' working and housing conditions, education, health, nutrition, and general welfare. The program works with an extensive network of local service providers.

Contact: Migrant Legal Action Program
        1001 Connecticut Avenue, N.W., Suite 915, Washington, DC 20036
        Telephone: (202) 775-7780, Fax: (202) 775-7784
        http://www.mlap.org/

Mexican American Legal Defense and Educational Fund (MALDEF)

A national non-profit organization that promotes the civil right of all Latinos living in the Unites States by providing advocacy, and educational outreach. The major areas MALDEF focusing on are employment, education, immigration, political access, language and public resource equity issues.

Contact: National Headquarters
        634 South Spring Street, Los Angeles, CA 90014
        Telephone: (213) 629-2512
        http://www.maldef.org

National Alliance for Hispanic Health

A national organization focusing on the health, mental health, and human services of the Hispanic community by representing and advocating for the health and mental health needs of Hispanic communities throughout the Unites States. The organization also provides the community based interventions to increase and enhance cancer control and conduct collaborative research with the Center for Disease Control.

Contact: 1501 16th Street, N.W., Washington, DC 20036
    Telephone: (202) 387-5000
    http://www.hispanichealth.org

National Association of Hispanic Nurses

NAHN is committed to toward the improvement of the quality of health and nursing care for Hispanic consumers and toward providing equal access to educational, professional, and economic opportunities for Hispanic nurses.

Contact: 1501 Sixteenth Street, N.W., Washington, DC 20036
    Telephone: (202) 387-2477, FAX: (202) 483-7183
    http://www.thehispanicnurses.org/

National Association of Latino Elected and Appointed Officials Educational Fund (NALEO Educational Fund)

NALEO is a non-profit organization that empowers Latinos to participate fully in the America political process, from citizenship to public service.

Contact: 1122 West Washington Boulevard., 3rd Floor, Los Angeles, CA 90015
    Telephone: (213) 747-7606, Fax: (213) 747-7664
    http://www.naleo.org/index.htm

National Association of Puerto Rican and Hispanic Social Workers (NAPRHSW)

NAPRHSW is interested and diligent in striving to make a difference toward the betterment of the Puerto Rican/Hispanic Communities. It provides scholarship monies to deserving students attending colleges/universities affiliated with NAPRHSW, co-sponsors conferences, offers workshops and social activities.

Contact: NAPRHSW
    P.O. Box 651, Brentwood, NY 11717
    Phone/Fax: (631) 864-1536
    http://www.naprhsw.com

National Council of La Raza (NALR)

A private non-profit organization providing organizational assistance in management, governance, program operations, and resource development to Hispanic community-based organizations in urban and rural areas nationwide.

NCLR applies research, policy analysis, and advocacy: providing an Hispanic perspective on issues such as education, immigration, housing, health employment and training, and civil rights enforcement.

Contact: National Council of La Raza
1111 19th, NW, Suite 1000, Washington, DC 20036
Telephone: (202) 785-1670
http://www.nclr.org

National Hispanic Council on Aging (NHCOA)

A national membership-based organization that works to promote the quality of life for Latino elderly, families and communities through advocacy, partnership activities with the Center for Disease Control (Cancer Prevention and Control), technical assistance, policy analysis and research. The partnership activities include the training of staff to conduct outreach and educational workshop for women about breast and cervical cancer.

Contact: 2713 Ontario Road, N.W., Washington, DC 20009
Telephone: (202) 265-1288, Fax: (202) 745-2522
http://www.nhcoa.org

National Hispanic Institute (NHI)

A nationwide institute providing leadership programs to Latino youth in high school and college with key learning experiences aimed at increasing their skills as future leaders in the Latino community.

Contact: P.O. Box 220, Maxwell, TX 78656
Telephone: (512) 357-6137, Fax: (512) 357-2206
http://www.nhi-net.org/home/default.asp

National Hispanic Medical Association

The National Hispanic Medical Association is a non-profit association representing 36,000 licensed Hispanic physicians in the United States. The mission of the organization is to improve the health of Hispanics and other underserved populations.

Contact: 1411 K Street, Suite 200, Washington, DC 20005
Telephone: (202) 628-5895, Fax: (202) 628-5898
http://www.nhmamd.org/about.htm

National Latino Behavioral Health Association (NLBHA)

NLBHA was established to fill a need for a unified national voice for Latino populations in the behavioral health arena and to bring attention to the great disparities that exist in areas of access, utilization, practice based research and adequately trained personnel.

Contact: NLBHA Headquarters
P. O. Box 387, 506 Welch Street, Berthoud, CO 80513
Telephone: (970) 532-7210, Fax: (970) 532-7209
http://nlbha.org/

National Latino Children's Institute (NLCI)

A national organization focused on enhancing the well being of Latino children by providing training, technical assistance and leadership development. NLCI also conducts ethnographic research on social policies and programs that affect Latino children.

Contact: 1325 N. Flores Street, Suite 114, San Antonio, TX 78212
Telephone: (210) 228-9997, Fax: (210) 228-9972
http://*www.nlci.org*

National Latino Council on Alcohol and Tobacco Prevention (LCAT)

A non-profit organization established to combat alcohol and tobacco problems and their underlying causes in Latino communities. LCAT concentrates its efforts on informing public opinion and promoting policy changes on the local, state and federal level that affect advertising, access, enforcement and consumption of these products by Latino youth.

Contact: 1616 P Street, N.W., Suite 430, Washington, DC 20036
Telephone: (202) 265-8054, Fax: (202) 265-8056
http://www.nlcatp.org/

National Network for Immigrant and Refugee Rights (NNIRR)

A national organization composed of local coalitions, immigrant, refugee, community, religious civil rights and labor organizations working to promote a just immigration and refugee policy in the U.S. and to defend and expand the civil rights of all immigrants and refugees regardless of immigration status.

Contact: *National Network for Immigrant and Refugee Rights*
310-8th Street, Suite 303, Oakland, CA 94607
Telephone: (510) 465-1984, Fax: (510) 465-1885
http://www.nnirr.org/

National Organization for Mexican American Rights (NOMAR)

A national non-profit organization working to promote and defend the civil rights of Americans of Hispanic Origin and their right to equal employment and educational opportunities.

Contact: *P.O. Box 681205, San Antonio, TX 78268-1205*
Telephone: (210) 520-1831, Fax: (210) 520-1831
http://www.nomarinc.org

National Puerto Rican Coalition, Inc. (NPRC)

A non-profit organization providing leadership in pubic policy, the growth and empowerment of Puerto Rican community organizations, and the transfer of knowledge to Puerto Rican advocates and emerging leadership.

Contact: *National Puerto Rican Coalition, Inc.*
1901 L Street, N.W., Suite 802, Washington, DC 20006
Telephone: (202) 223-3915, Fax: 202-429-2223
http://www.bateylink.org

Society for Advancement of Chicanos and Native Americans in Science (SACNAS)

The mission of SACNAS is to encourage Chicano/Latino and Native American students to pursue graduate education and obtain advanced degrees necessary for research careers and science teaching professions.

Contact: SACNAS
P.O. Box 8526, Santa Cruz, CA 95061-8526
Telephone: (831) 459-0170, Fax: (831) 459-0194
http://www.sacnas.org/

The National Latina/o Lesbian, Gay, Bisexual and Transgender Organization (LLEGO)

The National Latina/o Lesbian, Gay, Bisexual and Transgender Organization is the only national nonprofit organization devoted to representing

Latina/o lesbian, gay, bisexual and transgender (LGBT) communities and addressing their growing needs regarding an array of social issues ranging from civil rights and social justice to health and human services.

Contact: *1420 K Street, Suite 400, Washington, DC 20005*
Telephone: 1-888-633-8320, Fax: (202) 408-8478
http://www.llego.org/

U.S.-Mexico Border Health Association

The U.S.-Mexico Border Health Association promotes public and individual health along the United States-Mexico border through reciprocal technical cooperation. It focuses its technical cooperation resources on information dissemination on border health issues and the creation of effective networks. It also promotes and supports sister city relationships through its Binational Health Councils.

Contact: *5400 Suncrest Drive, Suite C-5, El Paso, TX 79912*
Telephone: (915) 833-6450, Fax: (915) 833-7840
http://www.usmbha.org/

For further information regarding resources specific to the Hispanic community, please refer to the following reference:

United States Department of Health and Human Services. (2003). *Pocket guide to mental health resources*. Washington, DC: Author.

Index

BOOK ORDER FORM!

Order a copy of this book with this form or online at:
http://www.HaworthPress.com/store/product.asp?sku=5470

Mental Health Care for New Hispanic Immigrants
Innovative Approaches in Contemporary Clinical Practice

____ in softbound at $24.95 ISBN-13: 978-0-7890-2308-7 / ISBN-10: 0-7890-2308-3.
____ in hardbound at $39.95 ISBN-13: 978-0-7890-2307-0 / ISBN-10: 0-7890-2307-5.

COST OF BOOKS _____

POSTAGE & HANDLING _____
US: $4.00 for first book & $1.50
for each additional book
Outside US: $5.00 for first book
& $2.00 for each additional book.

SUBTOTAL _____

In Canada: add 7% GST. _____

STATE TAX _____
CA, IL, IN, MN, NJ, NY, OH, PA & SD residents
please add appropriate local sales tax.

FINAL TOTAL _____

If paying in Canadian funds, convert
using the current exchange rate,
UNESCO coupons welcome.

❑BILL ME LATER:
Bill-me option is good on US/Canada/
Mexico orders only; not good to jobbers,
wholesalers, or subscription agencies.

❑ Signature _____

❑ Payment Enclosed: $ _____

❑ PLEASE CHARGE TO MY CREDIT CARD:
❑Visa ❑MasterCard ❑AmEx ❑Discover
❑Diner's Club ❑Eurocard ❑JCB

Account # _____

Exp Date _____

Signature _____
(Prices in US dollars and subject to change without notice.)

PLEASE PRINT ALL INFORMATION OR ATTACH YOUR BUSINESS CARD

Name

Address

City   State/Province   Zip/Postal Code

Country

Tel   Fax

E-Mail

May we use your e-mail address for confirmations and other types of information? ❑Yes ❑No We appreciate receiving
your e-mail address. Haworth would like to e-mail special discount offers to you, as a preferred customer.
We will never share, rent, or exchange your e-mail address. We regard such actions as an invasion of your privacy.

Order from your **local bookstore** or directly from
The Haworth Press, Inc. 10 Alice Street, Binghamton, New York 13904-1580 • USA
Call our toll-free number (1-800-429-6784) / Outside US/Canada: (607) 722-5857
Fax: 1-800-895-0582 / Outside US/Canada: (607) 771-0012
E-mail your order to us: orders@HaworthPress.com

For orders outside US and Canada, you may wish to order through your local
sales representative, distributor, or bookseller.
For information, see http://HaworthPress.com/distributors

(Discounts are available for individual orders in US and Canada only, not booksellers/distributors.)

Please photocopy this form for your personal use.
www.HaworthPress.com   BOF05